CRITICAL APPROACHES TO THE FICTION OF THOMAS HARDY

CRITICAL APPROACHES TO THE FICTION OF THOMAS HARDY

Edited by
DALE KRAMER

Professor of English
University of Illinois at Urbana-Champaign

MACMILLAN

First edition 1979
Reprinted 1990

Published by
THE MACMILLAN PRESS LTD
London and Basingstoke
Associated companies in Delhi
Dublin Hong Kong Johannesburg Lagos
Melbourne New York Singapore Tokyo

Printed and bound in Great Britain by
ANTONY ROWE LTD
Chippenham, Wiltshire

British Library Cataloguing in Publication Data

Critical approaches to the fiction of Thomas Hardy
   1. Hardy, Thomas, b. 1840 – Criticism and
   interpretation
   I. Kramer, Dale
   823.8   PR4754

   ISBN 0–333–23756–0

Dale Kramer; Critical Approaches
to the Fiction of Thomas Hardy

Contents

Textual Note

Quotations from Hardy's works are taken from the texts of the Wessex Edition (1912–31), published by Macmillan & Co. Ltd., of London. Most modern reprints use the text of this edition, the last edition supervised and proof-read by Hardy. Because the Wessex Edition is no longer in print, citations also are given to chapters for ease in reference by readers of such other editions as the New Wessex Edition, paperback and hardcover, published in recent years by Macmillan.

Notes on the Contributors

RICHARD C. CARPENTER. Professor of English at Bowling Green State University. Has published *Thomas Hardy* and essays in such journals as *NCF, MFS, Journal of Modern Literature,* and *Critique.* Is writing a book on the Romantic revival in late nineteenth-century fiction.

PETER J. CASAGRANDE. Associate Professor of English at the University of Kansas. Has published articles and reviews on Hardy and Wordsworth in *ELH, ELT, Criticism,* and the *Thomas Hardy Review.*

SIMON GATRELL. Lecturer in English Studies at the New University of Ulster at Coleraine, Northern Ireland. Has published several essays on Hardy, and, in collaboration with Dr Tony Bareham, *A Bibliography of George Crabbe.* Is working on a full-length study of Hardy from the point of view of the development of the texts.

MARY JACOBUS. Lecturer at Lady Margaret Hall, Oxford. Has published *Tradition and Experiment in Wordsworth's 'Lyrical Ballads'* and several essays on Hardy, and has in progress a book on Hardy.

W. J. KEITH. Professor of English at the University of Toronto. Born and brought up in England, now a Canadian citizen. Has published *Richard Jefferies: A Critical Study, Charles G. D. Roberts, The Rural Tradition,* and essays on Hardy in *NCF* and *ELN.* In the press is a book on rural poetry from Wordsworth to the present.

JAMES R. KINCAID. Professor of English at the University of Colorado. Has published *Dickens and the Rhetoric of Laughter, Tennyson's Major Poems: The Comic and Ironic Patterns,* and *The Novels of Anthony Trollope.*

DALE KRAMER. Professor of English at the University of Illinois at Urbana-Champaign. Has published *Charles Maturin, Thomas Hardy: The Forms of Tragedy,* and essays on Hardy's revisions of *The Woodlanders.*

DAVID LODGE. Professor of Modern English Literature at the University of Birmingham. Has published books of literary criticism (*Language of Fiction*, *The Novelist at the Crossroads*, *Graham Greene*, *Evelyn Waugh*, and *The Modes of Modern Writing*), novels (*The Picturegoers*, *Ginger, You're Barmy*, *The British Museum is Falling Down*, *Out of the Shelter*, and *Changing Places*), and numerous essays on Hardy and other writers.

MICHAEL RYAN. Assistant Professor of English and Comparative Literature at the University of Virginia. Has published essays on Pater, Newman, and Nietzsche, and is in the process of writing a book — *Victorian Ideology: Mill, Arnold, and Pater*.

DANIEL R. SCHWARZ. Associate Professor of English at Cornell University. Has published essays in collections and in such journals as *MFS, UTQ, Studies in the Novel*, and *Twentieth Century Literature* on narrative technique in Hardy, Conrad, and Lawrence.

ELAINE SHOWALTER. Professor of English at Douglass College, Rutgers University. Has published *A Literature of Their Own: British Women Novelists from Brontë to Lessing*, and other books and articles on women writers, Victorian fiction, and feminist criticism. Working on a book on insanity and the Victorian imagination.

LEON WALDOFF. Associate Professor of English at the University of Illinois at Urbana–Champaign. Has published a number of articles on the Romantic poets from the psychoanalytical perspective.

1 Making Approaches to Hardy

DALE KRAMER

Reading fiction and reading literary criticism are endeavours in common. In themselves, the two kinds of reading lead to quite dissimilar emotional and intellectual reactions, but the reactions support each other. Which of the two is the primary activity is obvious; but the importance of the secondary activity is attested by the evolution of novelists' reputations – and in a firm sense their readability – in pace with developments in literary criticism. Of course not every change in literary criticism affects every author's reputation in an even fashion. But understanding one novel in a fresh way often shakes our accustomed perceptions of other novels – especially those by the same author.

The authors of the essays in this book employ different theoretical approaches in response to Thomas Hardy's fiction. They write about specific issues, but the implications of their methods reach out to other novels, other problems. Although many of them employ recently developed, or recently redefined, methods, their essays are not abstract and dogmatic and revolutionary so much as concrete and personal and exploratory. Their footing in traditional approaches and evaluations, manifested more clearly in some essays than in others, suggests the efficacy of previous critical practices. For Hardy has not been badly served, in all, by commentators; and the terms in which he has been discussed in the past provide continuity to many of the essays here embodying suggestions as to how he might be read now and in the future.

Hardy has been classed variously as an old-fashioned novelist, the last great Victorian novelist, the first modern novelist, a crude writer whose shortage of formal education was fortuitously the cause of his freedom from constraints and novelistic conventions of his times, an autodidact, a recorder of rural customs and superstitions, a tragic interpreter of life's complexities, a displayer and shielder of his sensitive ego – the list could go on. The word 'Protean' is over-used in literary discussions; but still it is fair and accurate to say that, apart perhaps from Dickens, no novelist writing in English has appealed to so many different kinds of readers for so many differing reasons. Dickens' readers noticed mostly the humour, the social criticism, and the grotesqueries until Edmund Wilson's chapter in *The Wound and the Bow* (1941) alerted them to the darker driven qualities in Dickens' imagination. In a parallel manner, Hardy's readers from his own time until the Second World War were given to such reactions as delight in rustic manners and dialect, despair at the mechanistic operation of the universe, and annoyance at naive 'stylisms' and creaky plotting, until Albert Guerard (1949) inaugurated a long-developing shift in readers' attention by emphasising psychological patterns and oddities among Hardy's characters and the anti-realistic aspects of his imagination.[1]

Excitement at perceiving a range of previously unexplained qualities in Hardy has continued to the present, inspiring such books as those by J. Hillis Miller (1970) and Perry Meisel (1972). Of course, continually there have been studies of a more orthodox nature of such matters as Hardy's adaptation of the work of previous writers (Allan Brick [1963]), his views on responsibility (Roy Morrell [1965]), his ideas about time and chance (Bert Hornback [1971]), and his relationship to other nineteenth-century writers of tragedy (Jeannette King [1978]). From the early twentieth century there has been great interest in the reflection in Hardy's novels of events of his life; in recent years this interest has centred on his feelings about love and sex (Lois Deacon and Terry Coleman [1966]; J. O. Bailey [1972]; Robert Gittings [1975, 1978]). As Hardy's letters continue to appear in their full edition (Richard Little Purdy and Michael Millgate [1978 –]), such interest is bound to result in studies and conjectures; and the biography being written by Millgate may inspire still further biographical studies. Interest about Hardy's habits of revision (Laird [1975]) is increasing; and as his published works go out of copyright in England and the Commonwealth, definitive critical editions of his novels and poems are under way. General studies of the 'literary biography' sort (J. I. M. Stewart [1971]), informed less by their authors' interest in specific aspects of Hardy's works than by intelligent enthusiasm for the works as a whole, and buttressed by solid research in background documents (Michael Millgate [1971]), are staple items in many a publisher's list. And there have been a few fine briefer studies of Hardy's relationship with the large ideas of his times (DeLaura [1967]).[2]

To put it briefly, the appeal of Hardy as a novelist (and poet) has long been vital, increasingly so in recent years; he has never been more widely appreciated than he is at the present moment. He is read not only by hundreds of thousands of school and university students but by people who buy paperbacks for pleasure reading. His novels and stories are dramatised on radio and television, and made into movies. Again like Dickens, he is a classic who has not ceased to be popular. He has not been subject to swings of fad popularity and thus has been neither suddenly overexposed nor suddenly eclipsed.

For casual readers of Hardy, the nature of his reputation and the fact that people write about his works are not factors in their choosing his works to read. They read, are affected deeply by Hardy's art – or not; and go on to read another Hardy work, or not, as inclination leads. But for the Hardy aficionado, for the unusually interested reader, and for the professional or academic student, reading a novel even for a third or fourth time is only the primary step toward full understanding and satisfaction. The person who reflects upon the experience of reading – with its peculiar combination of aesthetic absorption and cognitive development – realises that discussion and self-query test initial reactions and bring into awareness aspects of literary works which had not been noted consciously during the first and perhaps not the third reading.

Readers have each their own 'way' of reading, a means of gaining to their own satisfaction a comprehension of features of the artefact which especially appeal to them, whether they are casual readers or dons preparing lectures. Individuals' ways of reading are developed without special effort and under the influence of chance occurrences – in the course of reading novels that attract them for unexamined reasons, by teachers emphasising different aspects of fiction, by parallels with popular media. Even with professional, trained readers the process varies only by intensity and, perhaps, by a greater degree of deliberateness. That is, in school, university, or first job a critic or teacher may emulate a teacher's or a colleague's method more or less intentionally before that method in course of time evolves to better suit his or her personality and professional intentions. And of course some people in university and early professional life decide, arbitrarily, to write studies of imagery or to emulate the humane goals and rhetorical tactics of an F. R. Leavis. If there is a strong pedagogical strain in a particular school or university, many pupils and students may almost literally be forced to commit themselves to an entrenched 'school' of criticism (and of life) which might be uncongenial to them, however admirable might be their principles and selflessly devoted their adherents. But in all, as experience tells us, in the practice of competent readers the principles of 'schools' are modified, combined, even rejected in part in favour of contradictory principles of other 'schools' (or of the reader's common sense). Attempts to understand correspond to the needs of the reader or critic and to the needs of the text in hand.

The point to be made is that, by and large, readers notice about a piece of literature what their ways of reading permit them to notice. Discoveries are implicit in premises. At obvious extremes, biographical critics (by whom I mean readers interested in biography) are not certain even to notice the repetitions and verbal cues and relationships in an artefact that formalist readers attempt to incorporate into a synthesis during the very moments of reading; nor is a formalist critic necessarily able to develop the sense of tact that seems so natural to the biographical critic in allowing him or her to judge what in the artefact is of a piece with its creator's own life and what is almost certainly wholly imaginary (or, again, what is intended to mask a bearing relevant to the creator's life). What this comes to mean is that readers with certain kinds of interests evolve into readers with certain kinds of skills, or, to invert the equation, certain methods of reading appeal to certain individuals. Readers without an interest in philosophy are not likely to become deconstructionists.

Although the essays in this collection employ identifiable general approaches in their addressing specific problems in novels or groups of novels or stories, it would be contrary to the foregoing sketch of 'ways of reading' to judge every one of these essays as representative of a school of criticism.[3] In an essential way, each essay is 'representative' only of its particular author's decision about the best way to resolve a specific problem or to explain an aspect of Hardy's work. How, for example, might one classify Peter Casagrande's examination of one of Hardy's best-liked heroines, Bathsheba Everdene? As the exploration of authorial attitudes through the detailed diagnosis of one character? As a study of techniques of characterisation? As a querying of stereotyped reader-judgement of a character? Of course, none of these is the statement of method of a 'school' – taken together, they may suggest the way Casagrande himself has felt it necessary to approach the explanation of a character he thought had not been accurately described before. And what about Mary Jacobus' casting Hardy against topical cultural and historical and aesthetic concerns? Is this an attempt to place Hardy's writing in the larger context of the relation between literature and ideas, or is it a study in the relation between fictional metaphor and novelistic form? Whatever category of critical approach these two essays could be shoehorned into – if forced to nominate I would myself opt for the first possibility of each of the two series – what is of clearer importance is that each essay embodies a 'way of reading' whose usefulness is not restricted to Bathsheba and myth-based stories or Romanticism. Elizabeth-Jane, Clym Yeobright, Eustacia Vye, and Fancy Day take self-contradictory actions that reveal Hardy trying to project basic values no less than does Bathsheba; and such topical concerns as urbanisation, the drive for universal education, and Utopianism await the sort of linking of general cultural milieu with specifics of the text that Jacobus gives to the background of *The Woodlanders*; and other more specifically literary influences on Hardy such as Anatole France offer obvious but still-uninvestigated opportunities for readers and critics with a bent toward literary history.

Defining features or qualities that appear, despite permutations that include ambiguities and contradictoriness, to characterise a significant dimension in an author's work is an essential approach to the reading of literature. Similar manifestations of a quality may affect readers differently, justifying further work, more subtle criteria. 'Tragedy' is one such quality, and James Kincaid briefly considers the need to define before giving judgement. W. J. Keith, in a more consuming effort to define, re-evaluates the 'regional' qualities in Hardy, using 'provincial' as a countering or comparable quality, and measures the distinctions between the two by evoking the standards of the 'cosmopolitan'. The unique qualities of Wessex become evident as the influence of London and a metropolitan culture begin to erode the distinctions. Through his consideration of several novels Keith further traces the applicability of the quality he is defining. As a 'way' of reading, definition requires an initial sense of the quality being discriminated, an ability to accommodate modifications of that initial understanding, and an assertiveness – not to mention an adequate memory – in the course of reading that keeps the reader's standards disentangled from those of the author. The employment of definition is by its nature continually evaluative. If a work is tragic or regional in part rather than in its entirety, the defining reader must recognise the difference and, if also a critic, be able to explain it. Obviously readers' creativity and knowledge determine the possibilities of 'reading by definition', a strategy as valid for a single novel or story as for an author's entire *oeuvre*.

Several of the critics employ in passing a kind of evidence to support their different cases which it is perhaps straining the common meaning of words to call a 'way of reading'. They cite changes Hardy made while literally penning the manuscripts of such novels as *The Return of the Native*, *Tess of the d'Urbervilles*, and *The Mayor of Casterbridge*. Clearly, this means of 'reading' is not open to casual admirers of Hardy but only to those with access to the monographs and scholarly journals that publish studies of such matters; and perhaps it is accurate to say that the only people who can truly 'read' in this fashion are those who handle the actual manuscripts or microfilm copies of the manuscripts and who take the trouble to compare earlier printed versions of a story side by side with the final version in the Wessex Edition (or, in the case of *A Pair of Blue Eyes*, in the Mellstock Edition). But this state of things will change as critical editions – which perhaps will print even minor deletions from and alterations in the manuscripts – are published in the next few years. (Still, of course, only those readers with access to these complex and costly editions will be able to 'read' the novels as they evolved over the decades of Hardy's revising them.) Simon Gatrell holds himself to examining only a few chapters of *Far from the Madding Crowd*, but even with this deliberate restriction is able to inform us not only about an important change in characterisation and class level, but about the kind of interference and censorship from editors that hampered Hardy's imagination all his life as a writer of fiction. (The censorship, and threat of censorship, may also have had a role in inspiring Hardy to challenge editors' and readers' reluctance to face what he saw as life's truth.) Most readers and interpreters take the text of a novel for granted, as if it were a 'given' that the creative impulse of their author would take the shape that it has in the particular artefact they are examining and confidently explaining. Textual criticism like Gatrell's brings up short such readers as these. While clearly textual criticism of Hardy is not an unlimited field – there are only so many novels, and not all their manuscripts survive – an immense amount of study is still in order, since just as in more conventional interpretative criticism different minds will interpret the same bits of evidence (rejected passages, substituted passages, rearrangements of passages, alterations in punctuation, and the like) in different ways; and more than one way may be 'correct' — just as in conventional interpretative criticism.

Whether psychological theories can be successfully used in literary criticism without reductionism is still an open question in many people's minds, despite decades of distinguished writing by the likes of Norman Holland, Simon Lesser, and Lionel Trilling — not to mention Sigmund Freud and Ernest Jones. The essential premise of psychological criticism is that creative writers consciously or unconsciously implant in their imagined characters traits, obsessions, predispositions of a kind not inherently different from those that can be identified in actual people. The critic's interpretation of personality can be based on specific clinical studies of presumably emotionally disturbed persons or on general studies of certain common features of everyday life (such as Freud's studies of dreams and slips of the tongue); or it can be developed from his or her own observations and common-sense judgement of people in everyday situations. In any event, the assumption is that universals of behaviour are revealed that are applicable to both sick and healthy individuals. (Indeed, a psychologist might avoid terms like 'sick' and 'well' in reference to mental states on the grounds that it is the relative success or failure of defence mechanisms that defines the degrees of social adjustment for each individual, the psychological nature of the human condition being so universal, yet so susceptible to particular circumstances.) In addition to applying its premises to characters in a work and to readers of a work, psychological criticism can extrapolate a theory drawn from the conditions in the work of art to the mind and life of the author — perhaps the reason it is one of the more controversial methods of literary study. Used with restraint and with knowledge of the present state of Hardy biography, however, psychology can confirm with added dimension the conjectures of sensitive biographers. Careful tracing of the relations between creator and the artefact through an intelligent deployment of the insights derived from a psychological theory can enhance our awareness of both creator and artefact, and point up relevances to our own being, as when Waldoff evaluates in *Tess of the d'Urbervilles* the interplay of the sensuous and affectionate feelings.

Feminist criticism is deeply concerned with the ways in which the experience of being male or female in a particular society is reflected through the literary imagination. It is possible to detect in Hardy residual signs of sexist thinking, including uncertain acquiescence in the Victorian double standard of sexual morality and condescension in allusions to the womanly attributes of female characters. But notwithstanding such indications of the influence upon him of his time and place, his sensitive portrayals of women and his use of their dilemmas as reflectors of his judgement on life have long been factors in Hardy's reputation. Because for Hardy full selfhood takes in more than the stereotypical qualities of one sex, Elaine Showalter's approach can lead her naturally not to female characters but to one of the notable males in English literature. In analysing Henchard's movement toward more complete humanity (as a relinquishing of male power and privilege) she makes a significant addition to the literature on Hardy as a tragic novelist. Further readings in this vein could well reshape our understanding of Clym and Eustacia in particular, as well as of John Loveday, Lady Constantine, and others. In all of Hardy's works tolerance and eager sympathy characterise the portrayal of members of both sexes; and as Showalter demonstrates, Hardy perceives sex-traits as psychological in origin, not as exclusive properties of one sex or the other.

Several of these essays address the related questions of the value of organisation and the possibility of meaning in fiction. David Lodge's essay on pessimism in *Jude the Obscure* instances the formalist approach, in which the reader develops generalisations about the author's vision of life from various indications of importance – repetitions of events or phrases, recurring substantive concerns, or patterns of any sort that highlight aspects of the artefact as being somehow special in the flow of, as Lodge puts it, 'apparently random . . . particularity'. The identification of formal concerns requires an active, sceptical, but participating reader, since authors are likely to attempt to disguise their pattern even while relying on it heavily. And authors seldom specify the purpose of the repetitions or the linguistically highlighted passages. That's the role of the reader: to experience the life conveyed in a sequence of words. Formalism is a particularly essential 'way of reading', especially for a professional or academic reader, for without at least a rudimentary capability to deduce an author's principal interests from a reading of a text by itself a reader or critic would of necessity have to rely on other readers' or critics' judgements of the special quality of a work of art.

The difference between formalism as reflected in Lodge's essay and the approach used by Richard Carpenter is partly in manner of explanation, partly in the degree of instantaneity of perception that is being proposed. The formalist critic makes no effort to disguise that a synthetic explanation is being drawn from a more or less obdurate text: mental diagrams are conceived to explain the stresses and points of high interest; and the number of times the critic has read the work is not an issue. What is attempted to be got at is the author's *meaning*, as clearly as possible. In the so-called 'reader response' approach, as Carpenter's essay reveals, the explanation is from the perspective of a single reader – that is, the ideal reader, possessing linguistic and literary 'competence' (to use a concept of linguists),[4] and behaving as the critic thinks a reader should when faced by the particular text. The intention is to explain how the text shapes the reader's response (thus the name of this approach) during a first, highly alert, reading. What is analysed is the action generated within the reader's mind by the organisation and expressiveness of words and sentences during the immediate act of reading. This mental action itself constitutes the 'meaning', one that is more important than logical propositions, one that changes from moment to moment as further words pass under the reader's eyes, shaped by the lexical and syntactical possibilities of language, use of irony, reversal of expectations, and the like. Meaning, then, is developmental and temporal, not static and spatial (as formalists often present it). The procedure of explanation is thereby necessarily sequential, and retrospective only up to the point in the narrative line the explanation has got to at any given time; leapfrogging ahead to the climax, or to high points in the narrative, in order to clarify an earlier crux of the story or of the author's presentation is illegitimate criticism – or at least is no longer 'reader-response' criticism – because the assumption of this approach is that the valid interpretation of or response to a piece of writing is that of the first-time reader in actual life. (*Anticipations* of future developments, on the other hand, reflect actual readers' efforts to get a handle on the artefact as it unfolds.) Since the author's intended reader must logically have been a contemporary, the reader-response critic can reconstruct the intended response by considering the meanings of words current at the time the work was written although obsolete at the time the criticism is being written, and also historical and cultural events familiar to the conjectured historical first-time reader.

The tradition of Anglo-American formalism embraces the concept of unity and coherence of novels' imagined worlds, worlds which reveal the author's identity and reflect the culture in which they were written. Critics who regard a novel as a discrete ontology, as does Daniel R. Schwarz, may be concerned how a work of fiction shapes a reader; but they are more concerned with the quality, integrity, and intensity of mimesis in the work – with the capacity of the work to

draw the reader into its own reality. Its view of the nature of reality in
art distinguishes Schwarz's ontological approach from the customary
formalist approach (Lodge) and the reader–response method (Carpenter). As is made especially clear by Carpenter, these non-
ontological approaches to form consider the work being read a
communication integral to the world that pre- and post-exists it, that
is, the real world, the stable world of the author and the reader. At
most, there is a mingling of real-world and imagined-world. Even
while taking heed of biographical and cultural matters, the ontologist
urges the special quality of the artefact's value-system. The ontological reading, then, is an intensification of the idea of unity. What one
method gains in interpretative flexibility may be offset by reduced
rigour in theorising; and the choice of one of these form-based 'ways
of reading' over the others most likely will fall to the one most
promising for the particular issue in the particular novel that is the
cause of the reader's or the critic's interest, the balance being tipped by
the individual critic's propensity to look for ultimate significances, to
decipher verbal and syntactic complexities, or to plumb larger
internal shapings of the novel.

If the purpose of Anglo-American formalism is to decipher the
figure in the carpet, that of recent Continental-inspired ways of
reading is to study the nature of the fibre in the threads and of the
spaces between them, and one of its recurring queries is whether the
carpet *has* a figure that one can finally locate. Structuralism and
deconstruction apply to literary issues the ideas and to some extent the
methods originally developed in such diverse disciplines as linguistics,
anthropology, philosophy, psychology, and social analysis. Although
it is mostly deconstruction that is reflected in two of the essays here,
for those not familiar with it deconstruction is perhaps most quickly
understood in light of its contrasts with structuralism. According to
structuralism, all features of life are significant because of the *relations*
they bear to each other. Through relations are expressed meanings
that may not be perceived or decipherable – or even present – in the
features observed in isolation. These relations can be within the text
entirely, or widely cultural and imaginatively extra-textual. For
example, Claude Lévi-Strauss has analysed features common to as
many versions of the Oedipus myth that he could collect; Roland
Barthes has analysed relations between diversified aspects of culture
and language, such as national feelings and photographs on the covers
of wide-circulation magazines; Michel Foucault has drawn relationships between such institutions as prisons and forms of

government.[5] Identifying these relations is the basis for model-building, in which the structuralist attempts to uncover implicit – and not necessarily conscious – strategies by tracing analogic relationships within the artefact, between the artefact and its author, between the artefact and the total milieu of the times that produced it, between words used by an author and the words in all their potentiality, or a combination of these and other fields of analogues. The resultant explanatory construct represents a system or set of ideas inhering in the actual (the literary text). In such a model important elements 'fit' according to artificial rules imposed by a consciousness which exists outside the phenomena, but which constructs the rules after analysing the totality of evidence. A model, then, in current terms, is both self-generating and self-explanatory. From its principle of relations and from its parallel notion that all human activity is part of a system of communication, a 'language' with its own 'grammar', it is obvious that according to structuralism one can't avoid expressing meaning, whether or not one understands what he or she is 'saying'.

The orientation of deconstruction diverges from these points, at some places sharply and at others subtly. Deconstruction rejects the concept of unity and system and coherence in art as in life; the core of each text expresses, through language and form, the indeterminacy of meaning. Structuralist analysis starts with the idea of synchrony – a concept of timelessness in which the structure of a set of phenomena is embedded in stable manifestations; deconstruction, on the other hand, acknowledges the consequences of time and change and movement in space. Because life is a matter of process, and 'meaning' a matter of continual production and thus never identical, it is impossible to call a halt to deconstructionist analysis. Each new insight, each different possible interpretation of a word, turns all of the interconnections of a text into a new, and itself inevitably impermanent, configuration; and that the author's life and the actual world are also 'texts' of equal status with the printed words, all to be comprised in the effort to 'read', increases the pace of changes in configuration. Deconstructionists do not rely on 'analogies' which search for identities to transcend and overcome differences, because analogies imply a system or structures of identity which are imposed upon the hererogeneity of the actual in order to tame it. Similarly, to a deconstructionist, points of contact are not 'relations' but 'references', points of some connection that can't be contained by the novel or by a version of an author's implicit or explicit meaning.

Once you try to put your finger on meaning – any structure of coherence in a book – it slips away like mercury, breaking up into ever smaller and smaller globules. Any cut-off point which ends that indefinite dissemination of references would be artificial. All the features of life refer to each other indefinitely, so that the trail of references has to be deciphered without the assurance that the trail will end, that the text will be fully interpreted, and that a plenitude of meaning will reveal itself.

Michael Ryan's essay traces manifold references affecting *The Well-Beloved* – possible influences, biographical details, literary history, contemporary cultural and social conditions, Hardy's textual revisions and even an editor's alteration (which clearly illustrate the impermanency of the text), and formal patterns in language and allusions. His reading suggests that the argument being conducted in the novel is much along the lines sketched above. Pierston is himself a model-builder, and the novel puts his enterprise in question. He wants to make all the Avises identical through the instrument of language – by calling them all Avis. Each is an analogy of the other. But according to deconstruction, difference always obtrudes to undo the identities Pierston constructs. Ryan shows how Pierston's identities are deconstructed – by the very language which would be a vehicle of identity-making, by the movement of time, by the frailty of the human body, and so forth. Ryan suggests that Hardy is criticising prudery through Pierston. Pierston wants everything to be ideal, always the same, above actuality. So also, above sex. He never makes love to any of the Avises. What Ryan is arguing, in effect, is that Hardy has carried out a proto-critique of structuralism in the novel: Pierston is a structuralist who wants to find unity and coherence in contingent, heterogeneous phenomena. Hardy argues against the structuralist 'search' sixty years before it began.

In turn, James Kincaid appraises deconstruction itself, questioning it in a context of such meaning-seeking approaches as formalism and Northrop Frye's system of archetypes (which is based on detection of similar underlying structures over centuries of writing). Kincaid holds to the existence of meaning in literature, and offers a substitute term, 'incoherence' (various meanings occurring simultaneously), for 'indeterminacy' (lack of ascribable meaning). In using the vantage points of, but refusing to concede ground to, either formalism or deconstruction, Kincaid promotes the exigencies of practical criticism over stringent ideological purity or theoretical criticism. Equally to the point, his refusal to seek univocal theme in Hardy suggests an alternative to the denigration of Hardy as artist and thinker because of his conflicting ideas.

As I have indicated at several points, these essays represent ways to read Hardy's fiction. (They don't represent all the modes of literary analysis being practised today, of course; for example, Marxist and biographical perspectives are lacking.) They may also point the directions Hardy's reputation may take in the foreseeable future, in keeping with, as I began by remarking, developments in literary criticism and allowing for developments that, like those expressed through Guerard's and Miller's books, are not anticipatable in their application to a particular writer.

Hardy's formal uses of the narrator have long appealed to readers; and aspects of his audaciousness strike one on every rereading of a novel. For instance, the opening of *The Mayor of Casterbridge* requires the narrator to ratchet back and forth to get just the right angle on the scene: at nearly the same instant he's so distant as to have to interpret their relationship from appearances and close enough to Henchard and Susan aurally to know they are *preserving* a perfect silence. Similarly, narrators' distortions of reality, as in the dormitory scene in *Jude the Obscure*, affect in complex ways the plausibility of novels that express in general Hardy's earnest concern for the real world.

Characterisation, one of the most appreciated facets of Hardy's stories, is likely to attract reinvigorated attention. Not only special perspectives such as psychoanalysis, but more traditional, broad character studies like Casagrande's reveal a range of discontent with platitudinous responses to famous characters. Seeing Hardy's people as symbols of elements of his cosmic philosophy becomes foreign to the experience of reading their performances in their uniqueness, sensitive to the fluctuations in their immediate situations as much as to the 'great web of human doings then weaving in both hemispheres from the White Sea to Cape Horn' (*The Woodlanders*: III; p. 21). If Hardy's characters are difficult to catch in a phrase and their roles in society to place in a verbal frieze, perhaps it is because only part of his imagination saw in his characters figments of general truths. Perhaps he also saw in them and tried to reproduce all of the characteristics of the real-life persons he had in mind as the story took shape (assuming more than one-real life person served as models for each character). Perhaps his imagination was large enough to project complex characters without needing to reach for abstractions to reduce them to explainable entities. In any event, none of Hardy's great characters is condensable to a mere role. For example, Giles is figuratively

'Autumn's very brother' (XXVIII; p. 246) – a woodlands god sym-
bolising the values of an idealised way of life. But he also expresses the
not unusual combinations of a strong sex-drive with a socialised
standard of purity and concern for the public appearance of things,
self-absorption with impracticality, and an awareness of human time
in relation to the imperturbability of natural processes – all stirred to
confusion by unacceptable opportunities to elevate his sense of his
own rights above his sense of the rights of everyone else. He possesses
these traits not in a generalised but individualised manner so that it is
at once appropriate and shocking that he should passionately embrace
Grace although he knows she cannot obtain a divorce from Fitzpiers
and that he allow himself to die rather than risk tempting Grace (the
sex drive of both is so strong, evidently, as not to be able to resist the
propinquity unavoidable in a one-room hut).

Valuable historical, biographical, and textual studies are certainties;
not only the need for them but their foundations are well established.
Critical editions of *Tess of the d'Urbervilles* and *The Woodlanders* have
been undertaken by the Oxford University Press; in time perhaps
other presses will see their way to commissioning adequately edited
full series of Hardy novels. Explorations of the relationships between
Hardy's works and the ideas he was coming across in reading and
social life should accompany the publication of the manuscript
materials in the Dorset County Museum and elsewhere. A high
standard for this kind of exploration has been set by Lennart A. Björk
in the 'notes' section of his first volume of the notebooks,[6] drawn
upon in the present essays by Mary Jacobus; Hardy's *Personal
Notebooks* have been edited by Richard H. Taylor for publication by
Macmillan.[7] Studies of Hardy's revisions will provide us with
evidence of Hardy's changed concepts and of his reactions to
censorship; and we will be able to theorise more soundly about his
'creative process' once we have detailed knowledge of his rearrangements of materials and of his seized and missed opportunities. Other
sorts of benefits – especially those pertaining to interpretative cruxes
in the works – which will accrue from textual or bibliographical
study depend upon the critic's perception of connected phenomena.
Even highly impressionistic criticism – although this may seem
distant from most people's perception of bibliographical work – can
be useful to a student of texts because many of the 'rough edges' in a
Hardy novel were no doubt caused by changes of plan which he failed
to carry through at all of the necessary points. We cannot of course
alter Hardy's text to make them smoother! – but even an author's

oversights are inescapably part of our phenomenological awareness of a novel, and by recognising ambiguities that may be unintentional we may be better able to understand what Hardy was getting at in intended or at least functional ambiguities. One modest example, to add to those in Gatrell's essay: the imaginative value of old families is announced as a discovery made by Angel in Brazil (XLIX; p. 436) although Angel had earlier argued this point, 'by no means a subtle one', to his father (XXVI; p. 213). I deliberately have not studied the manuscript and authoritative versions of *Tess of the d'Urbervilles* at these passages before writing this — but obviously there will be a difference in our judgement about Hardy's intentions in playing on the ideas of longevity and continuity according to whether any revisions that may be documentable at these locations are oriented towards altering the *narrator*'s views about antiquity, or *Angel*'s.

Apart from studies based on such documentary materials that we find in manuscripts and variant readings, and apart from firm biographical details, I believe that the most valuable interpretative criticism of Hardy for some time will be characterised by uncertainty, by hypotheses outside the range of empirical evidence as final authority, and by an emphasis on the presence of the reader or critic as a — perhaps the — central hermeneutic fact. This is in keeping with the stronger trends in today's theories about literature; there is no reason to think Hardy will be exempt. In fact, with his insistence that he recorded only impressions, not convictions, in his writings, Hardy invited kinds of criticism — such as psychoanalysis, structuralism, deconstruction, phenomenology — concerned with the multiple connotations of details and the virtually limitless interconnections within a novel, and the evasiveness of a single meaning when implications are pursued with ever more pertinacious operative questions. Whatever may be the fate of reading as it affects Thomas Hardy's novels and stories, we can be confident that the novels and stories themselves will survive, to be read in ways yet unimagined.

NOTES

1. Edmund Wilson, 'Dickens: The Two Scrooges', *The Wound and the Bow* (Boston: Houghton Mifflin, 1941); Albert J. Guerard, *Thomas Hardy: The Novels and Stories* (Cambridge, Mass.: Harvard University Press, 1949). An essay which may have helped prepare readers for Guerard's book was Morton Dauwen Zabel's 'Hardy in Defense of his Art: The Aesthetic of Incongruity' in *Southern Review*, VI (1940), 125–49; rev. and rpt. in Zabel's *Craft and Character in Modern Fiction* (New York: Viking, 1957) pp. 70–96.

2. J. Hillis Miller, *Thomas Hardy: Distance and Desire* (London: Oxford University Press; Cambridge, Mass.: Harvard University Press, 1970); Perry Meisel, *Thomas Hardy: The Return of the Repressed* (New Haven and London: Yale University Press, 1972); Allan Brick, 'Paradise and Consciousness in Hardy's *Tess of the d'Urbervilles*', *NCF*, XVII (1962), 115–34; Roy Morrell, *Thomas Hardy: The Will and the Way* (Kuala Lumpur: University of Malaya Press; London: Oxford University Press, 1965); Bert Hornback, *The Metaphor of Chance: Vision and Technique in the Works of Thomas Hardy* (Athens: Ohio University Press, 1971); Jeannette King, *Tragedy in the Victorian Novel: Theory and Practice in the Novels of George Eliot, Thomas Hardy and Henry James* (Cambridge, England, and New York: Cambridge University Press, 1978); Lois Deacon and Terry Coleman, *Providence and Mr. Hardy* (London: Hutchinson, 1966); J. O. Bailey, 'Ancestral Voices in *Jude the Obscure*', in *The Classic British Novel*, ed. Howard M. Harper, Jr., and Charles Edge (Athens: University of Georgia Press, 1972) pp. 143–65; Robert Gittings, *Young Thomas Hardy* (1975) and *The Older Hardy* (1978) (London: Heinemann; Boston: Little, Brown); *The Collected Letters of Thomas Hardy*, Vol. I: *1840–1892*, ed. Richard Little Purdy and Michael Millgate (Oxford: Clarendon, 1978); J. T. Laird, *The Shaping of 'Tess of the d'Urbervilles'* (Oxford: Clarendon, 1975); J. I. M. Stewart, *Thomas Hardy: A Critical Biography* (London: Longman, 1971); Michael Millgate, *Thomas Hardy: His Career as a Novelist* (London: The Bodley Head; New York: Random House, 1971); David DeLaura, '"The Ache of Modernism" in Hardy's Later Novels', *ELH*, XXXIV (1967), 380–99.

3. In the paragraphs following in the text, brief descriptions of the general approaches used in the essays express my own understanding of the critics' methods. In a few cases I have woven into my commentary authors' glosses about their essays occurring in letters to me; I owe special thanks to Michael Ryan. But I have used their self-descriptions only as I felt appropriate. In other words, any inconsistencies that may be felt between the essays and my remarks on them are my responsibility, not the critics'.

4. Stanley E. Fish, 'Literature in the Reader: Affective Stylistics', in *Self-Consuming Artifacts: The Experience of Seventeenth-Century Literature* (Berkeley, Los Angeles, London: University of California Press, 1972) p. 406.

5. Claude Lévi-Strauss, 'The Structural Study of Myth' (1955), *Structural Anthropology*, trans. Claire Jacobson and Brooke Grundfest Schoepf (1963; rpt. New York: Doubleday Anchor, 1967) pp. 202–28; Roland Barthes, 'Myth Today' (1957), in *Mythologies*, trans. Annette Lavers (London: Jonathan Cape, 1972) pp. 109–58; Michel Foucault, *Discipline and Punish: The Birth of the Prison* (1975), trans. Alan Sheridan (London: Allen Lane, 1977).

6. *The Literary Notes of Thomas Hardy*, Vol. I, ed. Lennart A. Björk (Göteborg, Sweden: Acta Universitatis Gothoburgensis, 1974).

7. *The Personal Notebooks of Thomas Hardy*, ed. Richard H. Taylor (London: Macmillan, 1979).

2 Beginnings and Endings in Hardy's Major Fiction

DANIEL R. SCHWARZ

What we call the beginning is often the end.
T. S. Eliot, 'Little Gidding', *Four Quartets*

Because of the length of a novel, our memory of it is disproportionately related to its opening and ending. In the opening chapters, the narrator creates for his readers the physical world in which the novel takes place and the first episodes of the story which begin to reveal the personalities of the characters. But more significantly, beginnings introduce the novel's cosmology and the standards and values by which actions will be judged. (Of course, since the reading of a novel is an ongoing process, as the reader experiences subsequent episodes, the moral terms on which the reader makes his or her judgement will be modified.) Each novel has its own Genesis and Apocalypse; when we open a novel, our world is closed off and the genesis of a new ontology begins. The opening chapters of the novel, that form which more than any other seeks to have the inclusiveness and specificity of the real world, mimes the process of Creation as the author's language imposes shape and form upon silence and emptiness. Imperceptibly, as we read the first sentences, our sense of time gives way to the internal imagined time of the novel. The ending is an apocalypse which reorders the significance of all that precedes; it is the moment when the imagined world is abruptly sealed off from us and we return to our diurnal activities.[1]

If, as I believe is true, on the first reading of a Hardy novel one has a sense that he has anticipated and almost experienced actions that occur for the first time, it is because Hardy has created a world where actions seem inevitable. Hardy's prophetic (and proleptic) openings in which every detail seems to foreshadow major themes, in conjunction with conclusions that confirm these openings, are responsible for this sense of inevitability. The openings take the reader into a world where man's aspirations are blunted, as external circumstances connive with man's hidden flaws, and where the well-meaning characters rapidly discover that they live in a world in which things are quite likely to turn out badly. By 'fulfilling' the promise of the beginnings, the endings imply that the world in which men live is closed and invulnerable to essential change. The title of Tess's last phase, 'Fulfilment', implies, I think, something about Hardy's world-view and aesthetic. By fulfilment, he means the inevitable bringing to fruition of the pattern that derives from the interaction of the central character's psyche with the world in which he (or she) is placed. After *Far from the Madding Crowd*, the endings fulfil the prophecies of the opening chapters. The ingredients of the destruction of central characters are implicit in the novels' beginnings. That the language, plot, and narrative comment of the opening are frequently echoed throughout, especially at the ending, enchances this sense of in-evitability. When the reader reaches the ending of a Hardy novel, it is as if a prophecy were fulfilled. Hardy's endings perpetuate conditions that have prevailed before his specific narrative has begun and will prevail as given conditions of the imagined world in which these events take place. Turning away from a traditional benevolent resolution, Hardy's endings confirm rather than transfigure what precedes and reject the notion that experience brings wisdom and maturity.

After *Far from the Madding Crowd*, 'fulfilment' of the novel becomes 'fulfilment' of the pattern of a character's demise; this fulfilment is ironically juxtaposed to the narrative that the protagonist tells himself in the form of hopes and aspirations for the future. As Hardy's career progresses, the central character's perspective re-plicates the narrator's at an earlier and earlier stage in the novels. Hence the ironic distance between the narrator and character disappears and the narrator becomes an empathetic spokesman, an apologist, and an advocate for those central characters whom he envisions to be victims. The gradual movement from innocence to experience that is so characteristic of English fiction before Hardy (except, perhaps, *Wuthering Heights* and *Tristram Shandy*) is, in Hardy, far less noticeable than the intensification of the central character's plight and the narrator's conclusion that the cosmos is antagonistic. The most significant movement is not the development of the central character's moral awareness, but the dwindling of his expectations and the consequent loss of mental and emotional vitality.

Hardy is the first English novelist who wholeheartedly rejects the conventional Christian myth of a benevolent universe. He shows the irrelevance of that myth within his imagined world and shows how his characters are educated by experience to adopt an alternative one. As a self-dramatising character who is a sceptical, gloomy, fatalistic presence, Hardy's narrator is an immanent presence whose pessimistic philosophical comments and bitterly ironic narration the reader feels on every page.[2] Hardy creates a malevolent world in which characters live not in light which is good, but in moral darkness which is bad. In an 1890 journal entry, he writes, 'I have been looking for God 50 years, and I think that if he had existed I should have discovered him. As an external personality, of course – the only true meaning of the word.'[3] Hardy's creation of a blighted star is his response to the premise that God's creation is a holy plan.[4] It is also his response to those Romantics and Victorians who, as M. H. Abrams remarks, fuse 'history, politics, and philosophy, and religion into one grand design by asserting Providence – or some form of natural teleology – to operate in the seeming chaos of human history so as to effect from present evil a greater good'.[5]

Hardy's novels are in part a response to the biblical myth of benevolent creation directed by a just and beneficent God. If only to correct the notion that Hardy 'wrote a fiction which presumed a commission to write about the world as he found it',[6] we should think of Hardy in the tradition of Blake and Lawrence, other great mythologisers who create their own world with its own rules and traditions. Hardy goes beyond mimetic narrative and presents a genuine anti-Genesis myth that exists beyond the usual nominalistic particularised world of fiction. Hardy's novels question the central postulates of the Christian cosmology by positing an imagined world where man cannot achieve salvation in a benevolent world created under the auspices of a just and merciful God. In the Wessex novels, Hardy's narrator is at times a ubiquitous, omniscient prophet who, anticipating Lawrence in *The Rainbow*, 'Present, Past, & Future, sees'.[7] After *Far from the Madding Crowd*, Hardy's prophecy of disaster contrasts with the biblical prophecy of the second coming of the Messiah, as well as with man's conventional expectation that his fictions will be fulfilled. Fulfilment in the biblical myth depends upon the Messiah, the Last Judgment, and the release of the eternal soul at death. But Hardy, although he liked to think of himself as a meliorist, creates a cosmos where moral improvement is ineffectual and spiritual improvement is impossible.

The opening chapters of the first of the major Wessex novels, *Far from the Madding Crowd* (1874), present a pastoral world and simultaneously invalidate the pastoral myth. These chapters are a kind of prologue in which the traditional pastoral world is de-mythologised as Gabriel, who had once seemed a 'pastoral king', becomes aware of the indifference of the cosmos to man's aspirations (VI; p. 43). In the early chapters, the narrator is divided between, on the one hand, nostalgically elegising rural life and comparing it favourably with urban life, and on the other, somewhat reluctantly acknowledging that the distinctions between town and country often prove apocryphal. But the first chapters illustrate that Bathsheba is as proud, vain, and emotionally self-indulgent as any townswoman might be. After presenting Gabriel's seeming idyllic existence as a shepherd, the narrator shows how the misfortunes of losing his sheep, near-suffocation, and disappointment in love permanently disrupt the illusion that place or profession can imply value. The memorable simile with which the novel opened (in which the 'diverging wrinkles' of his smile extended 'upon his countenance like the rays in a rudimentary sketch of the rising sun' [I; p. 1]) is no longer possible. The narrator registers Gabriel's instinctive non-verbal apprehension that the world is not what he thought it was. Gabriel's perception of the external scene after losing his sheep not only mirrors his internal state, but enables the narrator to provide an alternative to the pastoral myth: 'The pool glittered like a dead man's eye, and as the world awoke a breeze blew, shaking and elongating the reflection of the moon without breaking it, and turning the image of the star to a phosphoric streak upon the water. All this Oak saw and remembered' (V; p. 41).

Gabriel's sense of isolation and his concomitant instinctive movement towards an 'other' that will complete himself show the inadequacy and irrelevance of the pastoral myth to the particular needs of man in the nineteenth century: 'Having for some time known the want of a satisfactory form to fill an increasing void within him, his position moreover affording the widest scope for his fancy, he painted her a beauty' (II; p. 16). In this passage, Hardy identifies the underlying motive and often dimly acknowledged effective cause of every relationship in his Wessex novels. Lacking the sense of an

immanent, comprehending God, man seeks a responsive consciousness which he fictionalises upon the slightest evidence into an
omniscient, ubiquitous *alter ego*.

The marriage with which *Far from the Madding Crowd* ends is
hardly a fulfilment of what precedes. 'Fulfilment' of the *characters'*
aspirations occurs because the ending does not fulfil the pattern of the
opening and of subsequent episodes in which the possibility of idyllic
life has been evolved, treated, and discarded. As in an Austen or
Fielding novel, the central male and female characters marry,
presumably conditioned by society and modified by personal
experience. Hardy has not defined either an alternative cosmology to
the discredited pastoral myth or the traditional novel of manners with
its marriage and implied happy future; nor has he invented the formal
principles that will mime a new cosmology. In the early chapters,
Gabriel had been an unsuccessful fictionalist, unable to impose a form
on the recalcitrant material of his life. But ironically, after he passively
accepts his isolation, Bathsheba's visit and their subsequent marriage
fulfil the narrative that the central character had told himself. This
kind of fulfilment will no longer occur after *Far from the Madding
Crowd*. While the opening chapters dramatise Bathsheba's repeated
intrusion into Gabriel's consciousness and her subsequent rejection of
his suit, the ending (especially Chapter LVI) focuses on the intrusion of
Gabriel (who had suppressed his hopes in the face of social and
economic differences) into Bathsheba's consciousness. Not quite so
shy, diffident, and self-effacing, Gabriel has learned how to spar
with Bathsheba and how to monitor her solipsistic tendency to
create her own reality. Reversing the interview in which he has proposed, it is she who is the petitioner, claiming and believing that it
is merely her fear that she has offended him that brings her to his
cottage.

What is different from an Austen novel is that after Troy is dead
and Boldwood is imprisoned, Bathsheba, like Lydia in *The Rainbow*,
responds to a deeper physiological self beneath the conscious self:
'Bathsheba was stirred by emotions which latterly she had assumed to
be altogether dead within her' (LVI; p. 448). Bathsheba, who believes
herself a person of principle, is, in fact, a chameleonic character whose
constancy and stability are still very much in doubt. Bathsheba
foreshadows Hardy's mature belief that a man or a woman cannot
know his or her own psychosexual needs. Her behaviour discredits
the myth of moral education which the ending implies. The marriage
takes place within the context of a world where triumphs are

evanescent and where external circumstances – fire, storm, death – perpetually threaten to prevent the kind of resolution we find in an Austen or Fielding novel. The resolution of their love in marriage exists side by side with Joseph Poorgrass' closing comment: 'But since 'tis as 'tis, why, it might have been worse, and I feel my thanks accordingly' (LVII; p. 464). Our memory of Fanny Robin's tragedy, Troy's moral idiocy, Boldwood's madness, and Bathsheba's fickleness is stirred by that remark and makes us keenly aware that there is no idyllic life in *Far from the Madding Crowd*. 'Fulfilment' in such a world cannot but be ephemeral.

The opening of *The Return of the Native* (1878) presents the Genesis of the Wessex novels, the refutation of the Christian creation myth, and the proposal of an alternative one. Although in later novels the cosmos will become actively antagonistic, rather than merely indifferent, the heath contains the essential ingredients of the cosmos in which the Wessex novels take place. Its eternality and passivity are juxtaposed to the unrest and temporality of man. Although man has gradually emerged from 'Druidical rites and Saxon ceremonies' into the nineteenth century, the heath remains the same, and its permanence and monotony satirise the vanity of man: 'A person on a heath in raiment of modern cut and colours has more or less an anomalous look. We seem to want the oldest and simplest human clothing where the clothing of the earth is so primitive' (I, I; p. 6). By evoking Genesis in conjunction with the classical myth of Prometheus' rebellion, Hardy creates an alternative vision in which alienation and refusal to submit are plausible and dignified positions: 'Moreover to light a fire is the instinctive and resistant act of man when, at the winter ingress, the curfew is sounded throughout Nature. It indicates a spontaneous, Promethean rebelliousness against the fiat that this recurrent season shall bring foul times, cold darkness, misery and death. Black chaos comes, and the fettered gods of the earth say, Let there be light' (I, III; pp. 17–18). Throughout human history, mankind has organised community rites and rituals as an instinctive response to the world: 'The flames from funeral piles long ago kindled there. . . . Festival fires to Thor and Woden had followed on the same ground and duly had their day' (I, III; p. 17). As surely as those primitives who first lit a fire, the narrator is struggling with the effort to bring light to what for him threatens to become black chaos. In his effort to comprehend how to impose linguistic form on the illimitable heath, Hardy's narrator describes the heath as if it were alive: 'The place became full of a watchful intentness now;

for when other things sank brooding to sleep the heath appeared slowly to awake and listen' (I, 1; p. 4).

Paradoxically, the heath is not only a metaphor for the cosmos, but it mirrors mankind's common internal chaos: 'It was found to be the hitherto unrecognized original of those wild regions of obscurity which are vaguely felt to be compassing us about in midnight dreams of flight and disaster, and are never thought of after the dream till revived by scenes like this' (I, 1; pp. 5–6). As civilisation's enemy, as the scene of primitive rites and ceremonies, as 'the untameable, Ishmaelitish thing that Egdon now was [and] it always had been,' the heath corresponds to the atavistic and instinctive darker self which is within each of us (I, 1; p. 6). Not unlike Conrad's Congo, something within the heath summons man back to his primordial origins when passions were uncontrolled, when the pace of life was slower, and when the moral distinctions of ordinary life seemed anachronistic if not irrelevant. If the heath is what Auden would think of as a *paysage moralisé* for uncontrolled fantasies and undisciplined passion, then it is a fitting setting for the libidinous energy of Eustacia Vye, whose presence appropriately 'fulfils' the scenes.

The ending fulfils the prophecies of the beginning. Clym dupli- cates the narrator as a modern consciousness who understands the distinction between man's aspirations and the circumstances of his life. In *The Return of the Native*, unlike *Far from the Madding Crowd*, the plots that circumstances make of men's lives are incongruous with the fictions they tell themselves. Our last views of Clym are not of a man who has triumphed, but of one who has been defeated. Seemingly without passion or vitality after Eustacia's death, he is rather anxious lest Thomasin should propose to him. In an interesting anticipation of Paul Morel in *Sons and Lovers*, he is as dominated by his mother after her death as he had been before it and seems unable to cast off his sense of guilt for not preventing her death. Diggory and Clym change places; he becomes the Ishmaelite of the heath, and Diggory re-enters the community. When, as preacher, Clym takes Eustacia's place on Rainbarrow he is hardly an heroic figure. Clym has learned what the narrator knows: 'That old-fashioned revelling in the general situation grows less and less possible as we uncover the defects of natural laws, and see the quandary that man is in by their operation' (III, 1; p. 197). Clym's preaching is limited and self- indulgent. Yet, paradoxically, when Clym, the modern conscious- ness with whom the narrator empathises, acts upon this insight and willingly accepts his fate, he earns Hardy's ire. Hardy has become impatient with Clym's obsession with his mother, his passive and querulous response to vicissitude, and the surrender of his identity to Eustacia, his mother, and the heath. Surely, the emphasis on the penultimate sentence is upon his ineffectuality as a preacher: 'Some believed him, and some believed not; some said that his words were commonplace, others complained of his want of theological doctrine; while others again remarked that it was well enough for a man to take to preaching who could not see to do anything else' (VI, IV; p. 485).

The Mayor of Casterbridge (1886) begins by positing a world where civilisation's conventions and moral reason are in a state of suspension and where anything is possible. Before the reader is told anything much about the family that is introduced trudging to Weydon-Priors in an indefinite year 'before the nineteenth century had reached one-third of its span' (I; p. 1), the narrator describes a grotesque bargain: a drunken man sells his wife to the highest bidder. Such characters as the 'haggish' furmity woman and the 'short man, with a nose resembling a copper knob . . . and eyes like button-holes' take us into a nightmare world in which grotesque characters are depicted as cartoons which illuminate as they distort (I; pp. 5, 10). Gradually, the scene becomes transformed into something so strained and charged that a swallow who accidentally wanders in desperately wants to escape as if he, too, were shocked by the enormity of the horror. That his wife's misgivings are described as 'bird-like chirpings' equates her with the harmless swallow which escapes the tent and with the innocent bird which sings 'a trite old evening song' at Weydon-Priors 'for centuries untold' (I; pp. 6, 9, 3). In this atavistic scene, Henchard ritualistically casts off his wife as if she were the evil influence that has caused what he regards as his miserable plight.

The second chapter depicts the fetishistic effort of the still anonymous man to reverse his fatal act. Already the fabular ontology gives way to a nominalistic particular world. By Chapter III, Susan is embarked on the hopeless path of trying to reverse the past eighteen years, and the Walpurgisnacht atmosphere of the Weydon-Priors fair has entirely vanished. We are back in a world of shame, guilt, and recognisable motive. We begin to perceive that a sado-masochistic husband responds to unconscious psychic stimuli that he cannot even acknowledge, let alone understand. The restraint in Henchard's search for his wife ('a certain shyness of revealing his conduct prevented Michael Henchard from following up the investigation with the loud hue-and-cry such a pursuit demanded to render it effectual' [II; p. 19]) ironically anticipates the practical considerations invoked by Elizabeth-Jane and Farfrae when they plan to abandon their search for Henchard in the last chapter because a very slight financial sacrifice is called for.

In many ways, despite the conclusive ending of the plot of *The Mayor of Casterbridge*, the novel leaves unresolved its moral implications. Henchard's demise and the marriage of Farfrae and Elizabeth-Jane would seem finally to restrain and resolve the concatenation of events set in motion by Henchard's selling of his wife. Set against this consummate act of social anarchy by a man of unrestrained passion is the marriage of two people who have opted for traditional community values. But nevertheless the resolution is equivocal. For one thing, the novel comes full circle and makes Henchard, who had borne throughout the onus of moral opprobrium, the object of considerable compassion. When as a lonely man he reverses his journey of twenty-five years earlier, walking from Casterbridge to Weydon-Priors 'as an act of penance' (XLIV; p. 368), he engages our sympathy. Like Eliot's Bulstrode and Conrad's Jim, who continually experience a harrowing past as if it were the present, Henchard becomes obsessed with his past. His effort to leave the country is thwarted not only by his love for his stepdaughter but by a desire to humiliate himself hardly less strong than his earlier atavistic need to humiliate his wife. He decides to go to the wedding even though the likelihood of rejection is great. When Elizabeth-Jane unforgivingly rebukes him, he lacks the self-esteem to defend himself. As the novel progresses and as the punishment seems more and more disproportionate to Henchard's crime, the novel celebrates the magnitude of Henchard's immoderate and irrational emotions. Elizabeth-Jane's emotional balance and moderation are surely a comment on Henchard's, but his intense feeling in the closing chapters becomes a comment on our last impression of her. When she obeys his will and avoids the 'mournful pleasure' of an elaborate funeral, we cannot forget how easy it is for her to submit passively to social norms or personal idiosyncracies, and to tailor her emotions to fit the circumstances. Her perspective throughout is defined by her emotional limitations; recall how she had immediately felt a kinship with Farfrae, and created him into a fantasy *alter ego* on the flimsiest of evidence.

The closing remarks radically shift our sympathy towards the man that the narrative had discarded and emphasise the ironic nature of the resolution in which Farfrae and Elizabeth-Jane marry:

As the lively and sparkling emotions of her early married life cohered into an equable serenity, the finer movements of her nature found scope in discovering to the narrow-lived ones around her the secret (as she had once learnt it) of making *limited* opportunities endurable; which she deemed to consist in the cunning enlargement, by a species of microscopic treatment, of those *minute* forms of satisfaction that offer themselves to everybody not in positive pain; which, thus *handled*, have much of the same inspiriting effect upon life as wider interests cursorily embraced. (XLV; p. 385: emphasis mine)

The circumlocutious syntax, the emphasis on the limited and minute nature of these pleasures, her reliance on *cunning* enlargement of these emotions, and the comparison of her pleasures not to more substantive pleasures but to those pleasures that are '*cursorily* embraced' – all these demonstrate that the means by which she achieves her triumph and her 'unbroken tranquillity' (XLV; p. 386) question the desirability of that tranquillity as an end in itself. But Hardy wants us to see that *her* view is not that of the novel's dramatised experience. The alternative to Henchard's violation of social and moral norms need not be passive submission to whatever life brings and adoption of conventional morality. Elizabeth-Jane's final values are not those of Hardy. While Elizabeth-Jane's perspective parallels the narrator's for a time, she lacks the breadth of feeling, passionate intensity, and imaginative energy that are implied as alternatives to her final position.

Hardy patronises Elizabeth-Jane's bourgeois upward mobility from her first appearance as a young woman: 'The desire – sober and repressed – of Elizabeth-Jane's heart was indeed to see, to hear, and to understand. How could she become a woman of wider knowledge, higher repute – "better," as she termed it – this was her constant inquiry of her mother' (IV; p. 28). The novel concludes by the narrator presenting the views of someone who has experienced disappointment, and who because of this will accept willingly whatever comes her way since she felt 'happiness was but the occasional episode in a general drama of pain' (XLV; p. 386). But the narrator does not embrace passivity and stoicism. While in the opening chapter he had acknowledged man's potential for 'wilful hostilities' (p. 13) and shown its consequences, he increasingly protests against the nature of the cosmos which arouses man's expectations only to blunt them. If *The Mayor of Casterbridge* begins as Hardy's version of *Paradise Lost* where man is responsible for the evil in which he lives, it ends by affirming that whatever man's shortcomings, the cosmos is unjust to his aspirations.

The Woodlanders (1887) depicts a world in which moral and physical decay is rampant. Hardy posits the possibility that the world will gradually wear itself out. Nature is engaged in a melancholy struggle for survival within the woodlands: 'The trees dripped on the garden plots, where no vegetables would grow for the dripping, though they were planted year after year with that curious mechanical regularity of country people in the face of hopelessness' (XVII; p. 144). The fermenting cider, the 'scene of decay' from the 'perishing leaves', and the moths 'decrepit from late season' convey a sense of nature's disintegration. The struggle for survival intensifies on occasion to a macabre process in which one species seems to devour another: 'Owls that had been catching mice in the outhouses, rabbits that had been eating the winter-greens in the gardens, and stoats that had been sucking the blood of the rabbits . . . were seen and heard no more till nightfall' (IV; p. 24). Mrs Charmond and Fitzpiers unconsciously subscribe to a kind of sexual Darwinism by which those with strong sexual drives and few scruples manipulate and prey upon the weak in the interests of their own emotional gratification. Implicit in the narrator's perspective is a Darwinistic view that one creature lives off another. The desperation for human connection derives from each major character's understanding, based on his own experience, that he is involved in a pervasive struggle for physical or emotional survival. In the world of *The Woodlanders*, one person's emotional satisfactions and relationships are at the expense of someone else who is left excluded, suffering, or discarded. Just as Marty suffers from her inability to have Giles, Giles suffers from the loss of Grace and Grace suffers from Fitzpiers' desertion.

The road to Hintock seems to be a path not simply to a place but to an intensely melancholy and pessimistic state of mind. The narrator is the dramatised expression of that state of mind; he notices that 'the bleared white visage of a sunless winter day emerged like a dead-born child' (IV; p. 24). The spot on which the narrator first meditates is marked by 'tomb-like stillness', 'emptiness', and solitude (I; p. 1). The narrator's rhetorical effort to escalate a tale that is more bathetic than sublime to the level of classical Sophoclean tragedy derives from his desire to universalise the events that take place in Hintock.

The nostalgia that informs the narrator's every word is for an agrarian culture that has been displaced by the social pretensions of

Grace and her father and the emotional self-indulgence of Fitzpiers and Mrs Charmond. The corruption of an ancient way of life is to be a major motif. The first chapter of *The Woodlanders* dramatises the intrusion into Little Hintock of the pretensions and superfluities of urban life in the person of the barber who wants Marty South's hair for a wig. His intrusion foreshadows the continuing movement into Hintock of extrinsic social values and emotional and intellectual subtleties. Had Grace not been educated to patronise Giles's manners, she might have been satisfied married to him. Fitzpiers imports Byronic cynicism and worldliness into Hintock, contributing to the destruction of Grace's potential and the unhappiness of Giles and Melbury. Sophistication is anathema to the way of life epitomised by the straight-talking ingenuous Giles and the faithful, diligent Marty South, both of whom, while often self-conscious about their personal lives, can immerse themselves in their world and seem to have 'intelligent discourse with Nature' (XLIV; p. 399).

Whether it will be the simpler need of Marty or the rococo emotions of Fitzpiers and Mrs Charmond, the narrative gives validity to Fitzpiers' observation: 'Human love is a subjective thing − . . . it is joy accompanied by an idea which we project against any suitable object in the line of our vision' (XVI; p. 138). With each passing novel, the final marriage becomes a more ironic resolution, and human relationships become more strained. The conclusion shows how people desperately apotheosise those who reject their love. Ironically commenting upon how people will seek in personal relations surrogates for religious certainty, Hardy uses religious language to describe personal commitments at the close of *The Woodlanders*. The very name of Grace enables Hardy to play on the irony of the atheist Fitzpiers' quest for Grace's love: 'He longed for the society of Grace. But to lay offerings on her slighted altar was his first aim, and until her propitiation was complete he would constrain her in no way to return to him' (XLV; p. 407). The dénouement takes place under Timothy Tangs's eye rather than the Divine Eye that Grace hopes is blessing their relationship.[8]

To emphasise the disjunction between human events and the myth of a benevolent God directing events, the iterative plot stresses the impossibility of men's progress. The customs and values introduced by those exposed to urban life and those who have been highly educated demean rather than improve the quality of life among the woodlanders. The process of decay has extended to virtually every human relationship. The return of Grace to Fitzpiers,

given Fitzpiers' chameleonic nature and the clear implication that the
wooing of Grace is another demonstration that he is an emotional
gourmand, is the antithesis to the equilibrium achieved by a healthy
marriage. Melbury understands that this marriage is an emotional
disease and implies that their rapprochement may be another stage of
a macabre cycle: 'It's a forlorn hope for her; and God knows how it
will end!' (XLVIII; p. 440). Finally, the narrative returns to Marty
living in isolation. However, she is now encapsulated within her own
fictive world that is impervious to reality. Not only she, but the rural
culture that she represents have become anachronisms. The scene
where Marty stands over Giles's grave has perverse, even necrophiliac
overtones. There is a touch of fanatical madness in the final words of
this 'solitary and silent girl' who seems to have suffered 'continued
compression' like the legendary Chinese toys said to have been made
from human beings (XLVIII [p. 443]; VII [p. 60]). 'If ever I forget your
name let me forget home and heaven! . . . But no, no, my love, I can
never forget 'ee; for you was a good man, and did good things!'
(XLVIII; p. 444). She finds her fulfilment in the death of her beloved
when she can apotheosise him as her patron saint and finally possess
him.

In *Tess of the d'Urbervilles* (1891), Hardy creates a world in which
mankind seems to be devolving morally. The focus of the opening
chapter is the decline of the d'Urberville family. The chapter
introduces the theme of moral and physical decline and stresses how
modern life and its social and economic ramifications are affecting the
moral fabric of the folk culture. Apparently, man's consciousness (but
not his moral intelligence) has evolved to the point where even the
ordinary folk recognise the malevolent cosmology in which they
live and suffer acutely from that recognition. For Hardy, Tess is immune to conventional moral judgements because her motives are
beyond reproach. Finally, the freshness and vitality of her body seem
the most natural and instinctive aspect of the world in which she
lives. In no prior Hardy novel has the central character discovered
the nature of the world's quality before the action begins. The adolescent Tess and her younger brother anticipate Jude in perceiving
the disjunction between man's aspirations and the nature of
things.

Hardy's blood imagery (of which the characters are unaware)
intensifies the reader's sense of a creation where evil and darkness
proliferate. That Tess alone of the May Day walkers wears a red
ribbon and has a 'pouted-up deep red mouth' and that Prince's 'life's

blood' spouts from his injured breast and splashes Tess with 'crimson drops' subtly prefigures the breaking of Tess's hymen and her killing Alec (II [p. 13]; IV [p. 35]). In this world, innocuous details and mildly unsettling events are likely to foreshadow the most dire consequences. The prick on her chin from the rose anticipates the later violation which in turn anticipates the pool of blood created by her stabbing Alec – her desperate subconscious effort to revenge the original rape. No sooner does she consume the strawberries from Alec's hand than the bitterly ironic voice comments: 'Tess Durbeyfield did not divine . . . that there behind the blue narcotic haze was potentially the "tragic mischief" of her drama – one who stood fair to be the blood-red ray in the spectrum of her young life' (V; p. 47).

From the first encounter with Alec, Tess's world is a completely closed system where the plots she creates for herself inevitably remain unfulfilled fantasies. The final phase of *Tess of the d'Urbervilles* is entitled 'Fulfilment' to describe Tess's relationship with Angel and to comment ironically on its timing and brevity. The ephemeral nature of that relationship shows that man does indeed live on a blighted star and fulfils the expectations aroused by the novel's opening. We may recall Tess's perception that the wind (and Hardy might have added Nature's plan) is no more morally significant than 'the sigh of some immense sad soul, conterminous with the universe in space, and with history in time' (IV; p. 34). Her adolescent insight has been confirmed by the narrative. Even during their idyllic reunion, Angel does not recognise the quality of Tess's moral being, believing that it resulted from her 'moral sense' being 'extinguished' and from an 'aberration' 'in the d'Urberville blood' (LVII; p. 492). Tess might desperately wish for immortality in Liza-Lu's relationship with Angel. But the reader understands the pathos and desperation of this psychological need, and realises that Angel and Tess are participating in another futile effort to forestall the inexorable passing away of the d'Urberville family. Since the narrator has sympathetically traced Tess's attempt to be herself despite the accretion of family and personal history that keeps trying to shape her, the notion of Angel's transferring his love to her sister is bathetic. Such a mechanical transference of human affection characterises the stimulus-response, cause-effect of sociological determinism from which Tess has been trying to escape. Angel and Tess poignantly try to perpetuate her life through Liza because neither believes in the orthodox view that their reborn souls will meet in heaven. If Tess cannot escape the family history, why should we think that Angel and Liza-Lu are unencumbered by the onus of this new d'Urberville ignominy?

The juxtaposition of Angel's and Liza-Lu's final prayers with the previous scene at Stonehenge where Tess had been lying on the pagan altar stresses the impotence of traditional religion to forestall the 'inexorable'. Christianity can no more save Tess than the Druids could prevent their demise by their pagan rites. Since the massacre of the Innocent has social sanction Tess might as well have been a human sacrifice at the Druid altar. Hasn't the blood imagery prefigured her ritualistic death? When the narrator describes Liza-Lu and Angel as resembling 'Giotto's "Two Apostles"' and as 'bent . . . as if in prayer' (LIX; pp. 507, 508), he is ironically recalling not only Angel's erratic piety, but their need to embrace the kind of formalism that sentences Tess to death. The experience of the novel has shown that neither Druid pillar nor Christian belief provides the shelter 'from the wind' that Tess seeks before she is caught (LVIII; p. 502). Finally, Hardy's evocation of Aeschylus' 'President of the Immortals' deliberately proposes a pagan myth as an alternative to the discredited myth of the benevolent creator and the equally invalid myths of Apocalypse and human salvation (LIX; p. 508).

The first four chapters of *Jude the Obscure* (1895) are among the great openings in the English novel. In these chapters Hardy dramatises a young boy's discovery of the moral and metaphysical geography of the hostile world in which he lives. The purpose of the early chapters is to show that Jude's experience is universal rather than particular and idiosyncratic. The world in which Jude and Sue live does not *permit* fulfilment. Virtually every character's foreboding of evil is fulfilled, while hopes, dreams, and emotional and economic needs are not. That there is an inevitable disjunction between what a man would like to be and what he is, is the central philosophic premise of the narrator and the major metaphysical tenet of the novel's world.

Within the major novels, the time comes earlier and earlier when the characters begin to discover that there is a discrepancy between their narrative and the nature of the not-I world. By the age of eleven Jude knows that world in which he lives is antagonistic. In a rare moment of insight, Jude prematurely discovers the capriciousness of nature's logic when he is humiliatingly spanked for feeding the birds that he is supposed to chase off:

Events did not rhyme quite as he had thought. Nature's logic was too horrid for him to care for. That mercy towards one set of creatures was cruelty towards another sickened his sense of harmony. As you got older, and felt yourself to be at the centre of your time, and not a point in its circumference, as you had felt when you were little, you were seized with a sort of shuddering, he perceived. All around you there seemed to be something glaring, garish, rattling, and the noises and glares hit upon the little cell called your life, and shook it, and warped it. (I, II; p. 15)

Jude's melancholy is no mere childish moment, but encapsulates the narrator's mature wisdom, which shapes the entire telling and to which the latter had presumably been brought by adult experience. Jude seems to have prematurely reached an end. Jude anticipates not only his final death-wish, but the vision that caused Father Time to end his own life and that of his siblings. Yet, finally the biological, physiological self beneath Jude's modern consciousness recoils from this insight. Nevertheless, the momentary stasis, the 'fulfilment' reached even before his adolescence begins, remains a position to which the reader reverts. The boy's initial response is validated as Jude's aspirations are continually blunted by a combination of his psychic needs, a hostile social and economic structure, and the remorseless cosmology in which things inevitably turn out badly. While Jude's dreams are filled with scholarship and religion, his instincts respond to the tawdry sensuality of Arabella and his psyche to the sado-masochism of Sue.

Phillotson is as much Jude's double as Sue is. Phillotson anticipates Jude in the way he ambitiously formulates imprecise and ephemeral plans which he has little hope of fulfilling. Phillotson is a prototype of Jude as a hopeful, aspiring man trying to improve himself who when faced with unanticipated difficulty in mastering a hoped-for skill – such as playing a piano or getting an education – subsequently becomes disillusioned. He shares not only Jude's enthusiasm for learning, but his inconsistency and masochism. In the first chapter, Phillotson is leaving Marygreen, as Jude will years later, for the purpose of getting a university education so that he can be ordained. When Jude subsequently fictionalises Christminster into the new Jerusalem, it is in part because the one person who treats him like a human being has gone there. His efforts to create Phillotson into a father-figure reflect his isolation and loneliness. But Phillotson, like Jude, cannot fulfil his dreams; rather, he fulfils his intrinsic character and position in Marygreen. The correlative to Jude's desire to be upwardly mobile in professional and educational terms is his bent for travel. Hardy's novels show that when one moves from place to place, one cannot leave one's self behind. They debunk the Protestant myth of self-improvement that pervades English fiction since Defoe. Within a Hardy novel physical movement for a purpose, whether it be Clym's movement to Paris, Tess's in search of her relatives, or Jude's to Christminster, is ironic. The linear movement of the narrative – whether from beginning to end or from episode to episode – confirms that one's character rarely is changed fundamentally by experience.

That Jude remarries Arabella in an alcoholic stupor shows that he has not enlarged himself sufficiently to avoid compulsively repeating the past.[9] While his views remain enlightened, and consistently reflect what he has learned, his character and behaviour do not reflect personal growth. Whether he was intoxicated or not, his remarrying Arabella is the manifestation of his own self-destructive and masochistic strains and is hardly less pathological than Sue's conduct. He cannot leave Arabella because he has lost his will to live. Jude intuitively understands the parallelism of their fate and the mutual disintegration of their mental and moral energy. Widow Edlin's remark 'Weddings be funerals' applies to both of them (VI, IX; p. 481). Fanatically and obsessively, they both embrace their own destruction. Jude's quoting Job (who unlike Jude eventually rallied from despair) is an ineffectual exercise in self-pity. His willingness to die and his abandonment of principle are the fulfilment of his boyhood perception of 'nature's logic'.

The iterative structure – the remarriages, the return to Marygreen, the final interview between Gillingham and Phillotson, and the presence of Vilbert at the end – mimes man's fundamental inability to improve himself morally or spiritually. Jude and Sue reiterate the perverse errors of the past in their remarriage to those who are completely wrong for them. These remarriages – just as Father Time's fanatic and psychotic intensification of Jude's perceptions – underline the progressive diminution of man's stature in Hardy's novels. (In Tess of the d'Urbervilles, at least the title character retained her moral identity, even if she committed a murder.) Arabella's and Vilbert's survival, while better people are driven to neurotic and compulsive remarriage, madness, and death, reinforces our impression of man's devolution.

If The Rainbow is Lawrence's Bible, perhaps we should think of the Wessex novels as Hardy's Bible. Like Kafka and Lawrence, he intensifies some aspects of the world and distorts others to such an extent that he presents an alternative cosmology with its own mode of operation. His cosmos is not a benevolent pattern, moving towards the fulfilment of a divine plan in which the Apocalypse will bring the Heavenly kingdom to deserving souls, but is, to use Conrad's term, 'a remorseless process'.[10] Beginnings and endings 'rhyme' in Hardy's 'plan', but in a way which often makes it seem as if man were the butt of a cosmic joke. The very symmetry of his plots makes a statement about man's inability to progress. Man's condition is inseparable from the process which shapes him; but no moral or spiritual revolution will enable him to affect that process, nor his position within it. In Hardy's later novels, the human psyche becomes the principal means through which the malevolent process works. Increasingly, Hardy wrote about man's psychic needs, compulsions, and obsessions rather than his rational decisions and conscious motives. Anticipating Lawrence, Hardy saw that an unconscious, often libidinous self directs man's conduct, particularly his psychosexual behaviour. Like Conrad, he understood that an atavistic self lurks within each of us. While Hardy prepares the way for Conrad and Lawrence, he also marks a turning-away from the traditional resolution of Victorian novels. Not only in literary history, but in Hardy's career, what we call the beginning is often the end. For once Hardy completed the groundwork for the modern British novel, he abandoned fiction altogether.

NOTES

1. My understanding of endings has been influenced by Frank Kermode, *The Sense of an Ending* (New York: Oxford University Press, 1967) and by Alan Friedman, *The Turn of the Novel* (New York: Oxford University Press, 1966).

2. For further discussion of Hardy's narrators, see my 'The Narrator as Character in Hardy's Major Fiction', *MFS*, XVIII (1972), 155–72.

3. See Florence Emily Hardy, *The Early Life of Thomas Hardy, 1840–1891* (London and New York: Macmillan, 1928) p. 293.

4. As Scott Elledge indicates in his Norton Critical edition of *Tess of the d'Urbervilles* (New York: Norton, 1965) p. 19, when Hardy uses this phrase in the third chapter of the novel (p. 24 in the Wessex Edition), he is specifically responding to Wordsworth who, in line 22 of 'Lines Written in Early Spring', speaks of 'Nature's holy plan'.

5. M. H. Abrams, 'English Romanticism: The Spirit of the Age', in *Romanticism and Consciousness*, ed. Harold Bloom (New York: Norton, 1970) p. 103.

6. Ian Gregor, *The Great Web: The Form of Hardy's Major Fiction* (London: Faber

& Faber; Totowa, N. J.: Rowman & Littlefield, 1974) p. 232. I should stress that this remark is in no way central to Gregor's splendid study.

7. William Blake, 'Introduction' to *Songs of Experience*, 1. 2.

8. See Gregor, p. 164.

9. Although Friedman argues for a distinction between the two marriages ('The stream of Sue's conscience thus flows at the end into marriage; the stream of Jude's conscience flows beyond marriage into death' [Friedman, p. 70]), I would stress that remarriage and death are synonymous for both Jude and Sue.

10. *Joseph Conrad's Letters to R. B. Cunninghame Graham*, ed. C. T. Watts (Cambridge, England: Cambridge University Press, 1969) pp. 56–7.

3 A Regional Approach to Hardy's Fiction

W. J. KEITH

To suggest that little has been written about Hardy's regionalism may, at a first hearing, sound absurd, but if the term is used at all precisely such a statement is true. Most of the numerous studies of Hardy's Wessex have been primarily topographical (that is, dependent upon comparison with a known landscape) or else concerned in merely general terms with the rural background. However, the qualities that identify 'the regional novel' are much more specific, and it is worth while considering his work in this context since, for students of regionalism in fiction, Hardy is a supremely important witness.

In *The English Regional Novel*, Phyllis Bentley listed the following characteristics of the genre: 'Its first great merit is, of course, its brilliant illuminations of English landscape. . . . Its transcendent merit is that of verisimilitude. . . . Lastly, the regional novel is essentially democratic. It expresses a belief that the ordinary man and the ordinary woman are interesting and worth depicting.'[1] Particularity, realism, and a faithful, sympathetic presentation of life and labour: these may be accepted as essentials. But other factors are also involved. Since the characteristics of a distinctive community gradually develop over an extended period of time, the regional novelist will usually be concerned with historical – or even archaeological – customs and survivals. And above all, because of the importance of accuracy and detail, he is not likely to be successful unless he can claim what F. W. Morgan has called 'absorption in a particular locality: absorption and not merely interest'.[2]

The tendency to neglect Hardy's associations with regionalism probably stems from a widespread suspicion that to call a novelist 'regional' is somehow limiting. It could be argued, however, that

Hardy demonstrated his genius as a literary artist by the way in which he raised regional fiction to a much higher level than it had hitherto attained. He was able, in fact, to introduce two new elements into the genre which not only counteracted its limitations but even turned them into strengths.

With the exception of Trollope (who had different intentions), Hardy was the first English novelist to postulate a series of novels all focusing upon a particular locality. This has considerable implications for regionalism, since it enables the writer to evolve his regional awareness cumulatively. Thus an individual novel – *Under the Greenwood Tree*, for instance – may be too confined in its setting to qualify as regional in itself, yet it may ultimately take a legitimate place within a regional series. (The example is particularly apt in so far as *Under the Greenwood Tree* was written before Hardy thought of a series of local novels, and was only integrated into the Wessex scheme, after some revision, at a later date.) Moreover, Hardy's conception of Wessex can assist us in establishing more precisely what constitutes a region. It is significant that Morgan, who approaches regionalism from a sociological perspective, invokes Hardy as soon as he comes to consider the literary aspects of his subject:

> The heart of [Hardy's] Wessex, like the territories of most other regional authors, does not coincide with the boundaries of any region a geographer may draw, but there is no doubt that the Dorset of the novels is an individuality. The scenery varies from the clay lowland of the Vale of Blackmore to the chalk uplands of the centre and coastal regions and the heath country of the south-east. But there was unity in diversity, for the different geographical tracts were complementary to each other with their different products from meadow, arable, chalk pasture, woodland, or heath.[3]

Clearly, a regional analysis of this scope could only be attempted on the broad canvas that a novel-series provides.

The second of Hardy's contributions to the subject concerns the relation of his 'circumscribed scene' to the larger world. The chief case against regionalism lies in its undue emphasis upon the uniquely local which, almost by definition, leads to distortion. If a regional presentation confines itself to those aspects which distinguish it from other regions, no representative statement is possible. He who knows only his region, we might say, knows little of that. Raymond

Williams has argued the point most cogently: 'At its weakest, in what should be seen as a defensive reflex, the "regional" novel, in excluding all but its region, excluded not only other places but those deep social and human forces [i.e., the new social mobility and the ideas and education of an extending culture] which were explicitly active within it.'[4] But Hardy refuses to limit himself in this way. Indeed, it is part of his strength (part, moreover, of his unique contribution to Victorian fiction) that he placed at the centre of his novels the very factors which, as Williams points out, the average regional novelist tended to omit. Hardy's Wessex ('a modern Wessex of railways, the penny post, mowing and reaping machines', as he described it in the preface to *Far from the Madding Crowd*) is by no means cut off from outside pressures.

I would argue, however, that this development does not make his novels any the less regional. In according the relation between regional and universal so important a place in his fiction, he was drawing attention to one of the most significant trends of his age. He alludes to one aspect of the problem in his 'General Preface to the Novels and Poems'. He responded there to the view that 'novels that evolve their action on a circumscribed scene . . . cannot be so inclusive in their exhibition of human nature as novels wherein the scenes cover large extents of country'. Hardy denied this, insisting that 'the domestic emotions have throbbed in Wessex nooks with as much intensity as in the palaces of Europe', that his Wessex characters were 'beings in whose hearts and minds that which is apparently local should be really universal'.[5] This is not, of course, a specific defence of regionalism, but it shows how Hardy is intent to free himself from the possible limitation of the regional viewpoint without sacrificing its advantages.

But Hardy's main concern was not just the relation of regional and universal but the impact (even invasion) of the local by the cosmopolitan, and the subsequent effect of this upon regional customs and values. He was ideally suited, from the circumstances of his upbringing, for tackling this vexed question. Born and brought up in Dorset, when the traditional ways, though threatened, were still strong, he could claim that 'absorption' in locality which Morgan considered so vital. Even while working in Dorchester, he had sensed a contrast between the life of the bustling town and that of his native home:

Owing to the accident of his being an architect's pupil in a county-town of assizes and aldermen, which had advanced to railways and telegraphs and daily London papers; yet not living there, but walking in every day from a world of shepherds and ploughmen in a hamlet three miles off, where modern improvements were still regarded as wonders, he saw rustic and borough doings in a juxtaposition peculiarly close.[6]

Later, he had lived and worked in London, and thus came under the influence of more sophisticated cosmopolitan attitudes. As a consequence, the sense of being caught between two worlds was strong in him, and he naturally used it as a recurring element within his fiction. It is significant that when, returning to Dorchester in 1867 he began wondering 'how to achieve some tangible result from his desultory yet strenuous labours at literature', he should lay some stress on the fact that 'he knew fairly well both West-country life in its less explored recesses and the life of an isolated student cast upon the billows of London'.[7] Apparently *The Poor Man and the Lady* explored this dichotomy, and, after a number of experiments and false starts, Hardy ultimately recognised this tension as his overriding theme. Hence, the recurrent device of a stranger or alien visitant invading, and frequently dislocating, the traditional life of sheltered (but not necessarily 'innocent') Wessex. Hardy's novels, far from being confined to a regional locale, record the increasing confrontation of local and cosmopolitan, and derive much of their impact from the resultant clash. The regional question is actively debated within the novels; their subject and their dialectic become fully integrated.

One possible way of distinguishing a regional novelist from his merely provincial counterpart is to note how the former writes of a specific locality but for as wide an audience as possible (most of whom exist outside it), while the latter may be seen as writing primarily for the area itself. It would be wrong, I think, to look down on the provincial writer (Hardy himself considered 'provincialism of feeling' invaluable[8]), but he is obviously limited in scope. Too often, localism of any kind becomes a mere tactic for evasion, a means of avoiding contact with the broader, more dominant issues of the time. Hardy was clearly conscious of the problem. Thus, although he admired William Barnes, he considered that 'his place-attachment was strong almost to a fault'[9] — and one can see how studiously the novelist avoided the danger himself. Viewing Wessex from a more detached perspective than Barnes, Hardy never failed to see the macrocosm reflected in the microcosm. Moreover, his cosmopolitan experience enabled him to appreciate the ultimate (yet perhaps redeeming) irony concerning regionalism: that, although the sense of particularity is emphasised by reference to the local, only a cosmopolitan, with the generalising experience that renders comparison possible, is in a position to recognise the regional when he encounters it.

It may be argued, then, that regionalism involves far more than the mere description of a locality: it includes the depiction, in depth, of a whole community, and in addition, because narrative perspective is a central factor, it necessarily has profound implications for the novel as a literary form. Much recent Hardy criticism, undertaken with little concern for its relevance to a study of regionalism, can prove illuminating in this context. For example, J. Hillis Miller's presentation of a Hardy split in his attitudes between 'distance and desire' incidentally throws light on what may in fact be the ideal situation for a regional novelist. Moreover, his literary debt to Scott, his emphasis on what Raymond Williams calls 'the ordinary processes of life and work',[10] the importance he placed upon historical continuity and the preservation of local record, and the like – all these can be seen as converging aspects of his regional awareness. On the other hand, much more could be written about Hardy's relation to the regional movement. The way in which he compares with or differs from earlier regional writers like R. D. Blackmore or later ones like Eden Phillpotts represents only one possible line of further research. But I must content myself here with an attempt to look briefly at the major novels from a deliberately regional perspective. If we set Hardy within the context of regional fiction, rather than within the larger pattern of the Victorian novel, what aspects of his books are thrown into sharper focus? What qualities become manifest that we might otherwise fail to notice? Does such an approach explain what might otherwise seem anomalies in his work? I hope to throw light on at least some of these questions in the paragraphs to follow. Above all, we shall be able, I believe, to gain some insight into the varieties of regional presentation to be found within his novels.

Indeed, it is variety, more perhaps than any other factor, that distinguishes Hardy's Wessex fiction. There is no sense here (as there is, for example, in Eden Phillpotts' Dartmoor series) that the novelist is working to a regional formula. Each book presents a local community in a different manner, and the manner is invariably appropriate to the particular theme and approach involved. *Under the*

Greenwood Tree, for example, focused as it is upon Mellstock village, suggests the parochial rather than the regional, but, when examined with the advantage of hindsight as a segment of the Wessex series, it is seen as curiously representative — one is tempted to say proleptic — of the whole regional pattern. The Mellstock Quire becomes a rural community in miniature: it is a historical entity of which the individual members form a part, and within which they are defined. Much of the poignancy of the novel derives from the fact that the choir sees itself as the end of a tradition — that is, within a historical context. Dick Dewy, the central figure, gains a bride but at the cost of membership in a communal, rustic activity. He is originally introduced to us as a member of the choir, and it is through the traditional Christmas carolling that he sees and falls in love with Fancy Day. That Fancy with her 'educated ideas' (II, VI; p. 101) is the organ-player who will ultimately replace the choir is ironical, and she is also the first in a series of Hardy heroines to be educated out of the traditional communal ways. The novel is split, effectively, between the comic and the elegiac because our regret at the obliteration of the choir and all it stands for is mitigated, at least to some extent, by the successful union of the two lovers. Though set in a minor key, the novel presents one aspect of the basic tension that is to control and unify the whole of Hardy's fiction.

If *Under the Greenwood Tree* is seen as essentially a parochial novel, *Far from the Madding Crowd* might best be described as pastoral.[11] Here, of course, Hardy begins consciously to develop Wessex as a regional entity; as the well-known statement in the preface notes, 'the series of novels I projected being mainly of the kind called local, they seemed to require a territorial definition of some sort to lend unity to their scene' (p. vii). Although there is nothing uniquely local about the rural background, we gain a much greater sense of an organic rural community; Morgan describes Weatherbury as 'a perfect example of the nucleated settlement, with its farms, inn, malthouse, church, and great monastic barn'.[12] We find, moreover, a significantly greater social range here, from Boldwood the gentleman-farmer down to Fanny Robin. Above all, the regional emphasis on rural work is conspicuous, as the well-known sheep-washing and shearing scenes testify. It should be noted, however, that these scenes, excellent as they are, serve for the most part as background to the love-plot, which focuses on those characters at the upper end of the social scale — with Boldwood and Bathsheba, of course, but also with Gabriel Oak and Troy, both of whom are seen rising (by very

different methods) within the village hierarchy. Such figures as
Joseph Poorgrass, Cain Ball, and Liddy Smallbury, though memorable, are decidedly supernumerary. In this novel at least, to speak of
the choric function of the rustic characters is (*pace* Raymond
Williams) both legitimate and accurate.

I labour this point because one of Hardy's main contributions to
regionalism is a sense of the growing importance of social distinctions
that inevitably weaken the cohesion of a local community. The basis
of these distinctions is predominantly and increasingly presented in
terms not only of financial position but also of educational attainment
and social grace. This trend, implicit in the very title of *The Poor Man
and the Lady*, can be seen clearly enough in *Under the Greenwood Tree*,
especially in the scene where Dick Dewy asks Keeper Day for the
hand of Fancy (IV, II; pp. 162–4), though in this instance the
obstacle can be surmounted without undue difficulty. None the less,
Fancy's love of 'refinement' and her concern for 'respectability' (IV,
VII [p. 189]; V, I [p. 203]) are traits which will become more and
more conspicuous in Hardy's later heroines, and their implications for
regional customs and values are considerable.

In *Far from the Madding Crowd*, social distinctions are already more
prominent. Although at the time of Gabriel's first proposal Bathsheba
admits, 'you are better off than I', she adds, 'I am better educated than
you' (IV; p. 35). Later she tells Liddy, 'he wasn't quite good enough
for me' (IX; p. 85); but by this time, of course, Bathsheba has risen in
the class-scale (through succession to her uncle's farm) while Gabriel
has lost his independent status and slipped back into the role of
employed worker. True, the young Bathsheba places sophisticated
manners and sexual attractiveness in Troy above money and position
in Boldwood and uprightness and devotion in Gabriel, but my point
is that all these factors – financial position, educational standard,
social refinement (and, as we shall see later, even use of language) –
unite to complicate and often frustrate the traditional norms of
community life. I am not denying, of course, that the seeds of many of
these problems were always present in the rustic communities; it can
hardly be denied, however, that they were fostered and multiplied by
centralising, unifying pressures at the time of the Industrial Revolution. They represent, then, forces in the nineteenth century that
can legitimately be described as anti-regional. I believe we miss much
of the significance of Hardy's work if we fail to recognise the multi-
faceted ironies implicit in his presentation of increasingly anti-
regional elements within a developing regional series.

The Return of the Native can legitimately be described as Hardy's first full-scale regional novel, and the tension between regional and anti-regional is especially noticeable. Regional awareness is immediately stressed in the title. With *Under the Greenwood Tree* and *Far from the Madding Crowd*, the literary allusions in the titles implied sophisticated detachment; the rustic locale exists 'out there', and the attitude is reflected in Hardy's surprisingly condescending presentation of his rural characters in these early novels – what Frank Chapman described (with, alas, only slight exaggeration) as 'an unpleasant effect of performing animals going through their tricks'.[13] But *The Return of the Native*, on the contrary, presupposes 'here'; the novelist, like his protagonist, has returned home, and the rustic labourers are presented with amusement but also with respect. Hardy is at last speaking, we feel, from within his region.

The importance of the region is further stressed in the famous opening chapter; we begin with the immediate environment which is firmly established before 'Humanity appears upon the Scene, Hand in Hand with Trouble' (title of I, ii; p. 8). Egdon Heath dictates both the form of the novel and its boundaries. 'Every scene in the book', Joseph Warren Beach observes, 'takes place within the horizon of one standing upon Rainbarrow',[14] and John Paterson has shown how Hardy alters the geographical position of the tumulus, which in Dorset is located on the outskirts of the heath, so that 'it appears in the novel, for reasons which have to do with its symbolic meaning and with the focus of its action, at the heath's very center'.[15] (Later, as the regional series develops, we sense that, just as Rainbarrow forms the centre of Edgon, so the heath itself becomes a disturbingly unpredictable, untamed centre of Wessex.) Moreover, there is a deliberate emphasis on Egdon not only as a microcosmic image of an indifferent universe but as an image of life itself. So, for Clym, 'there was something in its oppressive horizontality which too much reminded him of the arena of life; it gave him a sense of bare equality with, and no superiority to, a single living thing under the sun' (III, v; p. 245).[16]

But there is a complicating irony about the regionalism of *The Return of the Native*. The same novel in which Hardy establishes the strongest feeling of a unique locality is the one in which regionalism is most surely challenged. That Egdon is the bleakest area in Wessex accounts to some extent for its memorableness, but for the first time words like 'isolation', 'loneliness' and 'solitude' become key concepts, and this militates against any sense of vital community. The inhabitants of Egdon are in the original sense of the word 'heathen'. The cohesive influence of the Church, prominent in *Under the Greenwood Tree*, is conspicuous by its absence, and there is no place to congregate like the Malthouse in *Far from the Madding Crowd* (the 'Quiet Woman' is significantly on the edge of the heath, and its character seems more divisive than communal). Egdon has no human centre – only the exposed Rainbarrow. Hardy specifically refers to 'the scattered inhabitants' of the Heath (II, IV; p. 142) and their 'remote cottages' (VI, IV; p. 484). Moreover, the attitudes of the rustics towards their environment are noteworthy. It is instructive, for example, to recall the scene in *Far from the Madding Crowd* in which Cain Ball reports upon the exotic sights of Bath (still, be it stressed, within the boundaries of Wessex). To the inhabitants of Weatherbury, his news is strange and doubtful: ' "Well, 'tis a curious place . . . ," observed Moon; "and it must be a curious people that live therein" ' (XXXIII; p. 253). By contrast, when Clym tries to explain the motives for his return to Fairway and his cronies, he finds it virtually impossible to persuade them that he prefers Egdon to Paris (III, I; pp. 201–2). It is as if the local populace has lost its regional cohesiveness and its regional morale – it sees itself as a backwater.

Against this equivocal regional background are set the two protagonists, Clym and Eustacia, one a native who returns, the other (and it needs to be stressed that Eustacia is a native of Wessex if not of Egdon) yearning to escape. Although we first see her as indistinguishable from Egdon, although her ability to follow the faint, indeterminate footpaths places her among 'the regular haunters of the heath' and shows that she is not 'a mere visitor' (I, VI; p. 63), yet she hates the place and has a passionate longing for 'all the beating and pulsing that is going on in the great arteries of the world' (IV, VI; p. 335). She is Hardy's most uncompromising anti-regional figure. Thus Clym and Eustacia represent diametrically opposed positions in the regionalist/cosmopolitan controversy.

In his detailed textual study, *The Making of 'The Return of the Native'*, John Paterson has drawn attention to some interesting changes in Hardy's conception of this novel – changes that prove highly relevant to my present concern. Originally, for instance, Clym did not go to Paris but only to Budmouth (and so, once again, remained within the Wessex boundaries); the cosmopolitan theme must therefore have increased in importance as the novel developed. And at an earlier stage the characters themselves were not so carefully differentiated in social terms. Virtually all the main characters,

Paterson shows, were elevated socially in the course of the writing, and part of the distinction is achieved through language. Whereas in the 'Ur-version', as Paterson calls it, all spoke at least to some extent in dialect, in the completed text there is a clear difference between the language of such people as the Cantles, Timothy Fairway and Olly Dowden, and that of the more central characters in the book.

This seems to me highly significant. It is true that such distinctions have occurred earlier. Fancy Day, educated outside Mellstock, speaks in 'National English' (as Barnes called it) like Mr Maybold, but Farmer Shiner and Fancy's socially-conscious father both speak in dialect. A similar split occurs in *Far from the Madding Crowd*, where Gabriel is differentiated from Bathsheba's other suitors by his speech and manners. In *The Return of the Native*, however, this split is decidedly more pronounced; only Diggory Venn, whose position as sometime dairy-farmer and sometime reddleman is continually equivocal, moves with any ease between dialect (in his conversation with Johnny Nunsuch, for instance) and standard English. This process is developed, almost relentlessly, in the later novels.

Hardy (and this distinguishes him from 'run-of-the-mill' regional novelists) does not reproduce local dialect merely in the interests of realism or verisimilitude – still less for the introduction of local colour. In fact, he is making a serious social point. In the older communities, the use of dialect did not necessarily imply a class difference. This is particularly clear in *The Mayor of Casterbridge*. Michael Henchard, holding the highest position of responsibility in the Wessex hierarchy, did not feel the need – for himself, at least – to adopt a standard English. But my qualification is needed, since in this novel (and the process is developed still further in *The Woodlanders*) Hardy catches a crucial shift in allegiances between acceptance of the old regional standards and insistence on the newer dictates of Victorian bourgeois society. The young Elizabeth-Jane has already been initiated into a sense of what is 'respectable' (she uses the word twice in Chapter III [pp. 23, 25], once in Chapters VI and VII [pp. 43, 49]), and Mrs Newson becomes known as the 'genteel' widow (XIII; p. 94). Yet Henchard, though 'uncultivated' himself (XX; p. 149), is determined that Elizabeth-Jane shall rise in the social scale, and the tension caused by this determination comes to a head in the brilliant but painful scene in which Henchard actually uses dialect in order to rebuke her for doing the same. Settling into Henchard's ways, she follows local precedent in what Hardy calls 'her occasional pretty and picturesque use of dialect words – those terrible marks of the beast to the truly genteel'. But Hardy's sardonic irony becomes deadly earnest in Henchard: 'Good God, are you only fit to carry wash to a pig-trough, that ye use such words as those?' (xx; p. 148).

The Woodlanders is positively dotted with words like 'genteel', 'respectable', 'fashionable', 'refined'. Melbury's obsession with his daughter's education and prospects is both pathetic and extreme, Grace's very name is eloquent in implication, and with the scene at Winterborne's hut an alien sense of 'propriety' derived from Victorian but not rural England becomes a focal point in the plot. In this novel, despite the sequestered situation of Little Hintock, class divisions have hardened. Mrs Charmond, the anti-regional figure corresponding to Eustacia Vye and Lucetta Templeman in earlier books, is a dictatorial lady-of-the-manor who, though owning an estate in a woodland area, can hardly tell 'a beech from a woak' (xxxiv; p. 298); Winterborne, once of yeoman status and close to Melbury, is slipping into the condition of a migratory labourer; Fitzpiers, looking down from a window in the 'Earl of Wessex' hotel, catches the trend of the times when he tells Grace: 'I feel as if I belonged to a different species from the people [Winterborne and his regional, dialect-speaking cider-makers] who are working in that yard' (xxv; p. 214).

Both *The Mayor of Casterbridge* and *The Woodlanders* can be studied with profit from a regional perspective. In the former, Casterbridge is described as 'the pole, focus, or nerve-knot of the surrounding country life' (ix; p. 70). In the latter, High-Stoy Hill provides a focal point not unlike that of Rainbarrow, which had been called 'the pole and axis of this heathery world' in *The Return of the Native* (I, ii; p. 13); High-Stoy dominates and as it were defines the regional setting, being described as 'the well-known hill, which had been the axis of so many critical movements [in the lives of Grace and Fitzpiers] during his residence at Hintock' (xlv; p. 407). Moreover, the setting of the novel, as the title suggests, is integral to the plot. Melbury's timber business, Winterborne's cider-making, Marty South's spar-making all depend upon the nature of the locality. The woodlands are as essential, economically, to the fortunes of the protagonists as they are, artistically, to the mood and texture of the whole novel. The famous passage in which Little Hintock is described as 'a sequestered spot outside the gates of the world' yet also a setting for 'dramas of a grandeur and unity truly Sophoclean' (i; p. 4) presents the regional/universal question in a nutshell. But Grace falls from 'the good old Hintock ways' (vi; p. 49), and Winterborne's decline and fall is emblematic of larger patterns of change. *The Woodlanders* presents 'a modern Wessex' with a vengeance.

It is not necessary, I think, to prolong this study with any detailed consideration of Hardy's later novels. Arnold Kettle and Douglas Brown have emphasised the wandering, increasingly migratory quality of rural labour as embodied in Tess and Jude, and, while we may wish to make certain qualifications, the basic pattern is clear enough. In choosing his protagonists from the humbler 'work-folk' of Wessex, Hardy is moving closer to the regional norms, but he does so only to demonstrate that, in the later Victorian period, their regional and communal backgrounds have been eroded. Tess knows only the fag-end of a regional village-community in Marlott; Blackmore Vale, which had been for Tess 'the world, and its inhabitants the races thereof' (I, v; p. 40), can no longer sustain her. Hardy, having by this time established Wessex as a coherent fictional entity, can present her wandering within it, from sub-region to sub-region, her family moving on Lady Day, her association with her native village finally snapped. And the extreme is reached in *Jude the Obscure*, which could legitimately be subtitled 'The Departure of a Native'. The preface, Ian Gregor has recently told us, 'announces . . . a world framed no longer by a remembrance of Wessex'.[17] Dispossessed of one way of life, Jude fails to establish himself in another. His dilemma is classified by Hardy as 'his form of the modern vice of unrest' (II, II; p. 98); Jude himself recognises Sue as 'a product of civilization' (III, II; p. 165). The issues raised by the novel are essentially those of 'modernism'. The break-up of regional society, its deliberate destruction in the interests of an alien process, is relentlessly chronicled in the opening chapter:

> Many of the thatched and dormered dwelling-houses had been pulled down of late years, and many trees felled on the green. Above all, the original church, hump-backed, wood-turreted, and quaintly hipped, had been taken down, and either cracked up into heaps of road-metal in the lane, or utilized as pig-sty walls. . . . In place of it a tall new building of modern Gothic design, unfamiliar to English eyes, had been erected on a new piece of ground by a certain obliterator of historic records who had run down from London and back in a day. (I, I; p. 6)

Here regionalism receives its *coup de grâce*; Jude is deprived of both his context and his roots.

The passage just quoted from *Jude the Obscure* describes the destruction of a regional locale. For an equivalent, concise account of the destruction of a regional personality we may turn to an important but rarely-quoted passage from *The Well-Beloved*. It is worth noting that although this is in most respects the least regional of his works, Hardy's preface stresses the regional uniqueness of Portland. His uncharacteristic and rather absurd theme has no necessary connection with Portland, and part of the weakness of the book derives from this lack of relation between plot and setting. Yet, as so often with Hardy, this awkward clash of elements within the novel is a significant part of his intention. Avice Caro's situation is representative, and brilliantly sums up the pattern of regional history as Hardy saw it:

> Every aim of those who had brought her up had been to get her away mentally as far as possible from her natural and individual life as an inhabitant of a peculiar island: to make her an exact copy of tens of thousands of other people, in whose circumstances there was nothing special, distinctive, or picturesque; to teach her to forget all the experiences of her ancestors; to drown the local ballads by songs purchased at the Budmouth fashionable music-sellers', and the local vocabulary by a governess-tongue of no country at all. . . .
>   . . . By constitution she was local to the bone, but she could not escape the tendency of the age. (I, II; pp. 13–14)

Hardy's twentieth-century readers are for the most part products of the educational process described here. The 'tendency of the age', continued and even stepped up in our own, has been so successful that our awareness of earlier regional differences and alternative attitudes is in danger of being expunged. If we are to understand the past and our own relation to it, we must take note of what has been lost. This is a final reason why a regional approach to Hardy's fiction can emphasise an important aspect of his work that we might otherwise overlook.

NOTES

1. Phyllis Bentley, *The English Regional Novel* (London: Allen & Unwin, 1941) p. 45.
2. F. W. Morgan, 'Three Aspects of Regional Consciousness', *Sociological Review*,

xxxi (1939) 84. This seminal article on the socio-political, geographical, and literary aspects of regionalism deserves far more attention from Hardy scholars than it has received.

3. Morgan, p. 79. For a later account of Wessex from a geographical viewpoint, see H. C. Darby, 'The Regional Geography of Hardy's Wessex', *Geographical Review*, xxxviii (1948) 426–43.

4. Raymond Williams, *The Country and the City* (London: Chatto & Windus, 1973) p. 253.

5. Published in the first volume of the Wessex Edition (London: Macmillan, 1912) pp. viii, ix.

6. Florence Emily Hardy, *The Early Life of Thomas Hardy, 1840–1891* (London and New York: Macmillan, 1928) p. 41.

7. *Early Life*, pp. 74–5.

8. *Early Life*, p. 189.

9. Hardy, 'The Rev. William Barnes, B.D.', *Athenaeum*, 16 October 1886, p. 502.

10. Williams, p. 211.

11. Perhaps I should state here that I use this word rather differently from Michael Squires in his recent study, *The Pastoral Novel* (Charlottesville: University Press of Virginia, 1974). Though Hardy's self-conscious, semi-humorous, essentially urban stance and the specific allusions to biblical and classical pastoral are both important, it is more strictly pastoral in the literal sense of being a novel about sheep and shepherding.

12. Morgan, p. 79.

13. Frank Chapman, 'Hardy the Novelist', *Scrutiny*, iii (June 1934) 31.

14. Joseph Warren Beach, *The Technique of Thomas Hardy* (Chicago: University of Chicago Press, 1922) p. 98.

15. John Paterson, *The Making of 'The Return of the Native'* (Berkeley and Los Angeles: University of California Press, 1960) p. 122.

16. That Hardy repeated much of this from an earlier passage in *Desperate Remedies* (xii; p. 254) indicates a curious determination on his part to develop the universal application of his regional settings.

17. Ian Gregor, *The Great Web: The Form of Hardy's Major Fiction* (London: Faber & Faber; Totowa, N. J.: Rowman & Littlefield, 1974) p. 38.

4 A New View of Bathsheba Everdene

PETER J. CASAGRANDE

It has become commonplace among critics of Thomas Hardy's *Far from the Madding Crowd* (1874) to say that Bathsheba Everdene, the novel's heroine, develops through misfortune and suffering from a vain, egotistical girl into a wise, sympathetic woman.[1] There is something to this view, for apparently at least Bathsheba changes for the better between the beginning and end of the novel. She learns to sympathise with Fanny Robin, seeks to make amends to Farmer Boldwood, and marries the exemplary Gabriel Oak. However, there is much in Bathsheba that this view does not account for. Take for example the following passage, typical of others:

> Bathsheba was no schemer for marriage, nor was she deliberately a trifler with the affections of men, and a censor's experience on seeing an actual flirt after observing her would have been a feeling of surprise that Bathsheba could be so different from such a one, and yet so like what a flirt is supposed to be.
>
> She resolved never again, by look or by sign, to interrupt the steady flow of this man's [Boldwood's] life. But a resolution to avoid an evil is seldom framed till the evil is so far advanced as to make avoidance impossible. (XVIII; p. 140)

One thing here is in basic conflict with a 'transformist' view of Bathsheba; she is an un-deliberate, inadvertent, unconscious agent of evil. Her actions are not within her control. This suggests that with her, moral growth, if possible, is always problematical. And Hardy's view of her is that of the surprised censor: he sympathises with her infirmity (for which she is not responsible) at the same time as he deplores her irrationality and its consequences.

The view of Bathsheba as one who progresses toward wider sympathy has gone unchallenged, probably because she is often described as an unambiguous character rendered in broad, sure strokes. 'Bathsheba', writes Douglas Brown, 'dominates the novel, not as a human personality created and explored with the searching art of the classical novelist, but as someone present to a balladist's imagination, confidently taken for granted as what she seems to be, recognized by the gesture of the hand, the inflexion of the voice; even the gradual transformation of her nature under the impress of suffering Hardy reveals in broad dramatic strokes.'[2] Hardy's alleged lack of interest in the subtler psychology of Bathsheba's career, deplored by Henry James in one of the first contemporary reviews of the novel, has come to be attributed to Hardy's preference for the art of the romance against the craft of the novel.[3] For several reasons then, not the least of which is the assumption on the part of most critics of the novel that Hardy accepted uncritically the developmental psychology prevalent in the fiction of his day, two closely related issues have been overlooked. First, little attention has been given either to Hardy's ambivalent attitude to Bathsheba (especially a misogynistic side to it) or to the ambiguous nature of Bathsheba's career. Second, an obliquity in Hardy's way of showing her at crucial moments in her career has gone unexamined.

Since an analysis of Bathsheba's career demands discussion of Hardy's method, by way of beginning I should mention the problems of delineation. First, Hardy's abbreviated handling of Bathsheba's childhood thwarts any attempt to understand her motives at the beginning of the novel. Our uncertainty about her motives is compounded by the nature of her career, which is not a gradual process of self-conscious growth, but exposure, sudden and violent, to murder, death, fatal disease, fire, storm, and uncontrolled passion. Third, there is Hardy's use, always ironical, of literary allusions to depict Bathsheba at the two most critical moments of her career – her recovery in the swamp after opening Fanny Robin's coffin and being rejected by Troy, and her recovery at Weatherbury after Troy's death. These problems, as well as one other – the dominance of Oak in a novel centrally concerned with Bathsheba's career – may be seen as emanating from Hardy's view of her as one infirm in nature. Oak's prominence is best seen, I think, as a function of Bathsheba's imperfection. Oak's ability to observe the defects of non-human nature (the loss of his flock, the fire, the storm, the bloated sheep) and to contrive amendment fits him to observe, minister to, and finally to marry the faulty Bathsheba. The novel thus associates the imperfect nature of its heroine with defective non-human nature and offers in Oak an example of how to cope with the unregenerateness of things. Hardy's view of Bathsheba as essentially flawed also explains his ironic allusiveness during her two great moments of recovery: he cannot imagine transformation in one of her nature and so invokes detached instances of it from other authors. Because he does not believe that an essential change in Bathsheba is possible, rather than depicting in her a gradual process of growth towards self-knowledge he subjects her, over a relatively brief period of time, to a series of violent, shocking, humiliating encounters with death, and keeps the patient, admonitory Oak present at all times. This is consistent with the view in the novel that defect in human and non-human nature cannot be eradicated – only studied, accepted, and made limited use of for the adaptation of means to ends.

We need only look to *A Pair of Blue Eyes* (1873), the novel which Hardy was completing when he began *Far from the Madding Crowd*,[4] for evidence of an almost clinical interest in the birth and growth of what there is disparagingly called 'womanly artifice'. Henry Knight, a fastidious London man of letters, shows to Elfride Swancourt, the novel's nineteen-year-old heroine, a description of her in his commonplace book:

> Girl gets into her teens, and her self-consciousness is born. After a certain interval passed in infantine helplessness, it begins to act. Simple, young, and inexperienced at first. Persons of observation can tell to a nicety how old this consciousness is by the skill it has acquired in the art necessary to its success – the art of hiding itself. Generally begins career by actions which are popularly termed showing off. Method adopted depends in each case upon the disposition, rank, residence, of the young lady attempting it. Town-bred girl will utter some moral paradox on fast men, or love. County miss adopts the more material media of taking a ghastly fence, whistling, or making your blood run cold by appearing to risk her neck. . . .
>
> An innocent vanity is of course the origin of these displays. 'Look at me,' say these youthful beginners in womanly artifice, without reflecting whether or not it be to their advantage to show so much of themselves. (XVIII; p. 196; ellipsis mine)

Elfride does not wish to be regarded as a mere girl, and so urges upon

Knight the view that 'the slower a nature is to develop, the richer the nature'. Knight advises, with some acerbity, that she should not take it for granted 'that the woman behind her time at a given age has not reached the end of her tether. Her backwardness may be not because she is slow to develop, but because she soon exhausted her capacity for developing' (*PBE*, XVIII; p. 198).

The vain Bathsheba who astonishes Gabriel Oak with her horsemanship undoubtedly owes something to Knight's vain and demonstrative country miss, though Bathsheba's aggressive coquetry is a distinct departure from Elfride's clinging. More important here, however, is the fact that Knight's scepticism about a woman's capacity for developing anticipates the view in *Far from the Madding Crowd* that Bathsheba cannot, in any essential way, change from a vain, foolish girl into a wise woman. It is Hardy's general view, maintained throughout the novels and the poems, departed from but not contradicted in *The Dynasts* (1903 – 8), that both nature and humanity are stained by what might be called ineradicable defects. The novels and poems before 1874 contain a melancholy sense of an unregenerateness in things. For Hardy, the good of the past is, in a phrase of Loren Eiseley's, 'unique and unreturning', the evil of the past ever-living. At the centre of the sensational *Desperate Remedies* (1871) is the story of Cytherea Aldclyffe's and Aeneas Manston's inability to escape from their sins of the past. Poems of the 1860s lament that 'the radiance has waned' ('Her Initials'), that 'bloom and beauty' are marred ('Discouragement'), that 'flowering youthtime' has faded ('The Temporary the All'), that 'excellencies' of a primal time have dwindled ('She, To Him: I'), and that – this is the crucial point – all is beyond recovery or restoration. *A Pair of Blue Eyes* urges much the same in triplicate: Elfride cannot undo the 'sin' of her flirtation with Jethway and elopement with Stephen Smith; Henry Knight cannot realise the lost glory and dream of his youth by marrying the flawed Elfride; Smith cannot return to his native Endelstow after a long absence. This sense of the irredeemable, the irretrievable, the unrestorable in human affairs, strong in Hardy's early writings, grew in strength throughout the later novels and poems. We need only look ahead to the agony of Grace Melbury and Clym Yeobright in their thwarted attempts to return to their native places, to the ineradicable weaknesses that slowly, inexorably destroy Henchard, Tess, and Jude, to late poems such as 'We Are Getting to the End', 'To Meet, or Otherwise', 'The Going', 'Christmas: 1924', and 'A Night of Questionings', to see how deep and lasting was

Hardy's sense of the unreturning and unregenerate nature of things.[5]

Among the major novels, *Far from the Madding Crowd* and *Under the Greenwood Tree* (1872), with their 'happy' endings, can be seen as attempts to show, in the comic mode, the possibility of amendment and regeneration. Fancy Day, the whimsical heroine of *Under the Greenwood Tree*, does return to her native place, and does marry her rustic lover under a greenwood tree, though the situation at the end of the novel is not without its grim irony. *Far from the Madding Crowd*, it might seem, is an attempt to show something similar – the growth of Bathsheba from impulsive folly to good sense and marriage to Gabriel Oak. But Bathsheba is subject to a more severe law than Fancy. Bathsheba is in Hardy's view an agent and a victim of the tragic unalterability of things, for she is afflicted by what he calls, in the first chapter, 'woman's prescriptive infirmity' (1; p. 5).[6] This, in turn, causes her entanglement in a series of events from which she cannot extricate herself.

Bathsheba comes to Norcombe as an orphan of twenty to live and work with an aunt. She is vain, haughtily independent in spirit, and recklessly flirtatious. Gabriel Oak, a Norcombe shepherd lately risen to the status of farmer, falls in love with her, courts her, and proposes marriage. But when Oak loses his flock and his new station his suit founders. At about the same time Bathsheba inherits a prospering farm at Weatherbury and moves to it as its mistress. Oak, falling back upon his old work as a shepherd, gains employment at Weatherbury Farm after saving its grain stores from fire. Bathsheba soon commits a grievous error. Allegedly as a joke, but in fact because he had ignored her at church and in the Corn Exchange, Bathsheba sends to Farmer Boldwood, a neighbour, a valentine on which she has written 'Marry Me'. The reclusive, repressed Boldwood comes courting in deadly earnest, and Bathsheba, pleased with her success, does not discourage him – at least not until Sergeant Troy, a dashing cavalryman with a winning tongue, completely entrances her. Boldwood is wild with jealousy, threatens violence against Troy, and Bathsheba sees that she has offended him deeply. Unbeknown to her she has offended him irremediably. If he could forgive her, all might be as it was. But he is too obsessed with the thought of having her to be able to understand her plea for forgiveness: her sin is his salvation, her childish joke his glorious dream of happiness come true. Far from relieving her of guilt, he seeks to bind her by it; later, in sheer desperation, he tries to bribe Troy not to marry her. But by then Bathsheba will have already wedded Troy, and Boldwood will be driven nearly mad. Bathsheba

soon discovers Troy to be irresponsible, deceitful, and worse — before
marrying her he had seduced Fanny Robin, a former servant of the
farm who now returns to her native spot to bear her child and to die.
Bathsheba and Troy part after a shockingly grotesque scene beside the
open coffin of Fanny and the child. Shortly after, Troy is reported
drowned. At this news, Boldwood is stirred to hope of recovering his
lost dreams. Deeply smitten with remorse for the earlier offence,
Bathsheba agrees to marry Boldwood 'as a kind of repentance' after
six years have passed. But this, her opportunity to make reparation, is
thwarted by Troy's unexpected return and his death by the hand of
Boldwood, who then tries to kill himself. Bathsheba is driven nearly
mad by the realisation that a childish act of two years before had
ignited a chain of events which now include a murder, a near suicide,
and a probable death by execution. Fortunately, however, Boldwood's death sentence is reduced to a term in prison. Bathsheba
recovers, and the novel ends with her marriage to her first lover, Oak,
who has remained loyal throughout. Bathsheba's moral history, it
must be noted, is paralleled by Troy's. As she injures Boldwood, he
injures Fanny. As his attempt to make amends is mockingly
overthrown by the working of the gargoyle on Weatherbury
Church, her attempt to atone is thwarted by events and personalities.
Both fail to 'undo the done', but their failures differ. Troy is
portrayed as one capable of better things but pushed into error by the
circumstances of his birth, his military profession, and even by the
susceptibility of women to his charm. Bathsheba, in contrast, is
portrayed as one who errs because innately flawed.

There can be little doubt of Hardy's view in *Far from the Madding
Crowd* that women are by nature infirm. Bathsheba's weakness, it is
said when she stubbornly refuses to pay a toll, is 'what it is always' in
women — Vanity. She feels no gratitude toward Oak when he pays
her toll because 'in gaining her a passage he had lost her her point, and
we know how women take a favour of that kind' (I; p. 6). She is
described as unusual among women because capable of finishing a
thought before beginning the sentence with which to convey it, thus
suggesting that most women speak before thinking (III; p. 23). But
she is no thinker, for hers is 'an impulsive nature under a deliberative
aspect. . . . Many of her thoughts were perfect syllogisms; unluckily
they always remained thoughts. Only a few were irrational assumptions; but, unfortunately, they were the ones which most frequently
grew into deeds' (XX; p. 149). In her presence, Oak is a Samson, in
danger of being unmanned, Boldwood an Adam, in danger of being

tempted (III [p. 23]; XVII [p. 133]). Faced with Boldwood's plea that she marry him, Bathsheba 'began to feel unmistakable signs that she was inherently the weaker vessel. She strove miserably against this femininity which would insist upon supplying unbidden emotions in stronger and stronger current' (XXXI; p. 232). A view of woman as the 'weaker vessel' permeates the novel (see, e.g., XII [p. 104]; XXIII [pp. 181]; XXXI [p. 235]); indeed even Bathsheba accepts this view of herself. As the newly installed mistress of Weatherbury Farm she warns the workfolk against taking the view of her as one of the weaker sex: 'Don't any unfair ones among you . . . suppose that because I'm a woman I don't understand the difference between bad goings-on and good' (X; p. 93: ellipsis mine). Confronted with the loss of Troy, she candidly admits inferiority: 'Tell me the truth, Frank. I am not a fool, you know, although I am a woman, and have my woman's moments. Come! treat me fairly' (XLI; p. 314). Nearly speechless before Boldwood's renewed ardour after Troy's disappearance, she acknowledges what may be the ultimate handicap: 'It is difficult for a woman to define her feelings in language which is chiefly made by men to express theirs' (LI; p. 405).

Henery Fray inveighs against the villainy of womankind, Laban Tall is nagged and humiliated by a domineering wife, the work-women Temperance and Soberness are, in spite of their names, 'yielding women', as, in fact, are Fanny Robin and Bathsheba herself. At one point Oak, mortified by Bathsheba's criticism for injuring a sheep he is shearing, murmurs to himself the bitter words of Ecclesiastes 7: 26: '"I find more bitter than death the woman whose heart is snares and nets"' (XXII; pp. 173–4). And so, when Bathsheba comes under the influence of the unctuous, deceitful Troy, his villainy can be made to seem less a function of his depravity than a response, almost excusable, to her infirmity:

> The wondrous power of flattery in *passados* at woman is a perception so universal as to be remarked upon by many people almost as automatically as they repeat a proverb, or say they are Christians and the like, without thinking much of the enormous corollaries which spring from the proposition. Still less is it acted upon for the good of the complemental being alluded to. With the majority such an opinion is shelved with all those trite aphorisms which require some catastrophe to bring their tremendous meanings thoroughly home. When expressed with some amount of reflectiveness it seems co-ordinate with a belief that this flattery

must be reasonable to be effective. It is to the credit of men that few attempt to settle the question by experiment, and it is for their happiness, perhaps, that accident has never settled it for them. Nevertheless, that a male dissembler who by deluging her with untenable fictions charms the female wisely, may acquire powers reaching to the extremity of perdition, is a truth taught to many by unsought and wringing occurrences. And some profess to have attained to the same knowledge by experiment as aforesaid, and jauntily continue their indulgence in such experiments with terrible effect. Sergeant Troy was one. (xxv; pp. 192–3)

What is interesting in this account of woman's (the 'complemental being's') helplessness before flattery is that it draws more of Hardy's censure than does Troy's deceit.[7] It is not, however, my primary purpose here to examine Hardy's anti-feminist tendencies, except in so far as they affect his view of Bathsheba's capacity for developing. His problem seems to have been this – how to show the growth of moral consciousness in a representative of the sex decreed infirm by long-standing custom? A degree of external improvement in her may be hoped for, but the logic of the governing initial premise – 'prescriptive infirmity' – is against transformation. Bathsheba is vain, changeable, domineering, impulsive, coquettish, and helpless before flattery. 'I want somebody to tame me; I am too independent' (IV; p. 34), she says to Oak during the courtship at Norcombe.[8] Bathsheba is tamed – that is, reduced from a state of wildness so as to be tractable and useful. Like a spirited animal, she is broken to harness. She submits to Troy's wiles, to Boldwood's claim upon her balky conscience, to Oak's example. Except in a limited sense, it is difficult to see this as moral growth, for rational self-awareness is conspicuously absent. Her irrationality is curbed, not transformed, by the end of the novel, for there we find her doing what she had done earlier, seeking an environment in which she is the enshrined centre. Her manner may change, but her instinct remains the same.

Hardy's scepticism about the possibility of essential change occurring in Bathsheba can be seen best in his oblique and allusive rendering of the two crucial moments in her career: her revival in the swamp at Weatherbury after the confrontation with Troy beside Fanny's coffin, and her response to the singing of 'Lead, Kindly Light' by the children at Weatherbury Church after Troy's death. The scene in the swamp follows immediately after Bathsheba's discovery that Fanny has borne Troy's child and that Troy is devoted to Fanny.

Significantly entitled 'Under a Tree – Reaction', the episode in the swamp shows not thoughtful, self-conscious amendment, but instinctive renewal of life-purpose, that is, 'reaction'. Though much has been made of this episode as an instance of the healing ministry of nature,[9] a close inspection of its tone and imagery does not bear this out. This is not a Wordsworthian interlude. In fact, the entire episode suggests that Hardy was unable to show Bathsheba vitally engaged in moral regeneration. Why, for example, does he choose to make the place of her 'reaction' the place of the sword demonstration and of Troy's first kiss (XLIV [p. 346]; XXVIII [p. 208])? Why is the place of her supposed regeneration the place, we might say, of her 'fall'? Mere irony? A hint, perhaps, that renewal must be accompanied by symbolic re-enactment of error? Whatever the intention of this suggestive recurrence, we are simply told that Bathsheba, 'neither knowing nor caring about the direction or issue of her flight', vaguely recalls seeing the place on a previous occasion. Why does she waken to the fluttering of Shelleyan leaves, '"like ghosts from an enchanter fleeing"' (XLIV; p. 347)? Is this phrase from 'Ode to the West Wind' used to evoke a vision of death and rebirth, sin and regeneration as being, like winter and spring, interdependent and recurring phases of the round of nature? Is this the point also, but in spatial rather than temporal terms, of Bathsheba's finding herself amidst 'pestilences small and great, in the immediate neighbourhood of comfort and health' (XLIV; p. 348)? It may well be so, since it suggests a kinship between Bathsheba's character and the unthinking, amoral working of external nature. But if this is so, it is also true that human nature is as active as non-human nature in her 'reaction'.

She wakens to the song of sparrow, finch, and robin, *and* to the sound of a ploughboy bringing horses to water. She hears still another boy, this a rather dull one, trying to learn a collect by repeating it aloud: '"O Lord, O Lord, O Lord, O Lord, O Lord":—that I know out o' book. "Give us, give us, give us, give us, give us":—that I know. "Grace that, grace that, grace that, grace that":—that I know." Other words followed to the same effect' (XLIV; p. 348). What is to be made of this modulation from 'pestilences small and great' into a half-comic image of a child straining to learn a plea for God's Redeeming Grace? It may recall the bewildered, childlike Bathsheba of the previous chapter;[10] it may anticipate the crucial scene in Chapter LVI in which Bathsheba, troubled by Troy's death, is deeply moved by the sound of children singing 'Lead, Kindly Light' (p. 448). If so, what is to be made of Bathsheba's faint amusement at

the boy's method? Is it her foolish forgetting of the lesson she seemed
to have learned by watching and imitating Oak at prayer in the
preceding chapter? Does she take seriously the collect,[11] if not the
boy or his method? These are legitimate questions raised by the text
and, once posed, suggest that neither non-human nature nor religion
is so important to Bathsheba in her recovery as plain humanity: 'her
heart bounded with gratitude' not at the song of birds or the sound of
prayer, but at the sight of Liddy and 'the thought that she was not
altogether deserted' (XLIV; p. 349). She is also hungry (p. 348).
Hunger – for love and for nutriment – moves her toward recovery.
She returns to the farm, decides defiantly that she will not retreat from
Troy and, with a 'faint gleam of humour' in her eye, decides to
immerse herself in *The Maid's Tragedy, The Mourning Bride, Night
Thoughts*, and *The Vanity of Human Wishes*. She suddenly decides,
however, to read something brighter, and so climbs to an attic to read
Love in a Village, Maid of the Mill, and some volumes of the *Spectator*
(p. 352). Bathsheba's shift from 'a vehement impulse to flee . . . not
stopping short of death itself' (XLIII; p. 345) to a whimsical retreat to
an attic with some light reading can hardly be accounted a significant
phase of her moral growth. Nor does Hardy treat it as such. He
portrays her as one involuntarily buoyant: her 'vitality of youth' has
been quenched by sorrow 'without substituting the philosophy of
maturer years' (XLVI; p. 367).

At this point of suspense, with Bathsheba dangling between
youthful vitality and mature philosophy, Hardy invokes a Wordsworthian model of female development in an attempt to define the
pattern of her career:

> To the eyes of the middle-aged, Bathsheba was perhaps ad-
> ditionally charming just now. Her exuberance of spirit was pruned
> down; the original *phantom of delight* had shown herself to be *not too
> bright for human nature's daily food*, and she had been able to enter this
> second poetical phase without losing much of the first in the
> process. (XLIX; p. 382: italics mine)

Hardy is paraphrasing and quoting Wordsworth's 'She Was a
Phantom of Delight' (1804), a poem which he clearly read as
depicting a woman's three-phase development from innocence
through experience to maturity.[12] I present it here in full because it
can be seen as an ironic analogue to his portrait of Bathsheba in the
novel.

She was a *Phantom of delight*
When first she gleamed upon my sight;
A lovely Apparition, sent
To be a moment's ornament;
Her eyes as stars of Twilight fair;
Like Twilight's, too, her dusky hair;
But all things else about her drawn
From May-time and the cheerful Dawn;
A dancing Shape, an Image gay,
To haunt, to startle, and way-lay.

I saw her upon nearer view,
A Spirit, yet a Woman too!
Her household motions light and free,
And steps of virgin-liberty;
A countenance in which did meet
Sweet records, promises as sweet;
A Creature *not too bright* or good
For human nature's daily food;
For transient sorrows, simple wiles,
Praise, blame, love, kisses, tears, and smiles.

And now I see with eye serene
The very pulse of the machine;
A Being breathing thoughtful breath,
A Traveller between life and death;
The reason firm, the temperate will,
Endurance, foresight, strength, and skill;
A perfect Woman, nobly planned,
To warn, to comfort, and command;
And yet a Spirit still, and bright
With something of angelic light. (my italics)

The Bathsheba of Norcombe and of the early days at Weatherbury is like the lovely, dusky-haired Phantom of the first stanza. The bold, independent Bathsheba who manages the farm, arouses Boldwood, succumbs to Troy, is rejected by him, and undergoes a 'reaction', is like the 'Spirit, yet . . . woman' of the second stanza, the creature 'not too bright' (note that Hardy drops the 'or good') 'for human nature's daily food'. At least this is what Hardy suggests when he tells us that she has entered a second phase of development without losing much of the first. There remains the 'woman . . . yet . . . Spirit' of the third phase, the Bathsheba who witnesses the violent death of Troy, knows piercing remorse for her treatment of Boldwood, and demonstrates (for a brief time) heroic self-control in the face of disaster. But the mature Bathsheba, unlike Wordsworth's mature Phantom, is no 'perfect Woman' or 'Spirit . . . bright / With something of angelic light'. She is viewed from the beginning as a flawed creature (Hardy's dropping the 'or good' reiterates this). The allusive, shifting style of these pages mirrors the difficulty of showing moral growth in a character conceived of as infirm.

However, what the style of the swamp episode does suggest – that Bathsheba's recovery from sorrow is as automatic as the turn of the seasons – is important, for it identifies Bathsheba's behaviour with the working of the non-human natural order, explaining in part Hardy's ambivalence toward her and making her a proper object for the ministrations of Oak, that knowing, resourceful student of nature. Hardy had been brutally explicit about Elfride Swancourt's naturalistic facility for getting rid of trouble: 'She could slough off a sadness and replace it by a hope as easily as a lizard renews a diseased limb' (*PBE*, XIV; p. 152). His way of associating Bathsheba's actions with Nature's is more general, and perhaps less sanguine. Her moral history, as illustrated in her attachments to Oak, Boldwood, Troy, and then to Oak again, is made analogous to the turn of the seasons. She is courted by Oak in December of the first and in January of the second year; she entices Boldwood with the valentine in February of the second year, witnesses the death of Troy on 24 December of the same year, and weds Oak on Christmas Day of the third. After the death of Troy, she is described as 'reviv[ing] with the spring' (LVI; p. 447), the season in which 'the vegetable world begins to move and swell and the saps to rise' (XVIII; p. 138). As winter and spring roll round, so for Bathsheba or for those associated with her renewal or death come round. Hardy leaves it tantalisingly uncertain whether the marriage of Oak and Bathsheba breaks the cycle.

Before going on to consider the climactic episode at Weatherbury Church, it is important to note Hardy's attempt to document this fatalistic nature-psychology of Bathsheba in more conventional psychological terms. We are told little about Bathesheba's childhood, but what we are told makes it clear that it was unhappy. Her father, a gentleman-tailor, loved his exceedingly beautiful wife best when pretending that he was not married to her and was 'commiting the seventh' (VIII; p. 69). Was Bathsheba expected to play the 'bastard' in this strange marriage, and is that an explanation for her puzzling statement to Boldwood that she is aloof toward him because 'An unprotected childhood in a cold world has beaten gentleness out of me' (XXXI; p. 233)? We cannot be certain. But we can be sure that at twenty she is a volatile mixture of girl and woman: now an 'unpractised girl' and now a cool woman (VII [p. 56]; X [p. 91]), now a model of 'aspiring virginity' (IX; p. 85), then, a few days later, a woman of 'full bloom and vigour' capable of 'alarming exploits of sex, and daring enough to carry them out' (XII; p. 102). Another striking aspect of Bathsheba's personality is her mannishness. She straddles a pony in masculine fashion, much to Oak's astonishment. Moved suddenly to the head of Weatherbury Farm by the death of her uncle, she assumes that masculine role. Finding bailiff Pennyways a thief, she takes on his duties as well. 'Let's toss, as men do', she urges Liddy, as she decides whether or not to send the fatal valentine, inscribed with an imperious 'Marry Me', to Boldwood. Hardy seems to have ordered the novel's main and subordinate plots in such a way as to place Bathsheba in the conventionally masculine role of aggressor and seducer. Troy's ruin of Fanny parallels Bathsheba's ruin of Boldwood, as later, in *Tess of the d'Urbervilles* and *Jude the Obscure*, Alec's seduction of Tess is re-enacted in Arabella's enticement of Jude. Bathsheba's valentine has, it seems, something in common with Arabella's pig's-pizzle. But the epicene Bathsheba is also like Sue Bridehead, Arabella's antithesis, in her alarm at Liddy's 'Amazonian picture' of her as a woman who would be a match for any man. 'I hope I am not a bold sort of maid — mannish?' she cries. Liddy replies: 'O no, not mannish; but so almightly womanish that 'tis getting on that way sometimes' (XXX; p. 227).[13]

Bathsheba is girlish, womanish, mannish, and also — though in her early twenties — very much a child, especially when in the presence of the three men whom she at once flees and pursues, perhaps because to her they are at once lovers and fathers. She entrances and rules Boldwood with her beauty, but in the face of his anger she describes herself as 'only a girl' (XXXI; p. 234). In the presence of the dashing Troy, there is 'a little tremulousness in the usually cool girl's voice' (XXVI; p. 198); her love for him is as 'entire as a child's' (XXIX; p. 215). When she sees him kiss the dead Fanny, there is 'childlike pain and simplicity' (Hardy calls it 'abnormal and startling') in her plea that he kiss her as well (XLIII; p. 344). Her 'coolness of manner' is, as Hardy says, only a 'trick' to mask her surprise and impulsiveness (XXXII [p. 244]; XLI [p. 311]). Her artfulness is understood by Oak from the moment, in the first chapter of the novel, when he steps forward to pay a toll which she stubbornly refuses to pay, and when, at the shearing, he teaches her to sharpen the clippers by guiding her hands with his own, 'taking each as we sometimes clasp a child's hand in teaching him to write' (xx; p. 150).

All this suggests that elements of Bathsheba's troubled childhood persist, undigested so to speak, into her young womanhood. This view differs significantly from the view of Wordsworth that the adult, with the aid of memory, can recall and preserve the pleasure and joy of childhood. Wordsworth views growth in 'She Was a Phantom' (and in 'Ode: Intimations of Immortality', which Hardy calls upon in the episode at Weatherbury Church) as a progress toward integration and compensation for loss. In Bathsheba, Hardy depicts growth as a fitful ebbing and flowing – on the one hand an improvement of externals, on the other a hopeless struggle against unalterable traits in an infirm nature and unalterable facts of experience. She cannot change her nature; she cannot change the past. The unalterability of things drives her into reminiscence and nostalgia, as in the unhappy days of her marriage to Troy:

> She was conquered; but she would never own it as long as she lived. Her pride was indeed brought low by despairing discoveries of her spoliation by marriage with a less pure nature than her own. . . . Until she had met Troy, Bathsheba had been proud of her position as a woman; it had been a glory to her to know that her lips had been touched by no man's on earth – that her waist had never been encircled by a lover's arm. She hated herself now. In those earlier days she had always nourished a secret contempt for girls who were slaves of the first good-looking young fellow who should choose to salute them. . . . Although she scarcely knew the divinity's name, Diana was the goddess whom Bathsheba instinctively adored. That she had never, by look, word, or sign, encouraged a man to approach her – that she had felt herself sufficient to herself, and had in the independence of her girlish heart fancied there was a certain degradation in renouncing the simplicity of a maiden existence to become the humbler half of an indifferent matrimonial whole – were facts now bitterly remembered. O, if she had never stooped to folly of this kind, respectable as it was, and could only stand again, as she had stood on the hill at Norcombe, and dare Troy or any other man to pollute a hair of her head by his interference! (xli; pp. 315–16: ellipses mine)

Bathsheba is filled with repugnance toward physical contact and near-hysteria at the thought of having lost her innocence. Sexual union with Troy has left her with a sense of 'spoliation', 'degradation', and pollution, the unalterability of which 'she would never own . . . as long as she lived'. Therefore she hates herself, regards herself a bloody victim, a fallen woman (the allusion to Goldsmith). Her instinctive affinity for Diana (so at odds with her fascination for men) reinforces this. Her idea of growing up is, in short, a nervous, panicky one requiring fulfilment of the impossible dream of regaining the lost 'simplicity of a maiden existence'. A similar paradisaic longing is behind her attempt to atone to Boldwood for her injury of him.

The culminating episode at Weatherbury Church begins when, at the news of Troy's death, Boldwood seeks to renew his courtship of her. Bathsheba welcomes Boldwood's devotion, for she is reminded of her original folly and wishes again 'as she had wished many months ago, for some means of making reparation for her fault' (LI; p. 403). Here she appears to be conscious of a capacity for self-amendment and eager to effect it. Where formerly she had pleaded with Boldwood to forgive her and free her from her moral debt, she now assumes full responsibility: 'My treatment of you was thoughtless, inexcusable, wicked! I shall eternally regret it. If there had been anything I could have done to make amends I would most gladly have done it – there was nothing on earth I so longed to do as to repair the error. But that was not possible' (LI; p. 405: see also p. 409). Like Sue Bridehead seeking by remarriage to Phillotson to punish herself for the death of her children, Bathsheba decides to marry Boldwood 'as a sort of penance'. Boldwood, half-mad in his passion to recapture through her his lost dream of happiness, encourages her moral masochism. 'Remember the past', he counsels, 'and be kind' (p. 406).

But Boldwood's desperate yearning for the irrecoverable past, as well as Bathsheba's nostalgic desire to make reparation to him, is blocked by Troy's return. 'Heaven's persistent irony' works through Troy to thwart Bathsheba in her attempt to atone just as it worked (in Troy's view) through the gargoyle on Weatherbury Church to thwart his attempt to make amends to Fanny by planting flowers on her grave. 'It may be argued with great plausibility', writes Hardy, 'that reminiscence is less an endowment than a disease.' Reminiscence, or 'projection of consciousness into days gone by', is the disease of Troy, of Boldwood, and of Bathsheba. 'Expectation', the only healthy attitude, is not easily come by; for 'in its only comfortable form – that of absolute faith – [it] is practically an impossibility; whilst in the form of hope and the secondary compounds, patience, impatience, resolve, curiosity, it is a constant fluctuation between pleasure and pain' (XXV; p. 190). Oak is of course the only character capable of expectation, though of the painful variety, and we may be inclined to think that in the critical moments after Troy's violent death, and in the months thereafter, Bathsheba imitates Oak by putting off reminiscence for expectation and undergoes thereby a gradual transformation. But not so. Hardy undercuts every sign of transformation with reminders of her infirmity. The spectacle of Troy's death 'made her herself again. . . . Deeds of endurance which seem ordinary in philosophy are rare in conduct, and Bathsheba was astonishing all around her now, for her philosophy was her conduct, and she seldom thought practicable what she did not practise.' That is high praise, but the next sentence – 'She was of the stuff of which great men's mothers are made' – makes it clear that it is limited praise (LIV; p. 437: ellipsis mine). With the appearance of three men, the parson, the surgeon, and Oak, she ends her brief moment of heroism with an appropriate feminine gesture: she collapses in a paroxysm of self-blame. 'O it is my fault', she cries; 'how can I live! O Heaven, how can I live!' (LIV; p. 440). Two months later she is even more worn down: 'Her eyes are so miserable that she's not the same woman', says Liddy. 'Only two years ago she was a romping girl [see the 'dancing shape' of stanza 1 of 'She Was a Phantom of Delight'], and now she's this!' (LV; p. 445). *This* is not the perfect woman 'bright / With something of angelic light' of stanza 3. Bathsheba's 'reviv[al] with the spring' (LVI; p. 447) reminds us that beneath her struggling moral consciousness lies an unalterable infirmity. It is in Hardy's view no more plausible to think her (or Troy, or Boldwood) capable of undoing the wrongs, or recovering the dreams, of days gone by, than it is to think her capable of recovering a prelapsarian state of perfection.

Bathsheba visits the grave of Fanny and the child, now the grave of Troy as well, and hears there the children of Weatherbury singing 'Lead, Kindly Light'. The lines from Newman's hymn are used, adroitly, to suggest, upon Oak's entry on to the scene, that Bathsheba hopes that he will forget the past ('"Pride ruled my will: remember not past years"'), and that she is prepared to forget Troy ('"Which I have loved long since, and lost awhile"'). 'Stirred by emotions which latterly she had assumed to be altogether dead within her', Bathsheba seems to be ready for the penultimate step in her transformation from egotism and crippling reminiscence to altruism and expectation. But Hardy quickly undermines this:

> Bathsheba's feeling was always to some extent dependent upon her whim, as is the case with many other women. Something big came into her throat and an uprising to her eyes -- and she thought that she would allow the imminent tears to flow if they wished. . . . Once that she had begun to cry for she hardly knew what, she could not leave off for crowding thoughts she knew too well. She would have given anything in the world to be, as those children were, unconcerned at the meaning of their words, because too innocent to feel the necessity for any such expression. All the impassioned scenes of her brief experience seemed to revive with added emotion at that moment, and those scenes which had been without emotion during enactment had emotion then. Yet grief came to her rather as a luxury than as the scourge of former times. (LVI; pp. 448−9: ellipsis mine)

Hardy's observation, wholly consistent with the 'weaker vessel' view of Bathsheba pervading the novel, that her feelings are *always* partly dependent upon her whimsy, blocks any attempt to take seriously this episode as a climactic moment in her moral transformation. Bathsheba's offences are neither forgiven nor atoned for; nor are they diminished by deep-felt contrition. They are made unimportant by the passage of time, and Hardy seems to agree that they must be. But the offences are also made slightly pleasing by Bathsheba's whimsical attitude to them. She weeps 'for she hardly knew what'. Hardy seems to find that reprehensible. She is as sorry as she, a woman, and therefore (in the view of the novel) a creature of inferior moral capabilities, can be.

Hardy marks her limited capacity for amendment by what I believe is a calculated use, in this same passage, of the language and sentiment of stanza 10 of Wordsworth's 'Ode: Intimations of Immortality From Recollections of Early Childhood' to create an aura of reconciliation and recovery in the face of loss. Stanza 10 begins 'Then sing, ye birds, sing a joyous song!' and continues with an assertion of the finality of loss ('Though nothing can bring back the hour . . .') and the certainty of compensation 'in the primal sympathy / Which having been must ever be; / In the soothing thoughts that spring / Out of human suffering; / In the faith that looks through death, / In years that bring the philosophic mind.' Bathsheba, listening to the singing children, recalling her past, wishing for the innocence of a child, reminds us of the poet listening to the song of birds and reflecting upon loss and gain. Hardy's 'crowding thoughts she knew too well' may echo Wordsworth's 'soothing thoughts that spring out of human suffering', the phrase which seems also to be the origin of Hardy's 'Yet grief came to her rather as a luxury than as the scourge of former times.' With the Wordsworthian analogue in mind, we can see that Hardy allows her only one consolation – 'soothing thoughts that spring out of human suffering', though even that is involuntary (the luxury of grief 'came *to* her'). She is deprived of 'primal sympathy' by an unhappy childhood, of faith that sees through death by irreligion, of philosophic understanding by her woman's, that is, her irrational consciousness. Her true gain, or 'strength', can come, within the masculine ethos of the novel, only through submission and marriage to an exemplary male. As in the use of 'She Was a Phantom of Delight' to describe the second stage of Bathsheba's career, Hardy's use of 'Ode: Intimations of Immortality' to describe the final stage creates ironic resonances which imply an incapacity for development more clearly than they imply a growth toward wider sympathy.[14] Bathsheba cannot be an embodiment of the vision of the Ode that the forever-lost can be compensated for by what remains behind. Oak, for all his solid strength, is not the dashing Troy. As for Bathsheba, even if she could regain a semblance of the state of maiden simplicity by marrying Oak, she could not root out the flaw of her nature; for her flaw is the flaw of maidens, of all daughters of Eve.

Hardy's use of Newman and (in my view) of Wordsworth suggests, however, a limited progress on Bathsheba's part. Her ability to find 'luxury' rather than a 'scourge' in grief, though suggestive of a degree of indifference toward Troy, Boldwood, and Fanny, is in Hardy's view 'right' because consistent with the relentless ongoingness of things. Here Hardy distinguishes between what might be called a moral and a sentimental function of memory. On the one hand, he clearly regards nostalgia or reminiscence as a disease that blinds its victims to the irretrievability inherent in change. In this he suggests that memory (in the form of excessive regret or remorse) constricts moral growth. Here the phrase from Newman, 'remember not past years' (overheard by Bathsheba) and the counsel of the Ode, grieve not and seek strength in what remains behind, concur in suggesting that Bathsheba is at this point seeking to begin anew, her past forgotten, if not forgiven. On the other hand, Hardy is

unsympathetic toward Bathsheba's capacity for sloughing off unpleasant memories, for 'reviving with the spring'. A ready capacity
for mending suggests a transientness of feeling which he perhaps
associates with the impassiveness of a natural order as likely, in the
words of 'Hap', to strew blisses about his pilgrimage as pain. He
seems, in short, to insist in this that memory is essential to moral
growth. He is not contradicting himself, but distinguishing validly
between recollective memory and nostalgia. But the interesting
distinction must be largely a moot one, for what Bathsheba overhears
is not what she can do. That is, she cannot make a new start, but
must — what else is possible? — revert to nature. If she can be cured of
the disease of reminiscence, of a moral masochism which would lead
her to a disastrous marriage or to prolonged graveside weeping, she
cannot be cured of the disease of kind. Hardy makes this abundantly
clear in the closing scenes between Bathsheba and Oak.

With Oak's re-entry into Bathsheba's life, reserve and funereal
sadness give way before a pleasing bit of male fantasy, the taming of a
shrew, when Oak's announced intention to emigrate moves Bathsheba to pursuit of him. However, Hardy does not allow the
playfulness in this to conceal the fact that Bathsheba's new manner,
characterised by humility and even mildness, cloaks the old instinct to
charm and possess a man. She is stung by the sensation that Oak, 'her
last old disciple', has abandoned her. On Christmas Day, exactly one
year after Troy's death and her great sorrow, she examines her heart
and finds it 'beyond measure strange that the subject of which the
season might have been supposed suggestive — the event in the hall at
Boldwood's — was not agitating her at all; but instead, an agonizing
conviction that everybody abjured her — for what she could not
tell — and that Oak was the ringleader of the recusants' (LVI; p. 452).
She is mistaking Oak's solicitousness for her delicate situation as a
widow for betrayal of an obligation to follow and worship her. The
language of the episode suggests even more. 'Disciple', 'abjured', and
'recusants' are the words of the religionist, in this case the once-
idolised woman longing for re-enshrinement. The words recall, with
grim precision, the fact that she sent Boldwood the fatal valentine
because she was somewhat annoyed by his 'nonconformity'. He was,
in her view, 'a species of Daniel in her kingdom who persisted in
kneeling eastward when reason and common sense said that he might
just as well follow suit with the rest, and afford her the official glance
of admiration which cost nothing at all' (XIII; p. 110). When she
receives Oak's letter announcing his departure in the coming March,

she weeps bitterly, but not at the thought of losing him. 'She was aggrieved and wounded that the possession of hopeless love from Gabriel, which she had grown to regard as her inalienable right for life, should have been withdrawn just at his own pleasure in this way' (LVI; p. 452). In essence she has altered little, it seems, since her earlier errors.

On the eve of the wedding there is 'a certain rejuvenated appearance about her: — "As though a rose should shut and be a bud again"':[15]

> Repose had again incarnadined her cheeks; and having, at Gabriel's request, arranged her hair this morning as she had worn it years ago on Norcombe Hill, she seemed in his eyes remarkably like the girl of that fascinating dream, which, considering that she was now only three or four-and-twenty, was perhaps not very wonderful. (LVII; p. 462).

There is considerable irony in Bathsheba's seeming to Oak 're-markably like' the girl at Norcombe, and even greater irony in Oak's indulging himself in a nostalgic attempt to recreate the girl of his dream, the girl, we will recall, whom he watched some three years before gaze so long upon herself in a mirror that 'she blushed at herself, and seeing her reflection blush, blushed the more':

> The picture was a delicate one. Woman's prescriptive infirmity had stalked into the sunlight, which had clothed it in the freshness of an originality. . . . She . . . observed herself as a fair product of Nature in the feminine kind, her thoughts seeming to glide into far-off though likely dramas in which men would play a part — vistas of probable triumphs — the smiles being of a phase suggesting that hearts were imagined as lost and won. (I; p. 5: ellipses mine)

Is Hardy suggesting that Oak is but another triumph for 'a fair product of Nature in the feminine kind'? The answer must be yes, in part. The old vanity, seeking the self's re-embodiment in others, rather than in a mirror, still governs Bathsheba. But it must be seen that Oak, knowing this from the start, is a willing victim who enjoys his own kind of victory. If Bathsheba has not changed essentially through some three years of severe schooling, her circumstances have changed significantly. Her circle of admirers has been reduced by two-thirds, and her 'absolute hunger' for affection, a genuine aspect of her flawed nature, can be satisfied only by Oak, the sole survivor of the original circle of worshippers. Oak has Bathsheba, so to speak, where he wants her – in a position in which she must turn to him for gratification of her infirm nature's deepest longing. The 'happiness' of this ending, and there can be no doubt that we have here happiness of a kind, grows up, as Hardy says, 'in the interstices of a mass of hard prosaic reality' (LVI; p. 456).[16]

I stated at the beginning of this essay that in *Far from the Madding Crowd* Hardy associates Bathsheba's prescriptive infirmity with the ineradicable defect he sees in non-human nature and presents in Oak an example of how to cope with the imperfection of things. Oak survives misfortune because he sees that he is subject, like all other living things, to the laws of nature, that is, to the stubborn, irreducible properties of things. He accepts the loss of his herd and works hard toward recovery. He confronts fire, storm, and disease among Bathsheba's flock, and uses a tarp, a lightning rod, and a surgical instrument to keep loss to a minimum. He attempts throughout to minimise the effects of Bathsheba's folly as well. In none of these does he succeed fully, but in all it is his achievement to accept loss and to make what improvement he can upon nature. He does not rebel against nature. Nor does he guide himself by or follow nature's laws. Rather, he studies nature's workings in order to know them and to use them to his ends. He attains his end with Bathsheba by seeing and accepting her infirmity, and suffering patiently the effects of it, until her infirmity and his purpose can be happily joined. His role is summed up metaphorically in a remark he makes while munching a piece of bacon which has fallen to the earth: 'I never fuss about dirt in its pure state, and when I know what sort it is' (VIII; p. 62).[17]

NOTES

1. See John Halperin, *Egoism & Self-Discovery in the Victorian Novel* (New York: Burt Franklin, 1974) p. 217: '*Far from the Madding Crowd* addresses itself basically to the question of how to live as painlessly as possible and answers that question by tracing Bathsheba's development from a state of moral solipsism and narrow vision to one of moral expansion and wider sympathy.' Dale Kramer, *Thomas Hardy: The Forms of Tragedy* (London: Macmillan; Detroit: Wayne State University Press, 1975) p. 31, writes: 'Bathsheba . . . definitely evolves from a flirtatious, light-hearted girl to a self-confident farmer, to a chastened but stubborn wife, . . . to a subdued female anxious for the protective strength of a Gabriel Oak' (ellipses mine). Albert J. Guerard, *Thomas Hardy: The Novels and Stories* (1949: rpt. New York: New

Directions, 1964) p. 140, says that 'the matured Bathsheba may have to depend on Oak at critical hours, but she is a courageous figure in her own right. She has been changed by responsibility and disaster.' My own view is nearer that of Richard C. Carpenter, 'The Mirror and the Sword: Imagery in *Far from the Madding Crowd*', *NCF*, XVIII (1964) 345: 'Without [its] imagery *Far from the Madding Crowd* would be merely a kind of melodramatic folk tale about the fair charmer who overplayed her capriciousness and came to insight and repentance almost too late.' The novel's imagery, argues Carpenter, reveals two aspects of Bathsheba's character, 'the respectable Victorian girl on the surface and the amoral Dionysiac underneath' (p. 343). J. I. M. Stewart (*Thomas Hardy: A Critical Biography* [London: Longman, 1971] pp. 89–90) takes brief notice of Hardy's 'sexual pessimism and inclination in misogyny' in the novel. Robert Gittings (*Young Thomas Hardy* [London: Heinemann; Boston: Little, Brown, 1975] p. 175) attributes 'the sharp aphorisms about the wiles of marriageable women' in the novel to the influence of Hardy's mother (in whose house he was living while writing it): 'One hears in them the voice of Jemima Hardy, providing, from the depths of folk-wisdom, a sexual philosophy for her favourite son.'

2. *Thomas Hardy* (London: Longman, 1954) p. 49. See also Irving Howe, *Thomas Hardy* (New York: Macmillan, 1967) p. 55: 'Bathsheba, by far the most striking figure in the novel, is presented almost entirely from the "outside": she is not, after all, a likely candidate for psychological probing.'

3. James's review (*The Nation* [New York], 24 December 1874) is reprinted in Laurence Lerner and John Holmstrom (eds), *Thomas Hardy and His Readers: A Selection of Contemporary Reviews* (London: The Bodley Head, 1968) pp. 28–33. James found Bathsheba 'alternately vague and coarse, and . . . always artificial' (p. 33). For Hardy as writer of romance, see John Paterson, *The Novel as Faith* (Boston: Gambit, 1973) pp. 40–68.

4. Hardy was still at work on *A Pair of Blue Eyes* in early 1873 when he outlined for Leslie Stephen, editor of *Cornhill Magazine*, 'a pastoral tale which I thought of calling "Far from the Madding Crowd" in which the chief characters would be a woman-farmer, a shepherd, and a sergeant in the Dragoon Guards' (quoted by Richard L. Purdy, *Thomas Hardy: A Bibliographical Study* [Oxford: Clarendon Press, 1954] p. 16).

5. *The Complete Poems of Thomas Hardy*, ed. James Gibson (London: Macmillan; New York: St. Martin's Press, 1976) pp. 13, 829, 7, 14; 929, 310, 338–39, 914, 726–8. A remark in a letter of 5 June 1919 to Florence Henniker is typical of Hardy's post-war view: 'I should care more for my birthdays if at each succeeding one I could see any sign of real improvement in the world – as at one time I had fondly hoped there was; but I fear that what appears much more evident is that it is getting worse and worse' (*One Rare Fair Woman: Thomas Hardy's Letters to Florence Henniker, 1893–1922*, ed. Evelyn Hardy and F. B. Pinion [London: Macmillan, 1972] p. 185).

6. See Henry Knight's Miltonic rebuke of Elfride when he learns of her past indiscretions: ' "Fool'd and beguiled: by him thou, I by thee!" ' (*PBE*, XXXI; p. 356; *Paradise Lost*, x: 880); also, the antique hymn, 'Remember Adam's Fall', with which Fancy Day is ushered into *Under the Greenwood Tree*. See also n.7.

7. This 'defence' of Troy lends unexpected strength to Troy's claim later that Bathsheba, and not he, is responsible for Fanny's plight: 'If Satan had not tempted me with that face of yours, and those cursed coquetries, I should have married her' (XLIII; p. 345).

8. Richard C. Carpenter, *Thomas Hardy* (New York: Twayne, 1964) p. 87, argues that Bathsheba is not ready for reform until she is 'dominated by a sexually aggressive man'.

9. Howard Babb, 'Setting and Theme in *Far from the Madding Crowd*', *ELH*, xxx (1963) 160, argues that the meaning of Bathsheba's experience in the swamp is that 'she has found refuge from Troy in nature and been morally regenerated by that world'.

10. At Bathsheba's plea that Troy kiss her after he kisses the dead Fanny, Hardy remarks: 'There was something so abnormal and startling in the childlike pain and simplicity of this appeal from a woman of Bathsheba's calibre and independence, that Troy, loosening her tightly clasped arms from his neck, looked at her in bewilderment. It was such an unexpected revelation of all women being alike at heart, even those so different in their accessories as Fanny and this one beside him, that Troy could hardly seem to believe her to be his proud wife Bathsheba' (XLIII; p. 344).

11. The Book of Common Prayer, the Collect for the 18th Sunday after Trinity (which falls in October, like the action at this point in the novel). What Bathsheba hears is probably a version of the following: 'Lord, we beseech thee, grant thy people grace to withstand the temptations of the world, the flesh and the devil, and with pure hearts and minds to follow thee the only God; through Jesus our Lord. Amen.'

12. Though the poem is usually read, I think, as a record of an observer's deepening knowledge of a woman throughout three views of her which occur in a short period of time, Hardy 'misread' it, to serve his immediate end, as a poem of growth describing in three stanzas a movement from childhood, to girlhood, to womanhood. Citations from Wordsworth throughout are from Thomas Hutchinson (ed.: rvd. Ernest de Selincourt), *Wordsworth: Poetical Works* (New York: Oxford University Press, 1969).

13. On one occasion Hardy uses imagery usually reserved for male sexual aggression to describe Bathsheba's attempt to attract Boldwood: 'All this time Bathsheba was conscious of having broken into that dignified stronghold at last' (XVII; p. 135).

14. My sense that Wordsworth's great Ode is at work in this episode is supported by the fact that Hardy quoted from it repeatedly during his career (see Frank B. Pinion, *A Hardy Companion* [London: Macmillan, 1968] p. 214; also Peter J. Casagrande, 'Hardy's Wordsworth: A Record and a Commentary', *ELT*, xx [1977] 210–37). Hardy quoted from it three times in *A Pair of Blue Eyes* (XV [p.162]; XX [p. 211]; XXXII [p. 366]), the novel on which he was at work when he undertook to write *Madding Crowd*. His use of it in *Tess* (LI; p. 456), in the scene in which Tess listens to her siblings singing 'Here we suffer grief and pain', is remarkably like his use of it in *Madding Crowd*: to assert that compensation for loss is not readily available.

15. The phrase is from Keats's 'Eve of St. Agnes', stanza 27. It is another example of Hardy's use of literary allusion to suggest regeneration when there is none.

16. See Carpenter, *Thomas Hardy*, p. 87: 'Although Hardy allows us the questionable sop to our feelings of a marriage with Oak as a dénouement, the novel does not really end "happily." The vibrant and proud girl we see at the beginning has been as thoroughly destroyed as Troy and Boldwood. Never again, we are sure, will she burst forth in a fine blaze of fury, her black eyes snapping and her cheek flushed; nor will she blush as furiously with love or at her temerity.' For similar views see Guerard, pp. 51–2; and Roy Morrell, *Thomas Hardy: The Will and the Way* (Kuala Lumpur: University of Malaya Press; London: Oxford University Press, 1965) p. 59.

17. Morrell (pp. 63–4) rightly describes this statement by Oak as 'a precise metaphor of what Oak has been doing in the wider sphere of his life'. I am indebted throughout this study to the graduate students of English 950: Seminar in Thomas Hardy, which gathered during the fall of 1974.

5 Hardy the Creator:
Far from the Madding Crowd

SIMON GATRELL

Most studies of the texts of Hardy's novels and stories concentrate upon the significant changes in structure and characterisation revealed by the manuscript and the various printed versions, and to a great extent this essay is no exception. But there is also another, not less important if less dramatic, element in the development of Hardy's fiction. This shows Hardy acting in ways that may be duplicated (generally speaking) in all his work. The full significance of these changes can only be shown through a comparative study of the whole range of his writing, which is hardly possible in a short essay. My intention is, however, to draw attention to examples in *Far from the Madding Crowd* of at least some of these kinds of activity and to suggest their significance as a first step towards a synthetic study of all Hardy's fictional prose.

I have chosen to concentrate, nominally at least, on Chapters XL to XLIII (pp. 302–45) of *Far from the Madding Crowd*.[1] The structure, though, is a loose one, and I have felt free to range over the whole novel where the material demanded it; digressions from the sequential run through the chapters are the rule. I have, for the most part, not discussed the early part of the book, since Professor R. C. Schweik has already analysed it in some detail;[2] though I have a few words to say in amplification of his conclusions, largely deriving from a feature of the manuscript which he has not reported.

Professor R. L. Purdy has described the final numeration, in three sections, which Hardy placed on each leaf of the manuscript of *Far from the Madding Crowd*,[3] but the earlier systems of numbering which are visible either as cancellations under the final version or else at the inner margin of the leaves have not so far been noticed. They provide much evidence about the composition of the novel which is not otherwise obtainable; indeed it is probable that were the manuscript disbound more information might be forthcoming, as it appears that some of these earlier numbers are at present lost in the gutter of the manuscript. One of the reasons that I have chosen Chapter XL as a starting point is that it inaugurates one of these earlier sequences of numeration, though its first leaf in the manuscript has only the final number 2–181 on it. The table on pp. 94–6 provides a comparative guide to the pagination of the four chapters that form the centre of this essay. For reference in the following analysis I shall prefix the earlier numeration on each leaf with the letter E; thus the leaf numbered 2–182 is also numbered by Hardy E2. I shall also be referring to various printed versions of *Far from the Madding Crowd*, and they will be identified by the following abbreviations:

> C = the serialisation in *Cornhill* (1874)
> 74 = the first edition in two volumes published by Smith, Elder in 1874
> 75 = the second impression revised of 74, published by Smith, Elder in 1875
> 77 = the first one-volume edition published by Smith, Elder in 1877
> 95 = its appearance in Hardy's first complete collected edition, published by Osgood, McIlvaine in 1895
> 02 = the revised plates of 95 issued by Macmillan in 1902
> 12 = its appearance in the Wessex Edition of Hardy's works, published by Macmillan in 1912

For convenience in tracing quotations through the versions, all page references are to 12; chapter numbers are also given where they are necessary. It will sometimes be found that quotations from the manuscript, identified by page numbers in the Wessex Edition, will differ from the text there present, since intervening revision may have taken place. All quotations from *Far from the Madding Crowd* are in italics.

Textually Chapter XL is relatively uncomplicated. The first leaf may be a later rewriting since it has no E number, but there is no evidence to suggest what is new in it. The single important narrative change in the chapter is the considerable augmentation of the role of the dog in helping Fanny to reach Casterbridge – the new leaves E7 and 7a contain the whole of this narrative. It is not likely that this was a completely new concept, since on E9 the dog is mentioned as having been stoned away, and there is no suggestion that this was a later leaf; it seems probable that Hardy wanted to heighten the sentimental appeal of an existing episode.

The only other detail that is worth noticing in this chapter is the phrase *the original amount of exertion* in the second paragraph on page 304; in manuscript this was *the original quantum of exertion*, and it reached its present form in 75. The change may be seen as the substitution of a simple for a slightly obscure word, and as of no further interest – but there were relatively few alterations made in this reimpression, and some at least are traceable to outside influences.

Two verifiable examples derive from criticisms in R. H. Hutton's review of the first edition of *Far from the Madding Crowd* in *The Spectator*.[4] Hutton says

> the repeater-watch which, it appears, . . . Jan Coggan carries in his waistcoat-pocket, seems to suggest a totally different world of physical belongings [than is appropriate to him]. (ellipsis mine)

In response to this Hardy added in 75:

> *Coggan carried an old pinchbeck repeater which he had inherited from some genius in his family. . . .*
>
> (XXXII; p. 241)

Later in the review Hutton quotes two paragraphs (run into one) beginning *The phases of Boldwood's life* (XVIII; p. 137), on which he comments

> The following passage strikes us as a study almost in the nature of a careful caricature of George Eliot.

Again Hardy's reaction was immediate; a sentence of the description of Boldwood was removed in 75 – and this time the impact of the criticism was so strong that he further abbreviated the passage when the novel was reset for 77 (though there was possibly another reason for this later change: see below pp. 84–5). Indeed Hardy's almost complete silence about George Eliot in the *Life* and his letters may well be the result of the continual repetition, in review after review, of comparisons with her as a writer; and it is easy to guess that *The Hand of Ethelberta*, the novel which followed *Far from the Madding Crowd* in *Cornhill*, was conceived not so much as an unpastoral novel as an un-George Eliot-like novel.

Another criticism generally made in reviews of *Far from the Madding Crowd* was directed at what was called the uncomfortably ingenious style, and some of the other alterations in 75 may be an attempt to tone down this element in the novel: *circumambient*, for instance, became *circling*, and it seems not impossible that *quantum* was changed for the same reason. One other feature of Hardy's receptivity to criticism, his reaction to the suggestions of Leslie Stephen, the editor of *Cornhill*, will be discussed later on.

E9, the final leaf of Chapter XL, is fragmentary, with a portion removed from the bottom; this by itself would be enough to suggest that Chapter XLI originally began in a different way, but a glance at the table of numerations will show that the whole chapter underwent considerable upheaval after the E numeration was first placed on the leaves. It was in fact expanded from an original seven leaves to its present fifteen; at one time it presumably began with E10 and ended with E16, since it is probable that the earlier first leaf of Chapter XLII was numbered E17 (see table of numerations). There appear to be four stages of development:

(i) 2–192 is the only leaf still bearing the original E numeration, though 2–195, which is a composite leaf, having a piece cut from the top and new material added in its place, also presumably dates from the first E numeration.

(ii) 2–199 to 202 and 2–205 belong to a second system of E numeration carried on into Chapter XLII, then abandoned.

(iii) 2–198, 2–203 and 2–204 are slightly later additions to that sequence.

(iv) 2–191, 2–193 and 2–196 to 197 are without E numbers at all and probably represent the latest stage of revision.

In contrast with the expansion in the rest of the chapter, the opening was shortened, two leaves making way for one; after this the main area of concern in the early part of the chapter up to 2–196 is the accidental revelation of Fanny's hair—and there are revisions still remaining on the new leaves which suggest that Hardy's view of this event and its consequences had altered. For instance, on 2–193 (p. 312) there are two additions to the first exchanges regarding the coil of hair, and on 2–196 we can see Hardy changing his mind as he writes. The MS reads (the passage within ⟨⟩ was cancelled):

"*You won't burn that curl. ⟨of hair, and you said "ties" just now, and Frank, that woman we met.*

O that's nothing, he said hastily.⟩ You like the woman. . . .

—then there is more dialogue about the hair and its owner until—

"*But just now you said 'ties'. . . ."* (p. 314)

Most likely, then, the importance of Fanny's hair was elaborated, so that Bathsheba would have no problem in recognising the corpse of the servant girl she had known so briefly, and so that she should have a more concrete reason for suspecting a connection between Fanny, Troy, and the girl she and Troy had met on the road.

It is probable that 2– 197 was originally E16a, for it is only sixteen lines long (whereas the average is twenty-five), and it contains the beginning (at *Her pride was indeed brought low* [p. 315]) of an extended analytical description of Bathsheba that occupies the whole of E16b and is only concluded on a small piece of paper jointed to the top of E17. This kind of analysis by the detached narrator is often an addition to the manuscript; additions of this kind of analysis are usually too long to write interlineally, so they mostly occur on the verso of the preceding leaf. There are two examples in the first chapter of the novel—on page 3—

He had just reached the time of life at which 'young' . . . *were clearly separated.* (ellipsis mine);

and on page 5—

Woman's prescriptive infirmity had stalked into the sunlight, which had invested it with the freshness of an originality.

And many other instances may be found throughout the manuscript. It is also true that some such passages of narratorial reflection which Hardy wished to add at a relatively late stage of the manuscript were too long to insert in this simple way, making it necessary to rewrite the leaves concerned. This probably happened at the beginning of Chapter v where 1 – 45 and 1 – 45a take the place of an original 1 – 45; the first new leaf has the paragraph beginning *It may have been observed* . . . and concludes with one of the descriptions of Oak's temperament, here in terms of lyrical natural imagery, that are often late additions to the text.

It is probable, then, that this long paragraph on page 315 describing

Bathsheba's instinctive allegiance to Diana was an afterthought, one in which he was trying to offer some counterbalance to the impression given by the early chapters of the novel to many contemporary readers that she was a selfish and thoughtless flirt; indeed the statement in the new paragraph that *she had never, by look, word, or sign, encouraged a man to approach her* seems hardly reconcilable with her early treatment of Oak, Boldwood, and Troy.

On 2–200 there is the first example in these chapters of something that concerned Hardy throughout the novel, exercising him perhaps more than any other topic – adjustment to the role of Gabriel Oak. He has with Gabriel a difficult problem of balance, and a similarly difficult one of placing: how to manage to keep him in the reader's mind while Bathsheba is primarily occupied with Troy and Boldwood, but yet not let him be too prominent; and, secondly, whereabouts exactly to pitch him in the available social scale. He is at the centre of the great set scenes of the fire and the storm, and in the first half of the novel he is involved in various shepherding occupations; but there is considerable evidence that Hardy wasn't satisfied, and at certain points in the climactic chapters I am concentrating upon, Gabriel's involvement is added or augmented.

Originally on 2–200 Farmer Boldwood gave a simple message about Fanny's death to Joseph Poorgrass, but this was cancelled, and in the consequent addition Gabriel became a confidant of Boldwood in the *earnest conversation* between them, and only after a *long time* did Poorgrass come by with his barrow to be informed of Fanny's death (p. 316). The purpose of the change is three-fold; firstly to reinforce Gabriel's relationship with Boldwood, which becomes more important as the novel goes on, secondly to maintain his connection with Fanny, established by their meeting early in the novel, and thirdly to begin his active involvement in this particular crisis of Bathsheba's life.

I would like for a while to look at how these three strands of intention in revision are arrived at, and where they lead. The first is the least important – there is only one previous revision which is related to this growth, on page 272 (XXXV) where Oak is added to Coggan in making a respectful nod to the farmer – primarily to emphasise his sense of inferiority in status at that stage in the novel. He then speaks to Boldwood after the storm, and the two men begin to be directly contrasted in their love for Bathsheba; the addition on 2–200 implies a closer connection between the men than heretofore, and this in the end leads to Gabriel's arrangement of partnership with

Boldwood; the change is signalled most clearly by the dialogue between Boldwood and Liddy Smallbury on page 384, in which Boldwood calls Gabriel *Mr Oak* (XLIX). The close of their relationship is on page 445 in a proof addition to C in which the narrator says of Boldwood *there had been qualities in the farmer which Oak loved* (LV; I shall have reason to recur to this particular addition later).

The second strand, the development of Gabriel's involvement with Fanny, begins with Chapter VII of the novel. Professor Schweik has said that the decision to add this chapter, indeed the decision to dramatise Fanny's story, was taken part of the way through the composition of Chapter X, citing cancelled numeration to help demonstrate his point.[5] He is clearly right to suggest that the leaves which now constitute Chapter VII in the manuscript were late additions, but I do not think he is correct in suggesting it was an entirely new idea. Professor Schweik believes that the cancelled numeration ended at 1–91 with a copying error on 1–112; in fact it extends to 1–125, the end of Chapter XI, which indicates that Hardy had got at least so far before he added the new Chapter VII.

At one time, according to a note on 1–125, Chapter XI was intended to end the second instalment of the serial, and so it would not be surprising if Hardy, reviewing the material for that episode, decided then to add the new chapter. In fact it seems certain that some encounter must have taken place between Gabriel and Fanny on the original two leaves which Chapter VII now replaces, for on 1–109, which has the cancelled number 104, it is mentioned that Gabriel has gone to look for Fanny at The Buck's Head; this leaf is not recopied, and so the inn must have figured in some original meeting; presumably a very brief encounter, which is very much more fully realised in the present version.

It is clear also from an examination of the manuscript that the leaves comprising Chapter XI, the scene outside the barracks in the snow, are a patchwork from perhaps three periods of conception. The earliest leaf is probably 1–123, which dates from a time when Hardy had not settled Troy's christian name; on this leaf it was *Alfred*, and only later was that cancelled and changed to *Frank* (with its ironic overtones);[6] on both 1–122 and 1–124 it is *Frank*, unrevised. There are four lines or so cut from the bottom of 1–119 leaving the vestiges of the words *If anything could*, and this phrase now occurs in the middle of the first paragraph on 1–120 (p. 96), showing that 1–120 dates from a later period than 119; 1–120 is in itself a leaf cut at the bottom, suggesting that there were at least two rewritings of the opening of the chapter

before any of the visible numerations were made (there is an E
numeration, but it too is consecutive). This is all strong evidence that
the scene was part of Hardy's early conception of the tale and not an
afterthought. It is, however, most probable that the close sympathy
felt by Gabriel for Fanny *was* a late thought on Hardy's part. This
connection between Fanny and Gabriel is further strengthened by a
small revision on page 260 (XXXIV) where Boldwood says in the MS
that he is the only person in the village *excepting one* who knows of
Troy's relation to Fanny; in proof for C *one* was changed to *Gabriel
Oak*. There are two further alterations in the chapters we are looking
at which carry on this concern still further: 2–203 and 2–204 (E 21
and 21a) are later additions to the manuscript, and following the
introduction of Gabriel in the addition in which Boldwood discussed
Fanny's death with him it is likely that the various details that
Poorgrass relates of Gabriel on these two leaves were new, and in
particular the paragraph on page 320 beginning

> *Perhaps he was busy, ma'am. . . . And sometimes he seems to suffer from
> things on his mind* (ellipsis mine) –

which may well have been added to prepare for the amplification of
Gabriel's unconscious influence over Bathsheba's mind in the next
chapters. Similarly in Chapter LXII on pages 331–2 the manuscript
originally read

> *But thanks to Boldwood's reticence very little more was known than this
> bare fact of death*

but was altered later to

> *. . . reticence and Oak's generosity, the lover she had followed had never
> been individualized as Troy.*

Indeed, at this stage of the novel Gabriel's involvement with Fanny
and with Bathsheba come together. Leaves 2–221 to 2–223 (E32–
32b) replace an original E32; the only satisfactory reason that can be
offered for such an expansion is an increase in the role of Gabriel Oak
in the last part of Chapter XLII, particularly in his anxiety to shield
Bathsheba as long as possible from the shock of discovering Fanny's
baby. E37 and 37a were also second thoughts and they contain a long
paragraph in which the narrator analyses Bathsheba's feelings

towards Gabriel, including a sentence of central importance: *What a way Oak had, she thought, of enduring things* (p. 338). There is no doubt of the significance of Bathsheba's new assessment of him at this point in the story; in it she is recognising him, almost for the first time, as an exceptional person, as more than an unwanted suitor or hired shepherd.

A particularly interesting change made in proof for C, which helps to prepare for this reported reverie about Oak, occurs during the immediately preceding potential catastrophe in her life, the threat of the destruction of her ricks by the storm. She has been telling Gabriel about her marriage, when he notices she has been tired out by the work of helping him thatch the ricks and tells her to go indoors. Her reply in the manuscript was:

> *If I am useless I will go. . . . But oh, if the wheat should be lost!* (ellipsis mine)

Hardy dramatically and economically transformed this selfish, or at best objective concern with her wealth into real anxiety about Gabriel, by altering *the wheat* to *your life* (XXXVII; p. 291). The speech represents in its altered form Bathsheba's first movement toward Oak; the episode itself shows the beginning of her disillusionment with Troy, and Hardy saw how important it was, if the ending of his novel was to be successful, that he should stress the presence of Gabriel close to her during the destruction of that relationship.

Indeed Gabriel grew gradually in stature as Hardy's conception of the novel developed, and to give some idea of how far Hardy may have come from his original version of the relationship between Gabriel and Bathsheba it is worth looking at the first six chapters of the novel. These early leaves at first glance have only one sequence of E numeration, and its absence from 1–8 and 1–9 at the end of Chapter 1 shows that Gabriel's first encounter with Bathsheba was rewritten after the E numeration was made. However, the chief interest lies in a discrepancy between leaves 1–44 and 1–46. Leaf 1–44 is numbered E44, 1–45 and 1–45a are later additions and have no E number, but 1–46 had E39, and this latter sequence carries on, with interruptions for later revised leaves, until 1–62 (E55). The only satisfactory explanation for this is to suggest that 1–24 to 1–44 (and possibly, though not probably, the earlier leaves of the novel) represent a newer stage of composition than 1–46 to 1–62, and that the later E number became the 1–number on the older leaves: 1–24 to 1−44 are those leaves that contain Bathsheba saving Gabriel's life, her flirtation with him, and his proposal of marriage. There is no way of knowing for certain what these leaves replaced but it is interesting in this context to notice that 1−49 (E42) has been cut to half its normal length and that a long addition to the beginning of 1−50 (E43) has been made on its verso, concluding with Gabriel's reflection

> *Thank God I am not married: what would she have done in the poverty now coming upon me!* (V; p. 41)

Apparently this passage replaced what was cut from the previous leaf, which might imply that in the original version no proposal of marriage had taken place. The only subsequent leaves up to the end of this E numeration – 1−53c, 1−57, and 1−63 – that bear any implication of Gabriel's desire to marry Bathsheba were added after the numeration was made: with 1−64 a different E numeration begins.

If Hardy did not originally intend Gabriel to propose to Bathsheba, then his idea of the character has come far. This development is also reflected in an elevation in the social/educational standing of the farmer-shepherd. In the original plan communicated to Stephen – if we may believe the account in *The Early Life*[7] – Gabriel had been thought of simply as a shepherd, closer to the other employees in the novel. The oldest leaves surviving in the manuscript, those with the earlier versions of the names of Oak and Poorgrass, contain some speeches by Gabriel that sound now rather inappropriate. As an example one might take his simpleminded response to some criticisms of Pennyways on page 71 (VIII) –

> "*Good faith, you do talk,*" *said Gabriel, with apprehension.*

– which, especially in the 'apprehension', seems a decisive contrast with his demeanour towards Bathsheba in the subsequent paying scene. This difference in tone is perceptible not only in dialogue, for later there is a vivid contrast between the jocular description of Gabriel's fist – rather smaller in size than a common loaf, laid as a threat on the table on pages 122−3 (XV), which is also on such an early leaf – and his ease with Mr Boldwood in the following discussion (on a leaf added later) of his letter from Fanny, in which he does not address him as Sir as the other workfolk undoubtedly would. Evidently there is a trace remaining still of a Gabriel Oak who was more akin to the habitués of Warren's than he appears in the rest of the novel, where even at his lowest ebb he is somewhat apart from them, and superior to them.

These distinctions are matters of tone, but more concrete evidence that Hardy's view of Gabriel tended towards making him more sophisticated can be derived from revisions to dialect in his speech. Early on in the novel Hardy removes some of the dialectal formations from Gabriel's speech in proof for C — as for instance in his final attempt to persuade Bathsheba to marry him on page 35 (IV), where *would ha' thought* is changed to *would have thought*, and *along wi' me* to *along with me*.

However, by the time the last two episodes of the novel were in Leslie Stephen's hands, Hardy's estimate of Oak's proper speech had changed to the extent that Stephen could write, on 25 August 1874:

> I will speak about the November proof tomorrow. I saw nothing to alter, unless that it seemed to me in one or two cases that your rustics — specially Oak — speak rather too good English towards the end. They seem to drop the dialect a little. But of this you are the best judge.[8]

Hardy in this matter, as in almost all others, responded vigorously to Stephen's prompting, and there are over thirty places where Gabriel had dialect added to his speech in the last two episodes. This extends to phrases like *the top and tail o't it* (LVI; p. 454) for *it amounts to* or *Surely, surely you be* (LVI; p. 455) for *you are necessarily* (where both versions have the identical number of characters, including spaces; presumably, one thinks, the second *surely* was added to save the compositors trouble in resetting the proof revision) as well as simple words such as *ye* for *you*. It may be right that Gabriel should retain the richness of dialect expression until the end of the novel, and indeed it is also added to in the general augmentation of dialect form that was made in all his novels during the revision for the Osgood collected edition of 1895 – 6; but the refinement in Gabriel's speech which he allowed, perhaps unconsciously, to creep into the latter part of the manuscript demonstrates (when all the other evidence I have offered is taken into account), the way in which Hardy's sense of his character changed as the novel progressed.

One final example shows it clearly. When, in the serial version of Chapter XVIII the narrator was analysing Boldwood's character, in the passage compared with George Eliot by R. H. Hutton (see p. 76) above), Hardy related the farmer's nature to that of Gabriel's:

> *Spiritually and mentally, no less than socially, a commonplace general condition is no conclusive proof that a man has not potentialities above that level.*
>
> *In all cases this state may be either the mediocrity of inadequacy, as was Oak's or . . . the mediocrity of counterpoise, as was Boldwood's.*
>
> (p. 137; ellipsis mine)

This passage remained in 74 and 75, and was only removed in 77, although it is manifestly inappropriate as a generalisation on the Oak who has a close relationship with Boldwood later in the novel, and who marries the heroine.

This glance at Gabriel has taken me rather far from the text that I am inspecting; I left it on 2–200 with the addition of Gabriel as the principal recipient of the news of Fanny's death; on the same leaf there occurs the first of two alterations connected with Fanny Robin that Hardy makes on artistic grounds (in contrast with some of those that come later); Poorgrass' reply to Bathsheba's question *What did she die from?* beginning *I don't know for certain, but I* originally continued in the manuscript *believe it was from inflammation of the lungs, though some say she broke her heart.* When reviewing this Hardy added a couple of sentences about her general weakness, but omitted all mention of consumption or love, adding in proof a further characteristically colourful detail *and 'a went like a candle-snoff, so 'tis said* (p. 317). There are two reasons for this alteration; one is that Poorgrass was, as a result of the addition of the Oak–Boldwood meeting (and his own later-added avowal to Bathsheba), not aware of the cause of Fanny's death, and Hardy would be anxious to avoid anything that might imply that he was; and the other, similarly dependent on the inclusion of Gabriel in this chapter, is that Hardy wished to postpone all direct hints at the true cause of her death till the end of the following chapter. This dual concern is also evident when Bathsheba repeats her question to Poorgrass on 2–203 (E21): *Died of what did you say, Joseph?* His reply, unrevised (thus showing that E21 is contemporary with E21a) is *I don't know, ma'am.* It seems that Hardy considered Bathsheba's question too suggestive despite Joseph's ignorance, for he altered it in proof for C to *Whose sweetheart . . .* (p. 319) though he didn't alter Joseph's subsequent narrative of his meeting with Boldwood and Oak in which Gabriel very self-consciously avoids the question of how she died. The proof change has the added advantage of

emphasising Bathsheba's anxiety about the colour of Fanny's hair
(newly stressed in the manuscript, as I have suggested), since her
preceding question to Poorgrass had been on that topic. His reply to
that was unhelpful, and the change from *Died of what* to *Whose
sweetheart* takes better account of her current concern.

The second of these revisions begins on the second leaf of Chapter
XLII (2–207), where Hardy originally let slip Fanny's secret un-
dramatically, through the writing that the Union man scrawled on
the coffin:

> *Fanny Robin and Child*
> *Died Oct 3 18—*

(It is interesting to note that *and Child* was a later addition to the MS,
and I shall be taking up this point later.) The next paragraph then
began:

> *Joseph then having learnt the sad truth concerning Fanny placed the*
> *flowers as enjoined.*

Hardy no doubt felt that by giving away his secret here he was
wasting valuable dramatic potential, and also that Poorgrass was
altogether the wrong person to act as intermediary for the reader,
especially since he had introduced Gabriel to knowledge of Fanny's
death in the previous chapter. So the inscription was replaced by *the
name and date* (Hardy changed *date* to the more appropriate *a few other
words* in proof). Poorgrass' learning the truth was omitted (p. 323),
and the last paragraph of the chapter was added, in which Gabriel's is
the consciousness through which the infant is explicitly revealed as he
wipes the *and child* from the inscription on the coffin – ending the
chapter and the September episode on a suitably tense note (p. 334).

This manipulation of the knowledge of Fanny's baby for artistic
reasons contrasts vividly with some of the alterations made in
Chapter XLIII. These, as is well known, respond to Leslie Stephen's
letter to Hardy of 13 April 1874, in which he wrote:

> I object as editor, not as critic, i.e. in the interest of a stupid public,
> not from my own taste.
>
>   I think that the reference to the cause of Fanny's death is
> unnecessarily emphasized. I should, I think, omit all reference to it
> except just enough to indicate the true state of the case; and

especially a conversation between your heroine and her maid, wh. is a little unpleasant. I have some doubts whether the baby is necessary at all and whether it would not be sufficient for Bathsheba to open the coffin in order to identify the dead woman with the person she met on the road. This is a point wh. you can consider. It certainly rather injures the story, and perhaps if the omission were made it might be restored on republication. But I am rather necessarily anxious to be on the safe side; and should somehow be glad to omit the baby.

However, these changes can easily be made when the story is in type and I shall send it to the printers now; and ask you to do what is necessary to the proofs.

We can talk about it when we meet. [9]

The extent to which Hardy was willing to be ruled by Stephen may be gauged by considering this list of C proof revisions to Chapter LXIII:

Fanny was at first called *innocent*, which was changed to *nesh young*.
Half a leaf of dialogue which explores the improbability of Fanny's consumptiveness was removed, in which it was mentioned that *she has only been away from us about eight months*.
Liddy's story about Fanny is amended from *there's two of 'em in there!* to *Liddy came close to her mistress and whispered the remainder of the sentence slowly into her ear. . . .*
A continuation of the same dialogue which included *We shall be sure to learn the rights of it tomorrow* is omitted.
I hate them was changed to *I hate her*.
features of the young girl and babe was changed to *features within*.
A page and a third of the manuscript is omitted which describes the appearance of Fanny and her baby in the coffin. Stephen must have objected to the lyrical and uncensorious treatment of the bastard and its erring mother; he can hardly have had other stylistic objections because the passage is characteristic of Hardy's high style throughout the novel, including as it does a literary quotation, a fanciful natural image comparing the baby's cheeks and plumb fists to *the soft convexity of mushrooms on a dewy morning*, and a painterly comparison between Fanny's hands and those in Bellini portraits. It is bad enough, but Stephen might as well have objected to the whole novel; and as a result of his advice we have also lost the extremely moving and delicately

expressed picture of the two in the coffin as companions of one kind, caught in incipiency rather than decadence: *they both had stood on the threshold of a new stage of existence.* The paragraph as a whole represents a central strand in Hardy's conception of states of being and becoming. And with this pasage we would also be able to enter much more readily into the impulse that later moved Troy to kiss Fanny, to sense that it was not purely one of remorse, as Hardy wrote: *The youth and fairness of both the silent ones withdrew from the scene all associations of a repulsive kind.* . . .

Thus almost every direct reference. to the baby has been removed. Curiously enough, Hardy himself may originally have conceived the episode as less explicit than it appeared in the final manuscript version, for the leaves that contain the description of the two in the coffin which was omitted in proof, were themselves late additions to the manuscript; and two passages that imply the baby's existence which still remain – *that there are two of you* and *beside the unconscious pair* – both appear on leaves added later. Two of the details altered in proof were written into the manuscript during a period of revision: *I hate them* and *dead woman and babe*; and I have already noticed the addition of *and child* to the inscription on the coffin.

At any rate Hardy was sufficiently concerned by the impact of this censorship on the scene that he took some steps to remedy the matter, not in 74 – which was published before the serial had finished in C – but in 75 (restoring *features of both mother and babe* for *features within*) and more extensively in 77, where seven small alterations were made, including the addition of *in maternity* to *forestalment, eclipse in maternity by another* (p. 344). But there was no attempt to restore either Liddy's whisper or the couple in the coffin; this is characteristic of Hardy as late as *Tess of the d'Urbervilles* and *Jude the Obscure*, where passages bowdlerised for the serial sometimes remain lost to the book versions.

There is other evidence of Stephen's censoring pencil (the passage describing Fanny and her baby was marked, not by Hardy, with pencil in the manuscript). One example, in Chapter XLII, may have been made on religious rather than moral grounds: after the paragraph of Jan Coggan's speech that ends at the top of page 329 there is in the manuscript the following passage, similarly marked with a pencil cancellation in a way that Hardy never used, and omitted from C.

"*The same here,*" *said Mark. If anything can beat the old martyrs who used to smoke for their principles here up on earth 'tis being willing to smoke for 'em hereafter.*"

"'*Tis the old feeling in a new way,*" *said Coggan.*

In a letter of 12 March 1874, Stephen admits to having

. . . ventured to leave out a line or two in the last batch of proofs from an excessive prudery of wh. I am ashamed: but one is forced to be absurdly particular.[10]

He then alludes to Troy's seduction of Fanny. Either April or May proofs are almost certainly meant here, and I have found two omissions presumably in proof that might represent the kind of editorial excision Stephen feels he had to apologise for. One is in Chapter XV, in the April episode: after Boldwood had read Fanny's letter to Gabriel, in the manuscript he ended his expression of anxiety over her fate with

"*She has now lost her character — he will never marry her — and what will she do?*"

This sentence, uncancelled in the manuscript, was left out of C. The second possibility occurs in the May instalment, at the end of Chapter XXIV: when Liddy was talking about Troy she calls him *a gay man*, and in the manuscript her speech continued *a walking ruin to honest girls, so some people say*. This too did not appear in C. Of course it is possible that Hardy overruled Stephen and the offending passage remains, undetectable; but this is unlikely in view of Hardy's ready acquiescence with Stephen's advice in other parts of the novel. Indeed when contributing to F. W. Maitland's *Life and Letters of Leslie Stephen*, Hardy related how Stephen had received a letter complaining of a passage in the serial from 'three respectable ladies', and said that his first reaction was to ask Stephen why he didn't strike out the passage.[11] Hardy later noticed the very sentences applauded in *The Times*'s review of the first edition of the novel, and suggested that he would 'never have taken the trouble to restore them in the reprint'. (The paragraph in question is that on page 69 [VIII] where Jan Coggan describes Levi Everdene's way of subduing his roving heart.)

One wonders whether Stephen also objected to a sheep's *buttocks* which was changed to *back* in proof (XXII; p. 167), or whether he was responsible for the new and rather unpleasant moral tone of Gabriel

Oak's attitude towards the murderer Boldwood in Chapter LV, where

> *Gabriel's anxiety was so great that he paced up and down, pausing at every turn and straining his ear for a sound*

became in C

> *Gabriel's anxiety was great that Boldwood might be saved, even though in his conscience he felt that he ought to die; for there had been qualities in the farmer which Oak loved.* (p. 445)

The first shows real agitation, the second a kind of patronising by Gabriel of Boldwood which is thoroughly nasty. Whether this was what Hardy wished, one has at least licence to doubt from Stephen's frequent Grundian interventions elsewhere.

Hardy was to suffer from this kind of advice or instruction or ultimatum from the editors of magazines throughout his career in fiction. It is fascinating to notice how, almost to a man, they claimed that it was not as individuals, but as editors that they made such suggestions or stipulations. Mowbray Morris belied this in his review of *Tess of the d'Urbervilles*,[12] and Leslie Stephen's recorded attitude to explicitness in sexual matters in contemporary French novels was to consider them 'prurient and indecent'.[13]

To return to Chapter XLIII, there is in it another characteristic feature of the way Hardy developed his texts; in 95 the details describing Casterbridge were altered to make them conform more closely to the existing topography of Dorchester. This kind of revision is common throughout the novel, and indeed a book might well be written about the changes in the complete Osgood and Wessex Editions that were made through this impulse in Hardy to preserve with scrupulous accuracy the localities and the customs, social activities and patterns of life of Dorset and the surrounding counties in the nineteenth century. The preface to *Far from the Madding Crowd*, largely written in 1895, discusses the first use of the word Wessex in the novel's serialisation and the subsequent development of the word's currency; numerous topographical alterations were thus made in order to bring each text into line with the now established Wessex landscape – semi-fictional, but self-consistent.

There is another interesting passage in the preface, in which Hardy describes

The game of prisoner's-base, which not long ago seemed to enjoy a
perennial vitality in front of the worn-out stocks. . . .

This detail may be taken as a measure of his increasing local-
historian's concern for such matters, for prisoner's base has its first
mention in the edition of 1895. Previously the game for which the
young men of Weatherbury had gathered *from time immemorial* was
fives.

The force that drove him to add in 1912 as a footnote to the end of
Chapter XLVI a reference to Puddletown Church –

The local tower and churchyard do not answer precisely to the foregoing
description (p. 368) –

was still operating later in his life, for in his own copy of the Wessex
edition of the novel,[14] he added in pencil, between *churchyard*
and *do*, the words *assumed to be those of 'Weatherbury'*. And in this
volume there is another interesting antiquarian note that never
reached print, attached to Gabriel Oak's call to his sheep, '*Ovey, ovey,*
ovey', in Chapter V:

It is somewhat singular – possibly a survival from the Roman occupation
of Britain – that the shepherds of this region should call to their sheep in
Latin.

Two more of these late, unadopted alterations to the Wessex text
touch on the major area of revision to the last chapters of the novel. At
some time between 1895 and 1902 (when Macmillan took over the
publication of his novels, and offered him the chance to make changes
in the plates of the Osgood text) Hardy decided to make Bathsheba
much less certain of Troy's death; and there is a sequence of passages in
Chapters LI and LIII which are altered to this effect in 02, and also one
word in Chapter XLIX, spoken by Liddy – *Mr. Troy's going* for *Mr.*
Troy's death (p. 383). Some of these passages were later changed
again in 1912. An example will show the effect:

MS   *time. Indeed the long time and the uncertainty of the whole thing*
       give . . .
02   *time, or Mr. Troy may even be back again! Such thoughts*
       give . . .

12   *time, even if Mr. Troy does not come back again, which he may not*
      impossibly do! Such thoughts give . . .

                                                    (LI; p. 408)

Hardy knew o2 was being reprinted from plates, and was anxious as
always to minimise type-shifting, so made his revisions as nearly
equivalent in length to what was removed as possible. There is a fine
example of this in the important final scene between Bathsheba and
Boldwood, just before Troy arrives to claim her. Hardy wanted to
add *If he does not return* to

> *She waited a moment. 'Very well, I'll marry you in six years from this*
> *day, if we both live.'*

So that the succeeding lines did not have to be disturbed, Hardy
calmly deleted the first sentence of the passsage in order to
accommodate his addition (p. 430). It may well be said that in this
and other places the text was manipulated for the benefit of the printer
alone. On the other hand, in 1912 the text was being reset, and so
Hardy could rephrase some of the awkwardnesses of the o2 revisions,
and add some more in the same vein. And, as I said, he was still
concerned with this matter in the annotated copy of 1912: one
addition in particular is interesting (though again, it appears in no
published text), in that it would be the earliest revision of this kind.
Soon after she has recovered from her fainting fit in Chapter XLVIII
Bathsheba says

> *death would have been different from how this is. I am perfectly convinced*
> *he is still alive!* (p. 377)

Hardy would have added between the two sentences *There may be*
some trick in it.

The motive for these changes, which were evidently important to
Hardy, is not very clear: it seems probable that he thought it more
likely that the independent-minded Bathsheba would not accept the
common interpretation of the evidence of Troy's death, which was
highly circumstantial; she would thus form more of a contrast with
Boldwood, who is clearly eager to believe in it. Also Boldwood's
mastery over Bathsheba is intensified if she is not convinced of Troy's
death, if he wins her consent to a prospective marriage against her
better judgement of the case. Perhaps Hardy did not like to see

Bathsheba proved wrong by events in company with most of the other characters in the novel. Moreover, the reader knows that Troy is not drowned (as he does not, for instance, with Newson in *The Mayor of Casterbridge*), and Hardy may have wanted to avoid any idea that he was even implicitly countenancing bigamy.

Even in a matter apparently so insignificant as punctuation a substantive differences is sometimes made by compositorial error, and there is one example in these chapters, on page 335, made in the resetting for the 77 edition. What had originally read

" . . . *there's a fire here. Liddy," she suddenly exclaimed . . . "have you heard . . ."*

became

" . . . *there's a fire here, Liddy." She suddenly exclaimed. . . . "Have you heard . . ."* (p. 335; ellipses mine),

which makes almost nonsense of the exclamation 'Liddy'.

Though such errors with substantive effect are rare, compositorial alteration of Hardy's manuscript punctuation is not less important in its overall impact on the novel than some of the changes I have already outlined. Elsewhere I have argued that the compositors who set Hardy's works for their first appearance in print destroyed a unique and valuable system of punctuation,[15] and nothing I have observed in *Far from the Madding Crowd* would lead me radically to alter that opinion. I do not want to labour the point here – three examples from the manuscript chapters under scrutiny will suffice (C punctuation is in brackets).

It was light [,] ma'am [;] but she wore it rather short [,] and packed away under her cap, so that you would hardly notice it. (p. 321)
Ah[,] well, [!] let me take . . . . (p. 331)
I cannot say – [;] let me go out – [.] I want air! (p. 343)

These examples are characteristic rather than exceptional; in every case Hardy's punctuation was less emphatic, and the distinction seems to be between one who writes with his inner ear attuned to a particular cadence of speech, and one who composes a printed text for the eye to read according, partly at least, to formal rules (though I

Wessex edition version of the words at the beginning of each MS leaf	Page	Final MS No.	E No.
CHAPTER XL	302	2–181	
passed the gate. It probably	302	2–182	2
of sound, or to the imagined	303	2–183	3
not cleared away; it was thrown	304	2–184	4
six hundred. Seventeen times that	305	2–185	5
her strength to come over half	305	2–186	6
From the stripe of shadow on	306	2–187	7
A thought moved within her	307	2–188	7a
Thus the town was passed	308	2–189	[8]
this wearied soul. A little door	308	2–190	9
CHAPTER XLI	310	2–191	
I was far sweeter than	310	2–192	[1]2
she said, with features between	311	2–193	
Bathsheba's eyes had been	312	2–194	
hair. People used to turn	313	2–195	
mingled tones of wretchedness	314	2–196	
me fairly,' she said, looking	314	2–197	
in arms, and the blood fired	315	2–198	16b
to folly of this kind	316	2–199	17
to futile dreaming, and her	316	2–200	18
to fetch her home here	317	2–201	19
churchyard gate, and take her	318	2–202	20
That will do, Joseph	319	2–203	21
Boldwood turned round to me	320	2–204	21a
Bathsheba, still unhappy, went	320	2–205	22

CHAPTER XLII			22a
his waggon against the high door	322	2—206	⟨18⟩ 23
of atmospheric fungi	323	2—207	⟨19⟩ 24
was audible anywhere around	323	2—208	⟨20⟩ 25
distinct species at this date	324	2—209	⟨ ?⟩ 26
but two copper-coloured discs	325	2—210	⟨22⟩ 27
tilted his head gradually	325	2—211	⟨ ?⟩ 28
Of course, you'll have another drop	326	2—212	⟨ ?⟩ 29
Oh, no no!	327	2—213	⟨25⟩ 30
"Yes," said Coggan.	328	2—214	⟨26⟩ 31
won't mind. He's a generous	328	2—215	⟨27⟩ 32
as if it were not a member	329	2—216	⟨28⟩ 33
Do hold thy horning	329	2—217	29
to my going down of the same	330	2—218	30
Gabriel hoped that the	331	2—219	31
Gabriel had his reasons	332	2—220	32
Perhaps Mrs. Troy is right	332	2—221	⟨33⟩ 32a
Bathsheba's life a shade	333	2—222	32b
	334	2—223	
CHAPTER XLIII			33
Why don't you sit	335	2—224	⟨35⟩ 34
has just heard something	335	2—225	⟨36⟩ 35
Bathsheba's face	336	2—226	36
the minutes of suspense	337	2—227	37
further speech would need	337	2—228	37a
injury to the occupant	338	2—229	38
More fevered now by a reaction	339	2—230	39
but which, when done	339	2—231	39a
	340	2—232	

Wessex edition version of the words at the beginning of each MS leaf	Page	Final MS No.	E No.
[Bathsheba's head sank	340	2—233	39b*
wound for wound	341	2—234	40
She knelt beside	342	2—235	41
He beheld it all	342	2—236	
volition seemed to leave her	343	2—237	44
for intense feeling is	343	2—238	45
There was something	344	2—239	46
Ah don't taunt me	345	2—240	47

⟨ ⟩ cancelled number
[ ] inferred number
* Most of this MS page was omitted from C and subsequent texts.

have shown that different compositors have different preferences in punctuation).

There are also a number of substantive compositors' errors in C which survive in current versions. For example, on page 276 (XXXVI) *a fine DD* should read *a final DD*; on page 414 (LII) *you have got quite cynical lately* should be *you have got quietly cynical lately*; and on page 451 (LVI) *Three weeks went on* is altogether too precise in context (in the manuscript it read *The weeks went on*).

I have tried to look in this essay at the whole range of differences that might be found between an edition of *Far from the Madding Crowd* that is read today and the earliest ideas that Hardy had of the novel; I have glanced, at least, at every substantively different edition of the novel (substantively different, that is, by authorial intention) and I hope I have given some idea of the variety of matters that Hardy was concerned with when revising a text.

The final claim that I want to make, one that I hope to substantiate in a series of essays along the same lines as this, is that in general terms everything said here about *Far from the Madding Crowd* can be applied to all of Hardy's fictional prose; and that from a comparative study of all his texts a new approach to Hardy as a creative writer may emerge. If we can make valid generalisations about the ways that Hardy approached his writing, the kinds of things he was interested in altering, heightening, deleting, augmenting, not only in the broad thematic or character concerns I have concentrated on here, but also in more detailed areas such as style or punctuation, then I think we will understand more clearly the nature of Hardy as a creative artist. Biographers and critics complain that he is an elusive man to pin down. I suggest that the most rewarding way to penetrate his amply shielded personality may be through the creative mind at work.

NOTES

1. Chapter XL contains Fanny Robin's journey to Casterbridge workhouse. Chapter XLI deals with Bathsheba's uneasiness regarding the relationship between her husband Troy and the woman, unrecognised by her, that they met on the road between Casterbridge and Weatherbury; and includes the news of Fanny's death. Chapter XLII has the delayed return of Fanny's coffin to Weatherbury, while Chapter XLIII presents the events leading up to the opening of the coffin by Bathsheba, and Troy's recognition and embrace of Fanny's body.

2. R. C. Schweik, 'The Early Development of Hardy's *Far from the Madding Crowd*', *Texas Studies in Literature and Language*, IX (1967) 415–28.

3. R. L. Purdy, *Thomas Hardy: A Bibliographical Study*, 2nd ed., rev. (Oxford: Clarendon Press, 1968) p. 14. The manuscript is in the possession of Mr Edwin Thorne to whom I am most grateful for permission to quote from it, as also to the Trustees of the Thomas Hardy Estate and the Trustees of the Estate of the late Miss E. A. Dugdale.

4. Quoted in *Thomas Hardy: The Critical Heritage*, ed. R. G. Cox (London: Routledge & Kegan Paul, 1970) pp. 21–6. The passages referred to are on p. 23 and p. 24.

5. Schweik, pp. 418–22.

6. In other leaves of the MS Oak was called first *Copeday* and then *Strong* (a characteristic early Hardy name salvaged from his abortive first novel *The Poor Man and the Lady*), and *Poorgrass* was *Poorhead*, which was perhaps considered rather too descriptive (it was not *Poorheed*, as Schweik suggests).

7. Florence Emily Hardy, *The Early Life of Thomas Hardy, 1840–1891* (London and New York: Macmillan, 1928) p. 125.

8. Purdy, p. 339.

9. Purdy, p. 339.

10. Purdy, p. 338.

11. *Early Life*, p. 130.

12. *Critical Heritage*, pp. 214–21.

13. F. W. Maitland, *Life and Letters of Leslie Stephen* (London, 1906) p. 266.

14. This volume is in the Dorset County Museum, and I would like to record here my hearty thanks to Mr Roger Peers, the curator of the Museum, for his great kindnesses to me over a period of years at work on this and other projects.

15. Gatrell, 'Thomas Hardy. House-style and the Aesthetics of Punctuation', in *The Novels of Thomas Hardy*, ed. Anne Smith (London: Vision Press, 1978).

6 The Unmanning of the Mayor of Casterbridge

ELAINE SHOWALTER

To the feminist critic, Hardy presents an irrestible paradox. He is one of the few Victorian male novelists who wrote in what may be called a female tradition; at the beginning of his career, Hardy was greeted with the same uncertainty that had been engendered by the pseudonymous publication of *Jane Eyre* and *Adam Bede*: was the author man or woman? *Far from the Madding crowd*, serialised in the *Cornhill* in 1874, was widely attributed to George Eliot, and Leslie Stephen wrote reassuringly to Hardy about the comparisons: 'As for the supposed affinity to George Eliot, it consists, I think, simply in this that you have both treated rustics of the farming class in a humorous manner — Mrs. Poyser would be home I think, in Weatherbury — but you need not be afraid of such criticisms. You are original and can stand on your own legs.'[1]

It hardly needs to be said that Stephen's assessment of Hardy's originality was correct; but on the other hand, the relationship to Eliot went beyond similarities in content to similarities in psychological portraits, especially of women. Hardy's remarkable heroines, even in the earlier novels, evoked comparisons with Charlotte Brontë, Jane Austen, and George Eliot, indicating a recognition (as Havelock Ellis pointed out in his 1883 review-essay) that 'the most serious work in modern English fiction . . . has been done by women.'[2] Later, Hardy's heroines spoke even more directly to women readers; after the publication of *Tess of the d'Urbervilles*, for example, Hardy received letters from wives who had not dared to tell their husbands about their premarital experience; sometimes these women requested meetings which he turned down on his barrister's advice.[3] Twentieth-century criticism has often focused on the heroines of the novels; judging from the annual *Dissertation Abstracts* (Ann Arbor,

Michigan) this perennial favourite of dissertation topics has received new incentive from the women's movement. Recent feminist criticism, most notably the distinguished essays of Mary Jacobus on Tess and Sue, has done much to unfold the complexities of Hardy's imaginative response to the 'woman question' of the 1890s.[4] Hardy knew and respected many of the minor women novelists of his day: Katherine Macquoid, Rhoda Broughton, Mary Braddon, Sarah Grand, Mona Caird, Evelyn Sharp, Charlotte Mew. He actually collaborated on a short story with the novelist Florence Henniker, and possibly revised the work of other female protegées; his knowledge of the themes of feminist writing in the 1880s and 1890s was extensive.[5]

Yet other aspects of Hardy's work reveal a much more distanced and divided attitude towards women, a sense of an irreconcilable split between male and female values and possibilities. If some Victorian women recognised themselves in his heroines, others were shocked and indignant. In 1890, Hardy's friend Edmund Gosse wrote: 'The unpopularity of Mr. Hardy's novels among women is a curious phenomenon. If he had no male admirers, he could almost cease to exist. . . . Even educated women approach him with hesitation and prejudice.'[6] Hardy hoped that Tess of the d'Urbervilles would redeem him; he wrote to Edmund Yates in 1891 that 'many of my novels have suffered so much from misrepresentation as being attacks on womankind.'[7] He took heart from letters from mothers who were 'putting "Tess" into their daughters' hands to safeguard their future', and from 'women of society' who said his courage had 'done the whole sex a service.'[8] Gosse, however, read the hostile and uncomprehending reviews of such women as Margaret Oliphant as evidence of a continuing division between feminist critics, who were 'shrivelled spinsters', and the 'serious male public'.[9] There were indeed real and important ideological differences between Hardy and even advanced women of the 1890s, differences which Gosse wished to reduce to questions of sexual prudery. Hardy's emphasis on the biological determinism of childbearing, rather than on the economic determinants of female dependency, put him more in the camp of Grant Allan than in the women's party. In 1892 he declined membership in the Women's Progressive Society because he had not 'as yet been converted to a belief in the desirability of the Society's first object' – women's suffrage.[10] By 1906 his conversion had taken place; but his support of the suffrage campaign was based on his hope (as he wrote to Millicent Garrett Fawcett) that 'the tendency of the women's vote will be to break up the present pernicious conventions in respect of manners, customs, religion, illegitimacy, the stereotyped household (that it must be the unit of society), the father of a woman's child (that it is anybody's business but the woman's own except in cases of disease or insanity)'.[11]

Looking at the novels of the 1890s, and at Hardy's treatment of his heroines as they encounter pernicious conventions, A. O. J. Cockshut has concluded that there were unbridgeable gaps between Hardy's position and that of *fin-de-siècle* feminism:

> Hardy decisively rejects the whole feminist argument of the preceding generation, which was the soil for the growth of the idea of the 'New Woman' à la Havelock Ellis and Grant Allen; and this is his final word on the matter. The feminists saw the natural disabilities as trivial compared with those caused by bad traditions and false theories. Hardy reversed this, and he did so feelingly. The phrase 'inexorable laws of nature' was no cliché for him. It represented the slowly-garnered fruits of his deepest meditations on life. It was an epitome of what found full imaginative expression in memorable descriptions, like that of Egdon Heath. The attempt to turn Hardy into a feminist is altogether vain.[12]

But the traditional attention to Hardy's heroines has obscured other themes of equal significance to a feminist critique. Through the heroes of his novels and short stories, Hardy also investigated the Victorian codes of manliness, the man's experience of marriage, the problem of paternity. For the heroes of the tragic novels — Michael Henchard, Jude Fawley, Angel Clare — maturity involves a kind of assimilation of female suffering, an identification with a woman which is also an effort to come to terms with their own deepest selves. In Hardy's career too there is a consistent element of self-expression through women; he uses them as narrators, as secretaries, as collaborators, and finally, in the (auto) biography he wrote in the persona of his second wife, as screens or ghosts of himself. Hardy not only commented upon, and in a sense, infiltrated, feminine fictions; he also understood the feminine self as the estranged and essential complement of the male self. In *The Mayor of Casterbridge* (1886), Hardy gives the fullest nineteenth-century portrait of a man's inner life — his rebellion and his suffering, his loneliness and jealousy, his paranoia and despair, his uncontrollable unconscious. Henchard's efforts, first to deny and divorce his passional self, and ultimately to accept and educate it, involve him in a pilgrimage of 'unmanning' which is a movement towards both self-discovery and tragic vulnerability. It is in the analysis of this New Man, rather than in the evaluation of Hardy's New Women, that the case for Hardy's feminist sympathies may be argued.

The Mayor of Casterbridge begins with a scene that dramatises the analysis of female subjugation as a function of capitalism which Engels had recently set out in The Origins of the Family, Private Property and the State (1884): the auction of Michael Henchard's wife Susan at the fair at Weydon-Priors. Henchard's drunken declaration that Susan is his 'goods' is matched by her simple acceptance of a new 'owner', and her belief that in paying five guineas in cash for her Richard Newson has legitimised their relationship. Hardy never intended the wife-sale to seem natural or even probable, although he assembled in his Commonplace Book factual accounts of such occurrences from the Dorset County Chronicle and the Brighton Gazette.[13] The auction is clearly an extraordinary event, which violates the moral sense of the Casterbridge community when it is discovered twenty years later. But there is a sense in which Hardy recognised the psychological temptation of such a sale, the male longing to exercise his property rights over women, to free himself from their burden with virile decision, to simplify his own conflicts by reducing them to 'the ruin of good men by bad wives' (I; p. 7).

This element in the novel could never have been articulated by Hardy's Victorian readers, but it has been most spiritedly expressed in our century by Irving Howe:

> To shake loose from one's wife; to discard that drooping rag of a woman, with her mute complaints and maddening passivity; to escape not by a slinking abandonment but through the public sale of her body to a stranger, as horses are sold at a fair; and thus to wrest, through sheer amoral willfulness, a second chance out of life – it is with this stroke, so insidiously attractive to male fantasy, that The Mayor of Casterbridge begins.[14]   ·

The scene, Howe goes on, speaks to 'the depths of common fantasy, it summons blocked desires and transforms us into secret sharers. No matter what judgments one may make of Henchard's conduct, it is hard, after the first chapter, simply to abandon him; for through his boldness we have been drawn into complicity with the forbidden.'

Howe brings an enthusiasm and an authority to his exposition of

Henchard's motives that sweeps us along, although we need to be aware both that he invents a prehistory for the novel that Hardy withholds, and that in speaking of 'our' common fantasies, he quietly transforms the novel into a male document. A woman's experience of this scene must be very different; indeed, there were many sensation novels of the 1870s and 1880s which presented the sale of women into marriage from the point of view of the bought wife. In Howe's reading, Hardy's novel becomes a kind of sensation-fiction, playing on the suppressed longings of its male audience, evoking sympathy for Henchard because of his crime, and not in spite of it.

In this exclusive concentration on the sale of the wife, however, Howe, like most of Hardy's critics, overlooks the simultaneous event which more profoundly determines Henchard's fate: the sale of the child. Paternity is a central subject of the book, far more important than conjugal love. Perhaps one reason why the sale of the child has been so consistently ignored by generations of Hardy critics is that the child is female. For Henchard to sell his son would be so drastic a violation of patriarchal culture that it would wrench the entire novel out of shape; but the sale of a daughter – in this case only a 'tiny girl' – seems almost natural. There may even be a suggestion that this too is an act insidiously attractive to male fantasy, the rejection of the wife who has only borne female offspring.

It is the combined, premeditated sale of wife and child which launches Henchard into his second chance. Orphaned, divorced, without mother or sisters, wife or daughter, he has effectively severed all his bonds with the community of women, and re-enters society alone – the new Adam, reborn, self-created, unencumbered, journeying southward without pause until he reaches Casterbridge. Henchard commits his life entirely to the male community, defining his human relationships by the male codes of money, paternity, honour, and legal contract. By his act Henchard sells out or divorces his own 'feminine' self, his own need for passion, tenderness, and loyalty. The return of Susan and Elizabeth-Jane which precipitates the main phase of the novel is indeed a return of the repressed, which forces Henchard gradually to confront the tragic inadequacy of his codes, the arid limits of patriarchal power. The fantasy that women hold men back, drag them down, drain their energy, divert their strength, is nowhere so bleakly rebuked as in Hardy's tale of the 'man of character'. Stripped of his mayor's chain, his master's authority, his father's rights, Henchard is in a sense unmanned; but it is in moving from romantic male individualism to a more complete humanity that he becomes capable of tragic experience. Thus sex-role patterns and tragic patterns in the novel connect.

According to Christine Winfield's study of the manuscript of *The Mayor of Casterbridge*, Hardy made extensive revisions in Chapter 1. The most striking detail of the early drafts was that the Henchard family was originally composed of two daughters, the elder of whom was old enough to try to dissuade Susan from going along with the sale: '"Don't mother!" whispered the girl who sat on the woman's side. "Father don't know what he's saying."' On being sold to the sailor Newson, however, Susan takes the younger girl ('her favourite one') with her; Henchard keeps the other. Hardy apparently took this detail from the notice of a wife-sale in the *Brighton Gazette* for 25 May 1826: 'We understand they were country people, and that the woman has had two children by her husband, one of whom he consents to keep, and the other he throws in as a makeweight to the bargain.'[15]

Hardy quickly discarded this cruel opening, and in the final text he emphasises the presence and the sale of a single infant daughter. From the beginning, she and her mother form an intimate unit, as close to each other as Henchard and his wife are separate. Susan speaks not to her husband, but to her baby, who babbles in reply; her face becomes alive when she talks to the girl. In a psychoanalytic study of Hardy, Charles K. Hofling has taken this bond between mother and daughter as the source of Henchard's jealous estrangement,[16] but all the signs in the text point to Henchard's dissociation from the family as his own choice. The personalities of husband and wife are evidenced in all the nuances of this scene, one which they will both obsessively recall and relive. Hardy takes pains to show us Henchard's rigid unapproach-ability, his body-language eloquent of rejection. In Henchard's very footsteps there is a 'dogged and cynical indifference personal to himself' (I; p. 1); he avoids Susan's eyes and possible conversation by 'reading, or pretending to read' (I; p. 2) a ballad sheet, which he must hold awkwardly with the hand thrust through the strap of his basket. The scene is in marked contrast to Mrs Gaskell's opening in *Mary Barton*, for example, where fathers and brothers help to carry the infants; Hardy plays consciously against the reader's expectation of affectionate closeness. When Susan and Elizabeth-Jane retrace the journey many years later, they are holding hands, 'the act of simple affection' (III; p. 21).

Henchard's refusal of his family antedates the passionate de-claration of the auction, and it is important to note that such a sale has been premeditated or at least discussed between husband and wife.

There are several references to previous threats: 'On a previous occasion when he had declared during a fuddle that he would dispose of her as he had done, she had replied that she would not hear him say that many times more before it happened, in the resigned tones of a fatalist'(II; p. 17). When Newson asks whether Susan is willing to go with him, Henchard answers for her: 'She is willing, provided she can have the child. She said so only the other day when I talked o't!' (I; p. 12). After the sale, Henchard tries to evade the full responsibility for his act by blaming it on an evening's drunkenness, a temporary breakdown in reason and control; he even blames his lost wife's 'simplicity' for allowing him to go through with the act: 'Seize her, why didn't she know better than bring me into this disgrace! . . . She wasn't queer if I was. 'Tis like Susan to show such idiotic simplicity' (II; p. 17: ellipsis mine). His anger and humiliation, none the less, cannot undo the fact that the bargain that was struck, and the 'goods' that were divided (Susan takes the girl, Henchard the tools) had been long contemplated. When it is too late, Henchard chiefly regrets his over-hasty division of property: 'She'd no business to take the maid — 'tis my maid; and if it were the doing again she shouldn't have her!' (I; p. 14).

In later scenes, Hardy gives Henchard more elaborated motives for the sale: contempt for Susan's ignorance and naiveté; and, as Henchard recalls on his first pilgrimage to Weydon-Priors, twenty-five years after the fair, his 'cursed pride and mortification at being poor' (XLIV; p. 367). Financial success, in the mythology of Victorian manliness, requires the subjugation of competing passions. If it is marriage that has threatened the youthful Henchard with 'the extinction of his energies' (I; p. 7), a chaste life will rekindle them. Henchard's public auction and his private oath of temperance are thus consecutive stages of the same rite of passage. Henchard's oath is both an atonement for his drunken surrender to his fantasies, and a bargain with success. In Rudyard Kipling's *The Man Who Would Be King* (1899), a similar 'contrack' is made, whereby Peachey Carnehan and Daniel Dravot swear to abjure liquor and women. When Dravot breaks his promise, they are exiled from their kingdom; so too will Henchard be expelled from Casterbridge when he breaks his vows. Save for the romance with Lucetta, in which he appears to play a passive role, Henchard is chaste during his long separation from his wife; he enjoys the local legend he has created of himself as the 'celebrated abstaining worthy' (V; p. 38); the man whose 'haughty indifference to the society of womankind, his silent avoidance of converse with the sex' (XIII; p. 94) is well known. His prominence in Casterbridge is produced by the commercialised energies of sexual sublimation, and he boasts to Farfrae that 'being by nature something of a woman-hater, I have found it no hardship to keep mostly at a distance from the sex' (XII; p. 89). There is nothing in Henchard's consciousness which corresponds to the aching melancholy of Hardy's poem 'He abjures love' (1883):

> At last I put off love,
>   For twice ten years
> The daysman of my thought,
>   And hope, and doing.

Indeed, in marrying Susan for the second time, Henchard forfeits something of his personal magic, and begins to lose power in the eyes of the townspeople; it is whispered that he has been 'captured and enervated by the genteel widow' (XIII; p. 94).

Henchard's emotional life is difficult to define; in the first half of the novel, Hardy gives us few direct glimpses of his psyche, and soberly refrains from the kind of romantic symbolism employed as psychological notation by the Brontës and by Dickens – dreams, doubles, hallucinatory illnesses. But the very absence of emotion, the 'void' which Hardy mentions, suggests that Henchard has divorced himself from feeling, and that it is feeling itself which obstinately retreats from him as he doggedly pursues it. When J. Hillis Miller describes Henchard as a man 'driven by a passionate desire for full possession of some other person' and calls the novel 'a nightmare of frustrated desire',[17] he misleadingly suggests that the nature and intensity of Henchard's need is sexual. It is an absence of feeling which Henchard looks to others to supply, a craving unfocused loneliness rather than a desire towards another person. Henchard does not seek possession in the sense that he desires the confidences of others; such reciprocity as he requires, he coerces. What he wants is a 'greedy exclusiveness' (XLI; p. 338), a title; and this feeling is stimulated by male competition.

Given Henchard's misogyny, we cannot be surprised to see that his deepest feelings are reserved for another man, a surrogate brother with whom he quickly contracts a business relationship that has the emotional overtones of a marriage. Henchard thinks of giving Farfrae a third share in his business to compel him to stay; he urges that they should share a house and meals. Elizabeth-Jane is the frequent observer of the manly friendship between Henchard and Farfrae, which she idealises:

> She looked from the window and saw Henchard and Farfrae in the hay-yard talking, with that impetuous cordiality on the Mayor's part, and genial modesty on the younger man's, that was now so generally observable in their intercourse. Friendship between man and man; what a rugged strength there was in it, as evinced by these two. (XV; p. 110)

Yet Elizabeth-Jane is also an 'accurate observer' who sees that Henchard's 'tigerish affection . . . now and then resulted in a tendency to domineer' (XIV; p. 104). It is a tigerish affection that does not respect that other's separateness, that sets its own terms of love and hate. Farfrae's passivity in this relationship is feminine at first, when he is constrained by his economic dependence on Henchard. There is nothing homosexual in their intimacy; but there is certainly on Henchard's side an open, and, he later feels, incautious embrace of homosocial friendship, an insistent male bonding.[18] Success, for Henchard, precludes relationships with women; male cameraderie and, later, contests of manliness must take their place. He precipitately confides in Farfrae, telling him all the secrets of his past, at a point when he is determined to withhold this information from Elizabeth-Jane: 'I am not going to let her know the truth' (XII; p. 92). Despite Henchard's sincerity, the one-sidedness of the exchange, his indifference to Farfrae's feelings if he can have his company, leads the younger man to experience their closeness as artificial, and to resist 'the pressure of mechanized friendship' (XVI; p. 117).

The community of Casterbridge itself has affinities with its Mayor when it is first infiltrated by Farfrae and the women. Like Henchard, it pulls itself in, refuses contact with its surroundings. 'It is huddled all together', remarks Elizabeth-Jane when she sees it for the first time. The narrator goes on: 'Its squareness was, indeed, the characteristic which most struck the eye in this antiquated borough . . . at that time, recent as it was, untouched by the faintest sprinkle of modernism. It was compact as a box of dominoes. It had no suburbs – in the ordinary sense. Country and town met at a mathematical line' (IV; pp. 29–30: ellipsis mine). The 'rectangular frame' of the town recalls Hardy's descriptions of the perpendicularity of Henchard's face; entering Casterbridge Susan and Elizabeth-Jane encounter the 'stockade of gnarled trees', the town wall, part of its 'ancient defences', the 'grizzled church' whose bell tolls the curfew with a 'peremptory clang' (IV; pp. 30–2). All these details suggest Henchard, who is barricaded, authoritarian, coercive. He has become, as Christopher Coney tells the women, 'a pillar of the town' (V; p. 39).

Deeply defended against intimacy and converse with women, Henchard is vulnerable only when he has been symbolically unmanned by a fit of illness and depression; his susceptibility to these emotional cycles (the more integrated Farfrae is immune to them) is evidence of his divided consciousness. His romance with Lucetta takes place during such an episode: 'In my illness I sank into one of those gloomy fits I sometimes suffer from, on account o' the loneliness of my domestic life, when the world seems to have the blackness of hell, and, like Job, I could curse the day that gave me birth' (XII; p. 90). Again, when Henchard is living with Jopp, and becomes ill, Elizabeth-Jane is able to penetrate his solitude, and reach his affections. At these moments, his proud independence is overwhelmed by the woman's warmth; he is forced into an emotionally receptive passivity. Yet affection given in such circumstances humiliates him; he needs to demand or even coerce affection in order to feel manly and esteemed.

In health, Henchard determines the conditions of his relationships to women with minimal attention to their feelings. His remarriage to Susan is the product of 'strict mechanical rightness' (XIII; p. 93); his effort to substantiate the union, to give it the appearance of some deeper emotion, is typical of his withholding of self:

> Lest she should pine for deeper affection than he could give he made a point of showing some semblance of it in external action. Among other things he had the iron railings, that had smiled sadly in dull rust for the last eighty years, painted a bright green, and the heavily-barred, small-paned Georgian sash windows enlivened with three coats of white. He was as kind to her as a man, mayor, and churchwarden could possibly be. (XIV; p. 99)

To Susan, his kindness is an official function, and although he promises her that he will earn his forgiveness by his future works, Henchard's behaviour to women continues to be manipulative and proprietary. He deceives Elizabeth-Jane in the uncomfortable masquerade of the second courtship; he has not sufficient respect for Susan to follow her instructions on the letter about her daughter's true parentage. When he wants Lucetta to marry him, he threatens to blackmail her; when he wants to get rid of Elizabeth-Jane he makes her a small allowance. He trades in women, with dictatorial letters to Farfrae, and lies to Newson, with an ego that is alive only to its own excited claims.

Having established Henchard's character in this way, Hardy introduces an overlapping series of incidents in the second half of the novel which reverses and negates the pattern of manly power and self-possession. These incidents become inexorable stages in Henchard's unmanning, forcing him to acknowledge his own human dependency and to discover his own suppressed or estranged capacity to love. The first of these episodes is the reappearance of the furmity-woman at Petty Sessions, and her public denunciation of Henchard. Placed centrally in the novel (in Chapter XXVIII), this encounter seems at first reading to have the arbitrary and fatal timing of myth; the furmity-woman simply appears in Casterbridge to commit her 'nuisance' and to be arraigned. But the scene in fact follows Henchard's merciless coercion of Lucetta into a marriage she no longer desires. This violation, carried out from rivalry with Farfrae rather than disappointed love, repeats his older act of aggression against human feeling. Thus the declaration of the furmity-woman, the public humbling of Henchard by a woman, seems appropriate. It is for drunk and disorderly behaviour, for disrespect to the church and for profanity that she is accused; and her revelation of Henchard's greater disorder is an effective challenge to the authority of patriarchal law. Hardy's narrative underlines the scene explicitly as forming the 'edge or turn in the incline of Henchard's fortunes. On that day – almost at that minute – he passed the ridge of prosperity and honour, and began to descend rapidly on the other side. It was strange how soon he sank in esteem. Socially he had received a startling fillip downwards; and, having already lost commercial buoyancy from rash transactions, the velocity of his descent in both aspects became accelerated every hour' (XXXI; p. 251). The emphasis at this point is very much on Henchard's fortunes and his bankruptcy; although the furmity-woman's story spreads so fast that within twenty-four hours everyone in Casterbridge knows what happened at Weydon-Priors fair, the one person from whom Henchard has most assiduously kept the secret – Elizabeth-Jane – unaccountably fails to confront him with it. Indeed, Hardy seems to have forgotten to show her reaction; when she seeks him out it is only to forgive his harshness to her. Retribution for the auction thus comes as a public rather than a private shaming; and Henchard responds publicly with his dignified withdrawal as magistrate, and later, his generous performance in bankruptcy.

The next phase of Henchard's unmanning moves into the private sphere. Hearing of Lucetta's marriage to Farfrae, he puts his former threat of blackmail into action, tormenting her by reading her letters to her husband. Henchard cannot actually bring himself to reveal her name, to cold-bloodedly destroy her happiness; but Lucetta, investing him with a more implacable will than he possesses, determines to dissuade him, and so arranges a secret morning meeting at the Roman amphitheatre, which is far more successful than even she had dared to hope:

> Her figure in the midst of the huge enclosure, the unusual plainness of her dress, her attitude of hope and appeal, so strongly revived in his soul the memory of another ill-used woman who had stood there and thus in bygone days, had now passed away into her rest, that he was unmanned, and his breast smote him for having attempted reprisals on one of a sex so weak. (XXXV; p. 288)

'Unmanning' here carries the significance of enervation, of a failure of nerve and resolve; and also the intimation of sympathy with the woman's position. The scene is carefully constructed to repeat the earlier meeting in the arena, when the wronged Susan came to Henchard in all her weakness; Henchard's 'old feeling of supercilious pity for womankind in general was intensified by this suppliant appearing here as the double of the first' (XXXV; p. 289). But Hardy does not allow us such simple sentiments; he intensifies the ironic complexities that make this meeting different. There is certainly a sense in which Lucetta is both touchingly reckless of her reputation, and weak in her womanhood; these elements will come together in the fatal outcome of the skimmington-ride, when her wrecked honour and her miscarriage provide the emotional and physical shocks that kill her. While the Victorian belief in the delicacy of pregnant women, and also the statistical realities of the maternal death rate, are behind this incident (no contemporary reader of *The Mayor of Casterbridge* found it difficult to believe), Hardy obviously intends it symbolically as a demonstration of female vulnerability.

But, in another sense, Henchard is still deceiving himself about women's weakness, and flattering himself about men's strength; his 'supercilious pity' for womankind is obtuse and misplaced. Lucetta's pathetic appearance, her plea of loss of attractiveness, is deliberately and desperately calculated to win his pity and to pacify his competitiveness. She is employing 'the only practicable weapon left her as a woman' in this meeting with her enemy. She makes her toilette with the intention of making herself look plain; having missed a night's sleep, and being pregnant ('a natural reason for her slightly drawn look') she manages to look prematurely aged. Skilled at self-production and self-promotion, Lucetta thus turns her hand success-fully to this negative strategy, with the result that Henchard ceases to find her desirable, and 'no longer envied Farfrae his bargain'. She has transformed herself into a drooping rag; and Henchard is again eager to get away. Lucetta's cleverest stroke is to remove the stimulus to Henchard's sense of rivalry by telling him that 'neither my husband nor any other man will regard me with interest long' (XXXV; pp. 287–9). Although he is defeated by a woman, Henchard's understanding of women is still constituted by a kind of patriarchal innocence; he is ashamed of himself but for all the wrong reasons.

It is out of this unmanning, out of his disturbed self-esteem which has been deprived of an enemy, that Henchard tries to reassert his legitimate authority, and rebuild his diminished stature, by invading the welcoming ceremonies for the Royal Personage. Defiantly clad in 'the fretted and weather-beaten garments of bygone years', Henchard indeed stands out upon the occasion, and makes himself as prominent and distinctive as Farfrae, who wears 'the official gold chain with great square links, like that round the Royal unicorn' (XXXVII; p. 306). The scene is the necessary preamble to the fight between the two men; Henchard's flag-waving salute to Royalty is really a challenge to Farfrae, the lion against the unicorn. He puts himself in the young mayor's path precisely in order to be snubbed and driven back, to be inflamed so that he can take his revenge in 'the heat of action'. The wrestling-match with Farfrae is the central male contest of the novel – rivalries over business and women resolved by hand-to-hand combat. But in mastering Farfrae, even with one hand tied behind his back, Henchard is again paradoxically unmanned, shamed, and enervated. The sense of Farfrae's indifference to him, the younger man's resistance to even this ultimate and violent coercion of passion, robs Henchard of the thrill of his victory. Again, it is the apparently weaker antagonist who prevails; and in the emotional crisis, roles are reversed so that Farfrae is the winner. As for Henchard,

The scenes of his first acquaintance with Farfrae rushed back upon

him — that time when the curious mixture of romance and thrift in
the young man's composition so commanded his heart that Farfrae
could play upon him as on an instrument. So thoroughly subdued
was he that he remained on the sacks in a crouching attitude,
unusual for a man, and for such a man. Its womanliness sat
tragically on the figure of so stern a piece of virility. (XXXVIII;
p. 316)

The rugged friendship between man and man, so impressive when
seen from a distance by Elizabeth-Jane, comes down to this regressive,
almost foetal, scene in the loft. Henchard has finally crossed over
psychically and strategically to the long-repressed 'feminine' side of
himself — has declared love for the first time to another person, and
accepted the meaning of that victory of the weak over the strong.
Thus, as Dale Kramer points out, 'In relation to the pattern of
tragedy, the "feminine" Henchard is by his own definition a
weakened man.'[19] But again, Henchard's surrender opens him for the
first time to an understanding of human need measured in terms of
feeling rather than property. In his hasty and desperate lie to Newson,
Henchard reveals finally how dependent he has become on ties of
love.

   Thus the effigy which Henchard sees floating in Ten Hatches Hole,
whence he has fled in suicidal despair after the encounter with
Newson, is in fact the symbolic shell of a discarded male self, like a
chrysalis. It is the completion of his unmanning — a casting-off of the
attitudes, the empty garments, the façades of dominance and
authority, now perceived by the quiet eye of Elizabeth-Jane to be no
more than 'a bundle of old clothes' (XLI; p. 343). Returning home,
Henchard is at last able to give up the tattered and defiant garments of
his 'primal days', to put on clean linen. Dedicating himself to the love
and protection of Elizabeth-Jane, he is humanly reborn.

   The final section of the novel fulfils the implications of Henchard's
unmanning in a series of scenes which are reversals of scenes in the first
part of the book. It is Elizabeth-Jane who assumes ascendancy: 'In
going and coming, in buying and selling, her word was law' (XLII;
p. 349). He makes her tea with 'housewifely care' (XLI; p. 334). As
the 'netted lion' (XLII; p. 349), Henchard is forced into psychological
indirection, to feminine psychological manoeuvres, because he does
not dare to risk a confrontation: 'He would often weigh and consider
for hours together the meaning of such and such a deed or phrase of
hers, when a blunt settling question would formerly have been his

first instinct' (XLII; p. 351). It is a humbling, and yet educative and ennobling apprenticeship in human sensitivity, a dependence, Hardy writes, into which he had 'declined (or, in another sense, to which he had advanced)' (XLII; p. 351).

In his final self-imposed exile, Henchard carries with him mementoes of Elizabeth-Jane: 'gloves, shoes, a scrap of her handwriting, . . . a curl of her hair' (XLIV; p. 366: ellipsis mine). Retracing his past, he has chosen to burden himself with reminders of womanhood, and to plot his journey in relation to a female centre. Even the circle he traces around the 'centripetal influence' (XLIV; p. 368) of his stepdaughter contrasts with the defended squareness of the Casterbridge he has left behind, the straight grain of masculine direction. Henchard's final pilgrimage, to Elizabeth-Jane's wedding, is, detail by detail, a reliving of the journey made by the women at the beginning of the novel. He enters the town for the last time as they entered at the first: the poor relation, the suppliant, the outsider. 'As a Samson shorn' (XLIV; p. 373) he timidly presents himself at the kitchen-door, and from the empty back-parlour awaits Elizabeth-Jane's arrival. As Susan and Elizabeth-Jane watched him preside over the meeting of the Council, so he now must watch his stepdaughter preside over her wedding-party. As Susan was overpowered by the sight of her former husband's glory, and wished only 'to go – pass away – die' (V; p. 37), so is Henchard shamed and overwhelmed by Elizabeth-Jane's moral ascendancy. What is threatened and forgotten in the first instance comes to pass in the second – the rejected guest departs, and neither Elizabeth-Jane nor the reader sees him more.

In a sense which Hardy fully allows, the moral as well as the temporal victory of the novel is Elizabeth-Jane's. It is she to whom the concluding paragraphs are given, with their message of domestic serenity, their Victorian feminine wisdom of 'making limited opportunities endurable', albeit in 'a general drama of pain' (XLV; p. 386). Casterbridge, under the combined leadership of Elizabeth-Jane and Farfrae, is a gentled community, its old rough ways made civil, its rough edges softened. We might read the story of Henchard as a tragic taming of the heroic will, the bending and breaking of his savage male defiance in contest with a stoic female endurance. In such a reading, Henchard becomes a second Heathcliff, who is also overcome by the domestic power of a daughter-figure; like Heathcliff, Henchard is subdued first to the placidities of the grange, then to the grave.[20]

Yet this romantic and nostalgic reading would underestimate

Hardy's generosity of imagination. Virginia Woolf, one of Hardy's earliest feminist critics, attributed the 'tragic power' of his characters to 'a force within them which cannot be defined, a force of love or of hate, a force which in the men is the cause of rebellion against life, and in the women implies an illimitable capacity for suffering.'[21] In Henchard the forces of male rebellion and female suffering ultimately conjoin; and in this unmanning Hardy achieves a tragic power unequalled in Victorian fiction. It may indeed be true that Hardy could not be accounted a feminist in the political terms of the 1880s, or the 1970s; but in *The Mayor of Casterbridge* the feminist critic can see Hardy's swerving from the bluff virility of the Rabelais Club, and the misogyny of Gosse, towards his own insistent and original exploration of human motivation. The skills which Henchard struggles finally to learn, skills of observation, attention, sensitivity, and compassion, are also those of the novelist; and they are feminine perhaps, if one contrasts them to the skills of the architect or the statesman. But it is because Hardy dares so fully to acknowledge this side of his own art, to pursue the feminine spirit in his man of character, that his hero, like the great heroines he would create in the 1890s, is more Shakespearean than Victorian.

NOTES

1. Letter of February 1874, given in Richard Little Purdy, *Thomas Hardy: A Bibliographical Study* (London: Oxford University Press, 1954) p. 338.

2. Havelock Ellis, 'Thomas Hardy's Novels', *Westminster Review*, LXIII n.s. (1883) 334.

3. See Florence Emily Hardy, *The Later Years of Thomas Hardy, 1892–1928* (London and New York: Macmillan, 1930) p. 5.

4. Mary Jacobus, 'Sue the Obscure', *EIC*, xxv (1975) 304–28; and 'Tess's Purity', *EIC*, xxvi (1976) 318–38.

5. For Hardy's personal need to have a 'literary lady – not his wife – whom he could mastermind, and who would appreciate him in return', see Robert Gittings, *The Older Hardy* (London: Heinemann; Boston: Little, Brown, 1978) pp. 77–81. Hardy had recommended Mona Caird's essay on 'The Evolution of Marriage' (eventually published in her *The Morality of Marriage* [1897]) to the *Contemporary Review* in 1890; he wrote to Florence Henniker about Sarah Grand's best-selling feminist novel, *The Heavenly Twins* (1893).

6. Edmund Gosse, 'Thomas Hardy', *The Speaker*, II (1890) 295. Gosse attributed this unpopularity to Hardy's unconventional conception of feminine character.

7. Letter of 31 December 1891, in *The Collected Letters of Thomas Hardy*, Vol. I: *1840–1892*, ed. Richard Little Purdy and Michael Millgate (Oxford: Clarendon Press, 1978) 250.

8. Letter to Edmund Gosse, 20 January 1892, in *Collected Letters*, I, 255.

9. Letter to Hardy of 19 January 1892, in Evan Charteris, *The Life and Letters of Sir Edmund Gosse* (London: Heinemann, 1931) pp. 225–6.

10. Letter to Alice Grenfell, 23 April 1892, in *Collected Letters*, I, 266.

11. Letter of November 1906, in the Fawcett Library (London); quoted in Elaine Showalter, *A Literature of Their Own: British Women Novelists from Brontë to Lessing* (Princeton: Princeton University Press, 1977) p. 185.

12. A. O. J. Cockshut, *Man and Woman: A Study of Love and the Novel 1740–1940* (London: Collins, 1977; New York: Oxford University Press, 1978) pp. 128–9.

13. See Christine Winfield, 'Factual Sources of Two Episodes in *The Mayor of Casterbridge*', *NCF*, XXV (1970), 224–31.

14. Irving Howe, *Thomas Hardy* (London: Weidenfeld & Nicolson, 1968; New York: Macmillan, 1967) p. 84.

15. Quoted by Winfield, p. 226.

16. Charles K. Hofling, 'Thomas Hardy and the Mayor of Casterbridge', *Comprehensive Psychiatry*, IX (1968) 431.

17. J. Hillis Miller, *Thomas Hardy: Distance and Desire* (London: Oxford University Press; Cambridge, Mass.: Harvard University Press, 1970) pp. 147, 148.

18. For a discussion of the homosexual implications of the relationship, see Dale Kramer, *Thomas Hardy: The Forms of Tragedy* (London: Macmillan; Detroit: Wayne State University Press, 1975) pp. 86–87. Kramer concludes that 'to stress the potentially sensational aspect of Henchard's character in this manner is to misunderstand seriously the reasons for the success of the novel as tragedy.'

19. Kramer, p. 87.

20. Frederick R. Karl has suggested that Henchard's domination of the novel is equivalent to the 'all-powerful Heathcliff' in *Wuthering Heights*; 'The Mayor of Casterbridge: A New Fiction Defined', *MFS*, VI (1960) 211.

21. Virginia Woolf, 'The Novels of Thomas Hardy', *The Common Reader*, Second Series (London: The Hogarth Press, 1932) p. 253.

7 Tree and Machine:
The Woodlanders

MARY JACOBUS

Igdrasil, the Ash-tree of Existence, has its roots deep-down in the kingdoms of Hela or Death; its trunk reaches up heaven-high, spreads its boughs over the whole Universe: it is the Tree of Existence. . . . Is not every leaf of it a biography, every fibre there an act or word? Its boughs are Histories of Nations. The rustle of it is the noise of Human Existence, onwards from of old. It grows there, the breath of Human Passion rustling through it. . . . It is the past, the present, and the future; what was done, what is doing, what will be done. . . . Considering how human things circulate, each inextricably in communion with all, . . . I find no similitude so true as this of a Tree. . . . The '*Machine* of the Universe,' – alas, do but think of that in contrast!

Carlyle, *On Heroes and Hero-Worship*[1]

Celebrating the Norse myth of Nature, Carlyle mourns the death of organicism. Igdrasil has become a fiction, the Tree of Existence displaced by a demythologised and mechanistic world: 'The "*Machine* of the Universe," – alas, do but think of that in contrast!' The same reduction of myth to machine haunts *The Woodlanders*. Hardy laments a lost mythology as well as the rape of the woods by rootless predators from the modern world. The novel is pervaded by elegy for which the death of Giles Winterborne is the declared focus, and trees the silent mourners – 'The whole wood seemed to be a house of death, pervaded by loss to its uttermost length and breadth. Winterborne was gone, and the copses seemed to show the want of him' (XLIII; pp. 393–4). To Grace's imagination, Giles becomes a tutelary spirit ('He rose upon her memory as the fruit-god and the wood-god in alternation' [XXXVIII; p. 335]); but his death also signifies the depletion of Nature by an anatomising scientific vision. Subjected to a post-Romantic gaze, Nature reveals the same defects, the same crippling evolutionary struggle, as urban industrial society.

The wintry woods in which Grace walks with her father, near the start of the novel, no longer constitute an idyllic refuge or a source of renewal:

> Here, as everywhere, the Unfulfilled Intention, which makes life what it is, was as obvious as it could be among the depraved crowds of a city slum. The leaf was deformed, the curve was crippled, the taper was interrupted; the lichen ate the vigour of the stalk, and the ivy slowly strangled to death the promising sapling. (VII; p. 59)

Behind this passage lies another, copied into Hardy's notebook during 1883 under the heading 'Galton on the defects, evil, & apparent waste on our globe' ('We perceive around us a countless number of abortive seeds & germs; . . . it is possible that this world may rank among other worlds as one of these').[2] As John South's brain tissue is dissected under Fitzpiers' microscope, so Nature has lost its soul to modern science. A malfunctioning world of Necessity and Circumstance replaces one of organic relationship, just as Grace and Fitzpiers are reunited at the end of the novel by the malfunctioning machinery of Tim Tangs's man-trap. The death of organicism marks the birth of compromise; life goes on, but its continuity is a matter of contrivance rather than regeneration.

Embarking on *The Woodlanders* in November 1885, Hardy described himself as 'in a fit of depression, as if enveloped in a leaden cloud'.[3] His depression beclouds the novel. After a night as dark and void as 'the ante-mundane Ginnung-Gap' (III; p. 15), the first dawn breaks with a 'bleared white visage . . . like a dead-born child' (IV; p. 24) — expressive of Marty South's still-born hopes (she has learned from overhearing Melbury's conversation with his wife that Giles is not for her) and foretelling the abortiveness of Melbury's plan to right an old wrong by marrying Grace to Giles. Later, on the foggy day when Grace breaks off her engagement to him, Giles retreats silently up John South's tree as he prunes its branches, 'cutting himself off more and more from all intercourse with the sublunary world' (XIII; p. 111); he answers Grace, as she wavers regretfully below, by continuing 'motionless and silent in that gloomy Niflheim or fogland which involved him' (p. 112). This is one of a number of references to Norse mythology scattered throughout the early part of the novel. Elsewhere, the wintry wood in which Grace walks with her father rustles 'like the sheet-iron foliage of the fabled Jarnvid wood' (VII; p. 59), while Marty's distress at the sight of her shorn head is compared to that of Sif 'after the rape of her locks by Loke the Malicious' (III; p. 20). In the guise of Percomb the barber, Loki – the mischievous evil principle of Norse mythology – sows the seeds of division which set awry all the relationships in the novel (Marty's hair makes Felice Charmond alluring to Fitzpiers, but it also causes the quarrel which sends him back to Grace at the end of the novel). Hardy may have known Mallet's *Northern Antiquities* and the Prose Edda; certainly he would have known the account of Norse mythology which Carlyle derived from it in the opening lecture of *On Heroes and Hero-Worship*. But there is a source nearer home for his allusions to Niflheim and Jarnvid wood – Arnold's 'Balder Dead' (1855).[4] In Arnold's poem, 'The plains of Niflheim, where dwell the dead' (i.172) is the region to which Balder is banished by the motiveless intervention of Loki the Malicious, who inhabits (in one of his guises) 'the wood / Of Jarnvid, . . . where the trees are iron' (iii.329–31). It is Loki who destroys an otherwise charmed life, and whose refusal to join in the universal mourning of Nature prevents Balder's restitution to the world of the living. A desolately contemporaneous reworking of Norse myth, 'Balder Dead' concerns the failure of Nature's renewing power and the loss of joy from a modern world. Like *The Woodlanders*, it is a pastoral elegy – but, importantly, an unreconciled one. Not only is there no restitution of the dead, but Arnold too mourns a natural world drained of significance; as for Carlyle's Teufelsdröckh, afflicted by 'The Everlasting No', Nature becomes a soulless machine – 'one huge, dead, immeasurable Steam-engine, rolling on.'[5]

Denial informs the frustrate world of *The Woodlanders*. Writing of the wood after Giles's death, 'pervaded by loss to its uttermost length and breadth', Hardy must surely have had in mind the futility of Nature's mourning in 'Balder Dead' –

> And all that lived, and all without life, wept.
> And as in winter, when the frost breaks up,
> At winter's end, before the spring begins,
> And a warm west-wind blows, and thaw sets in –
> After an hour a dripping sound is heard
> In all the forests, and the soft-strewn snow
> Under the trees is dibbled thick with holes,
> And from the boughs the snowloads shuffle down;
> And, in fields sloping to the south, dark plots
> Of grass peep out amid surrounding snow,

And widen, and the peasant's heart is glad —
So through the world was heard a dripping noise
Of all things weeping to bring Balder back . . . (iii. 306—18)

Arnold's elaborate simile is ironic in force; the coming of spring is not
to be re-enacted in the return of Balder, sun-god and source of natural
regeneration (as Giles is both fruit-god and wood-god). The
melancholy personal force of 'Balder Dead' comes partly from the
failure of pastoral, elsewhere a potent source of imaginative consolation for Arnold. As the natural world proves ineffectual, so, in
formal terms, the poem lacks the characteristic upward curve of
pastoral elegy.[6] Balder's own divided consciousness is allowed to
usurp on the closing movement to create a more complex lament. In
Arnold fashion, he prefers the spectral half-life of Hela — 'the
cheerless land /Where idly flit about the feeble shades' (ii. 181—2) —
to the violence of the world itself. '"I am long since weary of your
storm /Of carnage"', Balder complains to Hermod,

Mine eyes are dizzy with the arrowy hail;
Mine ears are stunn'd with blows, and sick for calm.
Inactive therefore let me lie, in gloom,
Unarm'd, inglorious . . . (iii. 503—4, 507—10)

Like Hardy, Arnold is preoccupied by the individual singled out for
misfortune and unable to withstand the struggle for survival in a
world of chance and crass casualty. Balder's quietism — the extinction
of will and withdrawal from the world of the senses — is Giles's also.
Defeated in love, he retreats up his tree and, later, into the solitude of
the wood itself. His merging into the rain-sodden landscape, as Balder
fades into the shadows of Hela, hints at a deeper longing. At the end of
Arnold's poem, Hermod is left yearning for transcendence, unable to
join the flight of Balder —

        as a stork which idle boys have trapp'd,
And tied him in a yard, at autumn sees
Flocks of his kind pass flying o'er his head . . . (iii. 559—61)

The same unrest within the confines of malfunctioning Nature gives
The Woodlanders its underlying elegiac disquiet.
  But for Hardy, the 'wars and broils, which make /Life one
perpetual fight' (iii. 505—6) are not martial but amorous; coupling,

the very birds fall to quarrelling among the embers: 'They speedily parted, however, and flew up with a singed smell. . . ."That's the end of what is called love," said some one' (XIX; p. 168: ellipsis mine). The speaker, of course, is Marty. At the start of the novel she pre-enacts Giles's withdrawal in her symbolic haircut, desexing herself in mourning as well as self-abnegation (Giles is not for her). Though her grief is personal here, she also interprets Nature's sorrow: 'It seems to me', she says of the newly-planted trees, 'as if they sigh because they are very sorry to begin life in earnest – just as we be' (VIII; p. 73). There is authorial prompting in this, as in Tess's unerring identification of her star as a blighted apple, not a sound one. But Marty's choric voice sounds the characteristic note of *The Woodlanders*. It is she who opens and closes the novel, and her role which most clearly expresses its modified relation to pastoral. Hardy himself said that *The Woodlanders* went back to a 'woodland story' of the same period as *Far from the Madding Crowd* (1874);[7] but the difference between earlier and later versions of pastoral ('the Fulfilled Intention . . . of his own imagination' as opposed to 'the Unfulfilled Intention of the actual world') is underlined by a contemporary reviewer:

> There is . . . a little of Gabriel Oak in Giles Winterbourne [*sic*]; but not enough to round off his life with domestic happiness. There is a little of Bathsheba Everdene in Grace Melbury – enough to make her marry the man of her fancy and not of her heart. As for Edred Fitzpiers, he is but a superfine (an intellectually, not morally superfine) Sergeant Troy. . . . But then we have an entirely new creation in Marty South, the poor girl who ascends from the ridiculous in the first chapter, in which she loses her hair, to the sublime in the last chapter, in which she loses her hero, and, standing by his tombstone, 'looks almost like a being who had rejected with indifference the attribute of sex'.[8]

Hardy's single addition defines the depletion of energy and chastened vision of *The Woodlanders* – its attentuation of vigour into quiescence, passion into elegy, endurance into renunciation. To a greater degree than in any other novel, his sensibility is diffused among his characters rather than focused on the consciousness of an individual; Giles and Grace, Fitzpiers and Felice, become elements in a larger pattern, just as plot becomes a network of cause and effect – 'the pattern in the great web of human doings then weaving' (III; p. 21). But the fullest expression of the Unfulfilled Intention devolves on

Marty. Her oblique presence is itself expressive of disjunction rather than relationship, making her less a participator than an observer throughout the novel; even her attempted interventions in the mechanics of the plot misfire as completely as Tim Tangs's man-trap. The consummation of her love for Giles can take place only after his death, in the sole possession of his memory as she lays fresh flowers on his grave — enacting the traditional rites of pastoral elegy in a context where they retain their beauty without their mythic power of consolation and renewal.

The changed relation of *The Woodlanders* to pastoral which makes Marty's so crucial a role is expressed elsewhere, in the novel's rendering of the seasonal pattern. In *Under the Greenwood Tree* (1872) the turning of the seasons had brought ritual celebration with the summer wedding of Dick Dewy and Fancy Day. Hardy disposes of the marriage of Grace and Fitzpiers rather differently. Occupying the exact mid-point of the novel (Chapter XXIV), it forms, not the resolution, but the pivot of the action — the fixed point about which the scales oscillate. The changing state of Grace's matrimonial case is not so much reflected as ironically counterpointed by the alternating seasons of three years. The first autumn brings her return to Little Hintock, winter the death of Giles's hopes, spring and summer her courtship and marriage to Fitzpiers; the second autumn and winter bring his infidelity with Felice Charmond, and spring the open breach with Grace. Early summer marks the renewal of Giles's courtship, this time followed, not by marriage, but by the news that there can be no divorce; with autumn comes his death, and winter, Grace's mourning, while spring completes her reconciliation with Fitzpiers. The seasonal pattern at once suggests human attunement to its cyclical movement, and records alienation from it; instead of fulfilment, we see the dual frustration of Melbury's intention. The 'drowsy content' (XI; p. 95) which might have been Grace's if she had married Giles is doubly aborted. Gentility and docility attenuate her instinctual preference for Giles, while social ambition makes Melbury deviate from his intention; later, divorce proves unobtainable on a legal technicality (Fitzpiers' infidelity has not been accompanied by cruelty). [9] While Grace herself becomes significantly more active and self-fulfilling during the course of the novel, Giles's decline expresses a contrary movement. Of his second courtship we are told, 'Though it was with almost the same zest it was with not quite the same hope that he had begun to tread the old tracks again' (XXXIX; p. 345). Loss of vital energy and optimism makes his second renunciation less stoic, more despairing, than his first. The seasonal cycle revolves and returns, but for humans it does not bring renewal; their consciousness of change effects a divorce between man and nature which is the pastoral equivalent of the Arnoldian 'ache of modernism' in Hardy's later novels.

Yet the mood of *The Woodlanders* is less one of discord than resignation. Nine months after beginning it, Hardy recorded that he had 'quite resigned himself to novel-writing as a trade, which he had never wanted to carry on as such. He now went about the business mechanically.'[10] His reversion to pastoral, and his resignation, are bound up with his agreement to provide a serial for *Macmillan's Magazine* – among the most respectable of the family magazines, and one for which he had not previously written.[11] In November 1885 he was working round the clock to get the details right, and it is clear that he was at pains to provide a novel precisely calculated to meet the demands of part-publication in *Macmillan's Magazine* – not only in subject and treatment, but in form. Although the serialisation was not always able to observe Hardy's own divisions,[12] *The Woodlanders* was conceived throughout in terms of monthly parts, each carefully plotted to maximise the opportunities for suspended action and ironic reversal provided by part-publication. At the same time, Hardy attempted to unify the twelve individual parts for which he had contracted with *Macmillan's Magazine*, apparently composing the novel in three blocks of four parts[13] – each comprising a crucial phase in Grace's marital adventures and creating a larger, tripartite structure. This careful overall plotting creates an effect of inelasticity in the finished novel; a rigid determinism constrains both situation and character. Instead of character appearing to shape plot, plot appears to 'work' the novel, serving as a formal expression of the frustration which is its theme. Checks and balances, stoppages and changes of direction, create the crab-like movement reflected in the three main units of the novel's structure. Beginning with Melbury's announcement of his plan for Grace and Giles (Part 1), the first section spans the lapse of his intention (Part 2) and the breaking off of the engagement (Part 3), and closes with Grace and her future husband brought face to face for the first time (Part 4). The middle section traces the progress of the relationship between Grace and Fitzpiers from courtship to engagement (Part 5), only for marriage (Part 6) to give way almost at once to Fitzpiers' affair with Felice Charmond (Part 7) and the revival of Grace's love for Giles (Part 8). The final section begins with the separation of Grace and Fitzpiers (Part 9), spans the unsuccessful attempt to obtain divorce, the return of Fitzpiers (Part 10), and the death of Giles (Part 11), and closes with Grace reunited with Fitzpiers (Part 12). The careful plotting is not so much satisfying as an emblem of dissatisfaction. Its completion involves a chain of circumstances working against the characters' natural alignments, setting askew the preconceived direction of pastoral romance and creating a subversive restatement of the traditional pattern. Instead of moving via courtship to marriage, *The Woodlanders* thus moves from unsuccessful courtship in the first section, to failed marriage in the second, and unobtained divorce in the third. Ousted from its traditional place at the end of the novel, marriage ceases to be a resolution and instead becomes a mid-point of instability and anti-climax.

The peculiar modernity and air of compromise in *The Woodlanders* derive from this subversion of conventional structure; though its setting is secluded and fresh, its plot creates a mood at once worldly and world-weary. The sense of baffled stasis is matched by an almost cynical determinism. The mechanism is set like a trap — part linked to part and section to section by a chain of cause and effect, suspense and consequence, making chance and mischance the fixed laws of the novel. A single triggering device connects the three larger sections: Marty's hair. Nothing could emphasise more clearly the triumph of machine over tree; plot itself becomes an index of meaning, functioning on a dual level of contrivance and metaphor. At the start of the novel, the rape of Marty's locks to satisfy Felice Charmond's vanity prefigures not just the casual appropriation of the sylvan Grace by Fitzpiers, but the rape of Little Hintock by outside forces — by the modernity to which Grace, Giles, and the wood itself surrender their capacity for instinctual life. Marty's hair also both sets going and sets awry the mechanism of the plot, constituting its Loki-like evil principle. As Hardy reminds us, Felice's abundant coiffure is part of her attraction for Fitzpiers, and she herself alludes playfully to her husband's collection of man-traps ('Man-traps are of rather ominous significance where a person of our sex lives, are they not?' [VIII; p. 67]). Grace replies primly: 'They are interesting, no doubt, as relics of a barbarous time happily past.' Clearly Hardy has in mind not only the hairy springes by which Felice ensnares Fitzpiers, but the man-trap set in primitive revenge for his philandering at the end of the novel. The middle section closes by recalling the device. As Grace goes home after Felice's impulsive confession that she and Fitzpiers are lovers, she observes Marty through her window, writing a letter. It is to

Fitzpiers. In an attempt to bring him back to his wife, Marty reveals that 'Mrs. Charmond's magnificent pile of hair was made up of the writer's more largely than of her own. It was poor Marty's only card, and she played it, . . . thinking her revelation a fatal one for a lover' (XXXIII; p. 295). It proves so. We learn retrospectively of the quarrel and separation provoked by Fitzpiers' later reading of the letter in Felice's presence, and of Felice's death at the hands of her jealous South Carolinian lover. But this is not the last of it. The hairy springe which has separated Grace and her husband is finally metamorphosed into a real, not metaphoric man-trap — set to punish Fitzpiers for his earlier entanglement with Suke Damson, but succeeding in pre-cipitating the petticoated Grace back into his arms when it catches her skirt instead of his ankles. The machine misfires as completely as the divorce laws, serving only to reinstate their marriage. As Hardy wrote later, the universe is not merely a machine, but an imperfect one.[14] The patched-up relationship and contrived ending lead to exile instead of the rebirth of love and the restoration of harmony in a village community; Grace leaves her woodland home for the world of small-town gentility in which, Hardy hints plainly enough, Fitzpiers will be no more faithful to her than before.[15]

Writing in 1886, Hardy saw the human race as 'one great network or tissue which quivers in every part when one point is shaken, like a spider's web if touched'.[16] A web of correspondences connects the rape of Marty's locks, Fitzpiers' purchase of Grammer Oliver's brain, and the felling of John South's tree. But there is more involved in all three than the casual appropriation of another's life-force, and it is John South's tree which testifies most strikingly to the existence of a deeper level of meaning in the novel. Like Marty's hair and Grammer Oliver's brain (the reason for Grace's first visit to Fitzpiers), South's death provides a crucial link in the working of the plot; by it, Giles loses both his cottages and Grace ('O Giles, you've lost your dwelling-place, / And therefore, Giles, you'll lose your Grace' [XV; p. 128]). But the pathology of his illness also probes at the relation of woodlanders to woods, man to Nature, body to soul, object to idea. South's illness ('Others have been like it afore in Hintock' [XIV; p. 121]) takes the form of an obsessive identification between himself and the elm which stands in front of his cottage; he keeps time to its movements — 'As the tree waved South waved his head, making it his fugleman with abject obedience' (XIII; p. 108) and believes that the tree which has grown old along with him will fall and crush him to

death: 'There he stands, threatening my life every minute that the
wind do blow' (p. 108). He is still more terrified of its gauntness after
Giles 'shrouds off' its lower branches, and falls dead when Fitzpiers'
kill-or-cure treatment reveals a 'vacant patch of sky in place of the
branched column so familiar to his gaze' (XIV; p. 122). The felling of
the tree is the most fatal instance of an outsider's unthinking
intervention in the closely-knit organism of woodland life, and – like
Fitzpiers' purchase of Grammer Oliver's brain – it has the fearfulness
of a broken taboo; Grammer Oliver tells Grace, 'John South's death
of fear about the tree makes me think I shall die of this' (XVII; p. 142).
But the unexplained prominence of the episode makes one return to it
as something more. On it Hardy pegs the obsessive quality – the
adherence to an *idée fixe* – which characterises life in Little Hintock as
described by the opening chapter: 'one of those sequestered
spots . . . where reasoning proceeds on narrow premises, and results
in inferences wildly imaginative' (I; p. 4).

Melbury's plans for Grace and Giles's love for her both contain
something of John South's fixation on his tree – an intensity which
Fitzpiers ascribes to the seclusion of woodland life: 'People living
insulated, as I do by the solitude of this place, get charged with
emotive fluid like a Leyden jar with electric, for want of some
conductor at hand to disperse it' (XVI; pp. 137–8); for Felice
Charmond, too, 'Hintock has the curious effect of bottling up the
emotions till one can no longer hold them' (XXVI; p. 228). John
South's tree is the conductor on which he discharges – what? Fear of
death or longing for it? The ambiguity is central to a novel whose
hero, like Balder, prefers the world of shadows to the world of the
living, and whose concern with love and death brings to light an
underlying unease about the self-sufficing, self-consuming solipsism
of inner life. It is not so much death-dealing illness as the idea of death
which kills South; it is not so much love as the idea of love that drives
Fitzpiers to self-immolation in the arms of Felice. Comparing him to
Tannhäuser when he rides off across country to see her, Hardy makes
him quote from Shelley's *Epipsychidion* (ll. 219–21) –

> – Towards the loadstar of my one desire
> I flitted, like a dizzy moth, whose flight
> Is as a dead leaf's in the owlet light. (XXVIII; p. 245)

As John South's tree is at once fugleman and executioner, so Felice is
at once Fitzpiers's 'loadstar' and the 'fiery sepulchre' which consumes

the moth. The plot of *The Woodlanders* may speak of 'the great web of human doings then weaving' – of the network of cause and effect described by John Addington Symonds in a passage which Hardy transcribed in his notebook ten years before ('Each act, as it has had immeasurable and necessary antecedents, will be fruitful of immeasurable and necessary consequents; for the web of the world is ever weaving, and to drop a thread in it is utterly impossible').[17] But the web gets its distinctive weave from isolated focuses of fear and desire. Love and death are the warp and weft; the pattern is one of fantasy and obsession. On its deepest level, the novel questions the status of the imagination itself in a post-Romantic context where Mind and Nature are irrevocably divorced. For all its geographical limitation, *The Woodlanders* opens on to the landscape of Hardy's own imagination, raising questions that are central both to his philosophical ponderings and to his skewed relation to Romanticism.

The Woodlanders is Hardy's most ambiguously Shelleyan novel. The intensely personal significance which Hardy himself attached to poems like *Epipsychidion* and *The Revolt of Islam* is countered by his ironic treatment of the Shelleyan temperament seen in Fitzpiers. The doctor is both an amateur idealist philosopher and a rationalist hewer-down of *idées fixes*. Popularly seen as in league with the devil, he is resolutely modern in his attitude to love and knowledge while being an old-fashioned sentimentalist and dilettante. Throughout the novel, his own self-conscious invocations of Shelley are deflated by the action. Catechising Giles about the identity of a young lady 'with a little white boa round her neck, and white fur round her gloves' (XVI; p. 137), Fitzpiers is moved to rhapsodise on the unknown Grace in the words of *The Revolt of Islam* (Canto II, stanza xxiii):

> She moved upon this earth a shape of brightness,
> A power, that from its objects scarcely drew
> One impulse of her being – in her lightness
> Most like some radiant cloud of morning dew
> Which wanders through the waste air's pathless blue
> To nourish some far desert: she did seem
> Beside me, gathering beauty as she grew,
> Like the bright shade of some immortal dream

Which walks, when tempests sleep, the wave of life's dark stream.

(XVI; p. 137)

But for all his sentimentality, Fitzpiers has a knowing cynicism.

When Giles remarks painfully after listening to these lines, 'You seem to be mightily in love with her, sir', the doctor furnishes him with a Spinozistic disquisition on the subjectivity of love:

> Human love is a subjective thing – the essence itself of man, as that great thinker Spinoza says – *ipsa hominis essentia* – it is joy accompanied by an idea which we project against any suitable object in the line of our vision, just as the rainbow iris is projected against an oak, ash, or elm tree indifferently. So that if any other young lady had appeared instead of the one who did appear, I should have felt just the same interest in her, and have quoted precisely the same lines from Shelley about her, as about this one I saw. Such miserable creatures of circumstance are we all! (p. 138)[18]

Ironic words to Giles, for whom the species of trees and the species of women are equally distinct; as he replies when Fitzpiers continues to speculate about the young lady's identity, 'What difference can it make, if she's only the tree your rainbow falls on?' (p. 139). Giles's wryness later becomes a more thoroughly undermining bathos on Hardy's part, literally toppling Fitzpiers from his Shelleyan pose. Confused by rum and concussion after a fall from his horse, he dramatises himself to his father-in-law as the Prometheus of Little Hintock:

> People don't appreciate me here! . . . except one – except one! . . . I say, old fellow, those claws of yours clutch me rather tight – rather like the eagle's, you know, that ate out the liver of Pro – Pre – , the man on Mount Caucasus. . . . People don't appreciate me, I say, except *her*! . . . (XXXV; p. 306: first ellipsis mine)

When Melbury loses patience and hurls Fitzpiers to the ground, the selfless Promethean rebel and frustrated quester after knowledge – in the words of Shelley's 'Preface', 'the type of the highest perfection of moral and intellectual nature, impelled by the purest and the truest motives to the best and noblest ends' – is cut down to size as erring husband and ungrateful son-in-law.

Though Fitzpiers' posturing travesties Shelley, the image of man writhing in the grip of cruel Necessity is one that Hardy himself would have found sympathetic; for him, as for John Addington Symonds, the Promethean myth was one of 'personified humanity struggling against the forces of niggardly nature',[19] and his own Spinozistic determinism tallies with the doctor's (he later wrote that his view approximated to Spinoza's, 'that neither Chance nor Purpose governs the universe, but Necessity'[20]). The peculiar ambivalence of Hardy's portrayal of Fitzpiers, like Carlyle's in writing of his own Teufelsdröckh, lies in his involvement with the ideas he parodies. Describing Fitzpiers to Grace as 'a projick, a real projick, [who] says the oddest of rozums', Grammer Oliver retails a garbled version of his philosophy – a mish-mash of Spinoza and subjective idealism.

> 'Ah, Grammer, . . . let me tell you that Everything is Nothing. There's only Me and Not Me in the whole world.' And he told me that no man's hands could help what they did, any more than the hands of a clock. . . . Yes, he's a man of strange meditations. (VI; p. 55: first ellipsis mine)

Hardy's source for the Idealist strain in Fitzpiers' thinking is almost certainly the thumbnail sketch of a 'German Idealist' in Carlyle's essay on Novalis:

> To a Transcendentalist, Matter has an existence, but only as a Phenomenon: were *we* not there, neither would it be there; it . . . depends for its apparent qualities on *our* bodily and mental organs; . . . being, in the common sense of that world, Nothing. The tree is green and hard, not of its own natural virtue, but simply because my eye and my hand are fashioned so as to discern such and such appearances under such and such conditions. . . . Bring a sentient Being, with eyes a little different, with fingers ten times harder than mine; and to him that Thing which I call Tree shall be yellow and soft, as truly as to me it is green and hard. . . . There is, in fact, says Fichte, no Tree there; but only a Manifestation of Power from something which is *not I*. . . . This, we suppose, may be the foundation of what Fichte means by his far-famed *Ich* and *Nicht-Ich* (I and Not-I).[21]

But what is for Fitzpiers a libertine's licence was for Hardy himself a matter of lasting philosophic concern. His own reading at this period lays the foundations for ideas which later find their way into *The Dynasts* – not only the image of the human race as 'one great network or tissue', but the replacement of material realities by 'the true realities of life, hitherto called abstractions'.[22] In this context Hardy noted his reaction to landscape painting in early 1887, when the serialisation of *The Woodlanders* was drawing to a close:

> I don't want to see landscapes, *i.e.*, scenic paintings of them, because I don't want to see the original realities – as optical effects, that is. I want to see the deeper reality underlying the scenic, the expression of what are sometimes called abstract imaginings.[23]

Behind Hardy's rejection of optical effects for abstract imaginings lies a dual preoccupation with transcendental philosophy on one hand, and the relation of mind to matter on the other. Committed to a Spinozistic monism – to Hume's 'hideous hypothesis' ('the unity of that substance, in which he supposes both thought and matter to inhere')[24] – Hardy shows particular interest at this moment in a subject of topical concern, the attempt to establish mind or consciousness in the context of scientific rationalism. If transcendental philosophy took him in one direction – towards Fitzpiers' 'Everything is Nothing' – contemporary reinterpretation of Spinoza as a scientific determinist took him in another, towards a physiological attempt to find the basis of mind in matter itself.

The duality surfaces in the curious scene which brings Grace and Fitzpiers face to face for the first time in a room containing both works of German transcendental philosophy and a microscope. Visiting Fitzpiers to intercede on Grammer Oliver's behalf, Grace finds him sound asleep in his study; going towards the bell-pull, she sees in a mirror that his eyes are open – but when she turns round, they are closed. She leaves, Fitzpiers wakes, and Grace returns. Their first interview is spiced with her consciousness of the oddity of the incident (can he have been playing a trick on her?) and his sense of having dreamed ' – what do you think? – that you stood in the room':

> I did not see you directly, but reflected in the glass. I thought, what a lovely creature! The design is for once carried out. Nature has at last recovered her lost union with the Idea! My thoughts ran in that direction because I had been reading the work of a transcendental philosopher last night; and I dare say it was the dose of Idealism that I received from it that made me scarcely able to distinguish between reality and fancy. I almost wept when I awoke, and found that you had appeared to me in Time, but not in Space, alas! (XVIII; p. 154)

The rationalist explanation (that Fitzpiers 'had opened his eyes for a few moments, but had immediately relapsed into unconsciousness' [XVIII; pp. 150–1]) undermines his effusion. Its fanciful self-indulgence is detected elsewhere: 'That the Idea had for once completely fulfilled itself in the objective substance (which he had hitherto deemed an impossibility) he was *enchanted* enough to *fancy* must be the case' (XX; p. 171: italics mine). His 'dose of Idealism' sounds like Schelling, whose philosophy of Nature, involving the concept of a fall from the Absolute or the 'real' to the limited reality of a finite world, allows for the possibility of evolution towards a recovery of the lost union. But Fitzpiers is also engaged in an attempt to bridge Idealist and rationalist stances – 'endeavouring', he tells Grace, 'to carry on simultaneously the study of physiology and transcendental philosophy, the material world and the ideal, so as to discover if possible a point of contact between them' (XVIII; p. 156). He goes on to show her 'a cellular tissue of some indescribable sort' – in fact a fragment of John South's brain. As Hardy indicates via Grace's response (wonder not aversion), he shares Fitzpiers' interest in this line of research. What he is looking for is the elusive substance which W. K. Clifford called 'Mind-stuff' – a hideous sub-teutonic coinage for the hypothesised material basis of consciousness. Hardy had read and annotated an account of Clifford in the *Edinburgh Review* for 1880 (where he is described as a scientist concerned not only with 'the structure of the nervous system, but with object and subject, the Me and the Not-me'),[25] and in 1892 he referred approvingly to 'Mind-stuff' in a metaphysical context: 'With Spinoza, & the late W. K. Clifford, you may call all matter mind-stuff (a very attractive idea this, to me).'[26] If dreaming could not recover Nature's lost union with the Idea, perhaps the microscope could.

Fitzpiers' dilettante studies, then, draw on ideas which preoccupied Hardy himself. But what emotional colouring did they have for the more serious student? The answer must lie in the mingled scepticism and nostalgia of *The Woodlanders*, and perhaps also in James Sully's *Pessimism* (1877), which Hardy seems to have read while working on this novel in 1886.[27] As Sully points out, the implications of Schelling's philosophy are dispiriting:

> Man . . . having stepped out of [his] original unity with God, nature has risen up against him in hostility and has, moreover, lost the initial stages of its perfection. . . . This view of the world gives room for much pessimistic complaint, and Schelling speaks now

and again of the sadness which cleaves to all finite life,' of the deep indestructible melancholy of all life, and of the veil of depression (*Schwermuth*) which is spread over the whole of nature.[28]

The same 'veil of depression' hangs over *The Woodlanders*, with its seasonal expression of the divorce between man and Nature, its deformed woods, and the limits of mortality defined by John South's tree. Fitzpiers' fanciful optimism about the reunion of Nature and the Idea is for Hardy contradicted at its very basis. Attracted though he was by the hypothesis of 'mind-stuff', he could find no rational justification for believing in a transcendental or unifying consciousness linking man to man, to Nature, or to God. Here lies his divergence from Shelley. In Act III of *Prometheus Unbound*, the unbinding of Prometheus brings the restoration of Nature through his marriage to Asia; in the words of Mary Shelley's 'Note', 'Nature resumes the beauty of her prime, and is united to her husband, the emblem of the human race, in perfect and happy union.' No such marriage can take place in the defective and frustrate world of *The Woodlanders*. Clifford's line of enquiry, too, leaves disquieting problems, not just for the rationalist, but for the imagination. Fitzpiers' inspection of John South's brain-tissue mirrors other depletions in the novel, representing a denial of soul — as Clifford puts it, 'the physical world . . . is made of atoms and ether, and there is no room in it for ghosts.'[29] But ghosts — the one means open to him of overcoming time and death — are indispensable to Hardy's imagination, as he later confessed: 'Half my time (particularly when I write verse) I believe . . . in spectres, mysterious voices, intuitions, omens, dreams, haunted places, etc., etc.'[30] Ultimately, he is left not only with the loss of Nature's soul, but, still more hauntingly, with the displacement of imagination itself. For Wordsworth, 'the homeless voice of waters' in Book XIII of *The Prelude*, though disembodied, was located with the stable 'under-presence, /The sense of God', uniting Mind and Nature (Book XIII, ll. 63–5, 71–2). But for Hardy there can only be a floating imagination anchored at random on a woman here, a tree there, and passing into nothing with the death of the individual consciousness.

It is through the figure of Marty that Hardy resolves, as far as he can, the imaginative and philosophic problems which trouble *The Woodlanders*. Earlier in the novel, we see her barking a tree, 'encaged amid the mass of twigs and buds like a great bird, running her ripping-tool into the smallest branches, beyond the furthest points to

which the skill and patience of the men enabled them to proceed'
(XIX; p. 160). Hardy is making an economic point here, for Marty's
time is worth less than the men's, and so she spends more of it on her
task. But the image also suggests that it is the cage of finite Nature
which transforms her into a great bird – an image recalling the
captive stork of 'Balder Dead', while implying that human life
necessarily takes its beauty from being confined by the tree of
existence. Marty's intimate observation of her woodland setting also
anchors Fitzpiers' floating and arbitrarily-projected imagination. For
her, as for Giles, Nature is a living, knowable, particularised
organism:

> From the light lashing of the twigs upon their faces when brushing
> through them in the dark either could pronounce upon the species
> of the tree whence they stretched; from the quality of the wind's
> murmur through a bough either could in like manner name its sort
> afar off. (XLIV; p. 399)

The tree of existence ceases to be a metaphor, becoming a reality
rendered intelligible by long association. The source of Fitzpiers'
rootlessness is for Hardy the absence of such knowledge, and
ultimately, of memory. Little Hintock means nothing to him because
he is ignorant of its past – of the 'invisible ones of the days gone by,
whose feet have traversed the fields . . . whose creaking plough has
turned those sods . . . whose hands planted the trees' (XVII; p. 146).
But to Marty the landscape is peopled with memories, and her daily
life becomes a memorial for the dead Giles – the tree of existence
ever-green in her planting and cider-making:

> Whenever I get up I'll think of 'ee, and whenever I lie down I'll
> think of 'ee again. Whenever I plant the young larches I'll think
> that none can plant as you planted; and whenever I split a gad, and
> whenever I turn the cider wring, I'll say none could do it like you.
> If ever I forget your name let me forget home and heaven! . . . But
> no, no, my love, I never can forget 'ee; for you was a good man,
> and did good things! (XLVIII; p. 444)

Marty's fidelity partially heals the breach between Nature and
Imagination, making available the only source of immortality
permitted in a depleted and demythologised world. Rooted in
experience, memory displaces the floating obsessions with love and

death that impel Fitzpiers' quest for Felice and John South's obedience to his tree. It alone transcends the limitations of Nature and mortality — providing the post-Romantic substitute for Imagination which makes Hardy's characteristic mode the backward-looking, elegiac vision of *The Woodlanders*, while allowing him a necessary arboreal ghost in the '*Machine* of the Universe'.

NOTES

1. *The Works of Thomas Carlyle*, ed. H. D. Traill (London: Chapman & Hall, 1896–99), V, 20–1.

2. *The Literary Notes of Thomas Hardy*, Vol. I, ed. Lennart A. Björk (Göteborg, Sweden: Acta Universitatis Gothoburgensis, 1974) I, 160, item 1311; ellipsis mine.

3. Florence Emily Hardy, *The Early Life of Thomas Hardy, 1840–1891* (London and New York: Macmillan, 1928) p. 230.

4. See David DeLaura, '"The Ache of Modernism" in Hardy's Later Novels', *ELH*, XXXIV (1967) 384n.

5. *Sartor Resartus*; in *The Works of Thomas Carlyle*, I, 133.

6. For a consideration of the novel's generic relation to pastoral elegy, see David Lodge's introduction to the New Wessex Edition of *The Woodlanders* (London: Macmillan, 1974) pp. 24–9 (paperback edition).

7. *Early Life*, p. 135.

8. William Wallace, *Academy*, 9 April 1887, p. 252.

9. Hardy has in mind the Divorce and Matrimonial Causes Act of 1857; see Michael Millgate, *Thomas Hardy: His Career as a Novelist* (London: The Bodley Head; New York: Random House, 1971) p. 246.

10. *Early Life*, p. 239.

11. 'A high-toned periodical', in the words of the outraged vicar's wife from Crewkerne who wrote to complain of *The Woodlanders* on the score that the story hinged on conjugal infidelity; see *Letters to Macmillan*, ed. Simon Nowell-Smith (London: Macmillan; New York: St. Martin's Press, 1967) p. 131. Hardy had already been warned by his editor, Mowbray Morris, 'not to bring the fair Miss Suke to too open shame' for fear of 'pious Scottish souls' (19 September 1886; given by Dale Kramer, 'Revisions and Vision: Thomas Hardy's *The Woodlanders*', *BNYPL*, LXXV [1971] 207).

12. As published in *Macmillan's Magazine*, only Parts 1–4 and Part 9 followed Hardy's own part-divisions in the manuscript.

13. Argued by Kramer in his account of the novel's composition and textual evolution, 'Revisions and Vision', pp. 205–9.

14. 'The Universe is to [Nietzsche] a perfect machine which only requires thorough handling to work wonders. He forgets that the universe is an imperfect machine' (Florence Emily Hardy, *The Later Years of Thomas Hardy, 1892–1928* [London and New York: Macmillan, 1930], p. 160).

15. The hint was strengthened by revisions made for the one-volume edition of 1887 and for the Osgood edition of 1895; see also *Early Life*, p. 289.

16. *Early Life*, p. 232.

17. Symonds, *Studies of the Greek Poets*, Second Series (London: Smith, Elder, 1876) p. 398; see Hardy's partial transcription in *Literary Notes*, I, 67, item 638.
18. See Spinoza, *Ethics*, III. xiii: "*Love* is nothing else but *pleasure accompanied by the idea of an external cause.*'
19. Symonds, p. 380.
20. *Later Years*, p. 128.
21. In Vol. II of *Critical and Miscellaneous Essays*; in *The Works of Thomas Carlyle*, XXVII, 24–5; see also *Literary Notes*, I, 193, item A215; and I, 407, item A215n.
22. *Early Life*, p. 232; see also W. F. Wright, *The Shaping of 'The Dynasts'* (Lincoln: University of Nebraska Press, 1967) p. 7.
23. *Early Life*, p. 242.
24. David Hume, *A Treatise of Human Nature*, Book I, Part IV, section V.
25. *Edinburgh Review*, CLI (April 1880) 485; see *Literary Notes*, I, 363–5, item 1215n.
26. To Roden Noel, 3 April 1892; given in *Literary Notes*, I, 365, item 1215n.
27. See Wright, p. 40.
28. Sully, *Pessimism: A History and a Criticism* (London: Henry S. King, 1887) pp. 68–9.
29. Clifford, *Lectures and Essays*, ed. Leslie Stephen and Frederick Pollock (London: Macmillan, 1879) II, 66–7; the sentence is also quoted in the account annotated by Hardy from the *Edinburgh Review*, p. 489.
30. To Dr Saleeby, 2 February 1915; given in *Later Years*, p. 271.

8 Psychological Determinism in *Tess of the d'Urbervilles*

LEON WALDOFF

The conception of tragedy in *Tess of the d'Urbervilles* rests on an assumption of inevitability. 'The best tragedy – highest tragedy in short', Hardy thought, 'is that of the WORTHY encompassed by the INEVITABLE.'[1] Throughout *Tess of the d'Urbervilles* Hardy invokes several discrete yet interrelated forms of determinism to make his heroine's fate seem inevitable. Heredity is the most obvious of these. Tess's ability to see or hear the d'Urberville Coach of the legend and her resemblance to the d'Urberville women of the portraits in the farmhouse at Wellbridge ('her fine features were unquestionably traceable in these exaggerated forms' [XXXIV; p. 277]) suggest that she has the fateful blood of the ancient d'Urbervilles in her veins. A somewhat different form of determinism is in Hardy's use of the laws of Nature, particularly in the great pastoral scenes in which Angel and Tess first discover and resist their love for each other. 'All the while', we are told, 'they were converging, under an irresistible law, as surely as two streams in one vale' (XX; p. 165). Tess, with her sensuousness, is an embodiment of the principle in Nature of irresistible sexual attraction. Her flower-red mouth, her pretty face, her fine figure, and her unselfconscious affinity with all that is natural suggest how Nature is a force in her character and determinant of her fate. Still another form of determinism may be seen in the use of omens to indicate the presence of a supernatural power behind the scenes: the text-painter, the cock that crows the afternoon of the wedding, the allusions to Satan in the characterisation of Alec, and so forth. The scene at Stonehenge is particularly evocative of a supernatural presence and seems to set the stage for the ironic suggestion of a divine hand in Tess's fate: '"Justice" was done, and the President of the Immortals, in Æschylean phrase, had ended his sport with Tess.'

In considering these as well as other forms of determinism in the novel (the social code, for example), a question naturally arises as to what notion of psychological inevitability contributes to the design of the tragedy. For one thing, any determinism that has implications for human behaviour, as heredity, Nature, and the social code do, assumes some kind of psychology, though the rationale for it may not be made explicit. For another, a discussion of Tess's character and motivation would in any case involve psychological considerations. The great strength of the novel, it is widely acknowledged, is the characterisation of Tess. She haunts our imagination long after whatever confusions or inconsistencies we may find in the plot or narration have ceased to seem important. She ranks, with Elizabeth Bennet, Jane Eyre, Becky Sharp, and a few others, among the great female characterisations in nineteenth-century English fiction. In a novel where the heroine is so central to every important consideration, an understanding of how her character shapes her fate is essential for an interpretation of the meaning of her tragedy.

To a large extent the psychological considerations in the novel seem to resolve themselves into a paradoxical question of responsibility: Does Tess co-operate in her fate to an extent that makes her responsible for it? It is true that Hardy is less concerned in this novel than he was in *The Mayor of Casterbridge* with the idea that character is fate. In the earlier work the concern seems to be with the tragedy of character, ruin brought upon oneself; in the later, with the tragedy of fate, disaster brought upon one by blood, passion, circumstance, and something far more darkly interfused. Still, as Lionel Johnson felt, it seems impossible to read the novel with a complete disregard of the idea that Tess is somehow responsible for her fate.[2] Hardy, it is well to remember, thought that 'A Plot, or Tragedy, should arise from the gradual closing in of a situation that comes of ordinary human passions, prejudices, and ambitions, by reason of the characters taking no trouble to ward off the disastrous events produced by the said passions, prejudices, and ambitions.'[3] In what way, it may be asked, does Tess fail to take the necessary trouble to ward off disaster? Is it her pride, her passionate nature, her passivity, or some combination of these that makes her fate inevitable?

Unfortunately, it is not possible to answer these questions about Tess's responsibility with anything like certainty. In fact, the uncertainty or indeterminacy in the novel is a major obstacle in the way of interpretation. There is an unresolved tension between the rhetoric of inevitability in Hardy's editorial commentary and a basic ambiguity at the heart of several crucial episodes. Because of the repeated emphasis on inevitability one expects a sense of certainty about the qualities in Tess's character that make her end tragic. Hardy is painstaking in his effort to link the forms of determinism to her character and fate. She is said to possess a 'slight incautiousness of character inherited from her race' (XIV; p. 114) and her pride is thought to be 'a symptom of that reckless acquiescence in chance too apparent in the whole d'Urberville family' (XXXVII; p. 324). In addition, the narration is everywhere buttressed by words such as 'doomed', 'destined', and 'fated'. But the crucial linking is never made and one remains uncertain about why Tess's fate is inevitable.

The ambiguity in two early episodes suggests the nature of the difficulty. Take, for example, the first occasion when the problem of responsibility becomes an important consideration, the scene in The Chase. It is a matter of some surprise to discover that there is still no general agreement about exactly what takes place after Alec returns from the slope. He finds Tess asleep. Most critics refer to the next event as a seduction, suggestive of a degree of responsibility on Tess's part, but others take it to be a rape.[4]

Even in summary form the case for seduction is strong. When Car Darch's mother remarks 'Out of the frying-pan into the fire!' (X; p. 84) after Alec's rescue of Tess from the hostility of the other women on the way home from Chaseborough, she seems to assume that Tess will be seduced by Alec and become his mistress. Car Darch's envy of Tess as the 'first favourite with He just now' (X; p. 82) suggests that the mother's comment means that Tess will soon be dazed by Alec, as her daughters have been. Of course, her expectation is not necessarily an indication of what happens. But one of the functions of the scene, aside from establishing a situation in which Tess will have to be more receptive to Alec's affectation of concern for her than she so far has been, seems to be to foreshadow what will happen. With his cigar, black moustache, rolling eye, and provincial Byronism ('Well, my Beauty, what can I do for you?' [V; p. 44]), Alec fascinates and seduces cottage girls. Tess is to become one of these.

Seduction also seems to be foreshadowed in the scene when Alec insists on placing the strawberry in Tess's mouth. She continues to eat 'in a half-pleased, half-reluctant state whatever d'Urberville offered her'. When he gives her roses to put in her bosom, 'she obeyed like one in a dream' (V; p. 47). The various scenes with Alec prior to the one in The Chase seem designed to show how Tess eventually 'succumbed to adroit advantages he took of her helplessness' and how she could be 'stirred to confused surrender awhile' (XII; p. 104).

It is worth noting that Tess's remaining with Alec 'some few weeks' (XII; p. 95) after the night in The Chase seems to fit better with the idea of seduction than with rape. In a cancelled version of the scene in which Tess returns to Marlott and Alec insists on giving her a farewell kiss, Hardy had written that 'only a month had elapsed since she had ceased to defend herself against him.'[5] That she had 'ceased to defend herself' (presumably after his long pursuit of her, not merely after the loss of innocence) suggests an actual though reluctant acquiescence. In what seems to be Tess's painful awareness that she had become Alec's mistress there is an implicit suggestion that she had given something up rather than that she had had something forced upon her. She may even have felt that she had become part of the 'whorage' (X; p. 83) of the Darch sisters. In another cancelled passage, again part of the scene in which Tess takes leave of Alec, she remarks that 'They called me your – your – I won't say the horrid word.'[6] It may be that the 'they' was intended to refer to the Darch sisters or their friends and that the unspoken epithet was 'whore'. In any event, the prelude to the resumption of the relationship a few years later is the occasion of Tess's return from the unsuccessful trip to Emminster, when she sees Alec in the role of preacher. At this point she has the conviction that she confronts her 'seducer' (XLIV; p. 386). The renewed relationship seems to make the most sense as an extension of an initial seduction. Would she have become his mistress earlier and been willing to resume the relationship years later if he had raped her?

Seduction, however, seems impossible to reconcile with a comment made by one of the women who works in the field with Tess when the baby is brought to be suckled: 'A little more than persuading had to do wi' the coming o't, I reckon. There were they that heard a sobbing one night last year in The Chase; and it mid ha' gone hard wi' a certain party if folks had come along' (XIV; p. 114). Equally significant seems to be the narrator's reference to an 'illegal surrender' (XLIX; p. 435) in the tracing of Angel's thoughts while in Brazil, though admittedly 'illegal' is not necessarily synonymous with physical force. Finally, Pinion makes a strong case for an influence on the design of *Tess of the d'Urbervilles* by Richardson's *Clarissa*, a novel Hardy had read and admired in 1888, not long before he began to write his novel. One of the verbal similarities he

identifies is between 'Once subdued, always subdued' in *Clarissa* and
'Once victim, always victim – that's the law!' in *Tess of the
d'Urbervilles* (XLVII; p. 423).[7]

Nevertheless, much of the evidence used to support one view can
usually be used to support the other. A few examples will suffice: the
question Tess puts to the text-painter, 'suppose your sin was not of
your own seeking?' (XII; p. 101); her complaint to her mother that
she had been ignorant: 'Why didn't you tell me there was danger in
men-folk? . . . Ladies know what to fend hands against, because they
read novels that tell them of these tricks' (XII; p. 104: ellipsis mine);
her later comment about 'the trap [Alec] set for me in my simple
youth' (LVII; p. 491); Alec's admission of a 'trick' (XLVI; p. 402) and
his comment, 'I saw you innocent, and I deceived you' (XLVII;
p. 420); the narrator's references to Tess as one of the 'betrayed' (XVI;
p. 135), to her having been 'made to break an accepted social law'
(XIII; p. 108), and to the idea that hers 'were not sins of intention, but
of inadvertence' (LI; p. 455). One could easily extend the list, but
perhaps the depth of the ambiguity is best suggested by a sentence
deleted from Chapter XXVII. It was part of the narrator's description of
Tess's reaction to Angel's proposal. Deletions are designated by angle
brackets (⟨ . . . ⟩). Additions are given above the line, as they appear
in the manuscript:

exercised

To be sure, the heartless coercion ⟨ practiced ⟩ upon her ⟨in these⟩
inexperienced ⟨days of⟩ girlhood was sufficient excuse ⟨for her⟩
w[ith] her own conscience: but Angel Clare's fastidiousness
could, she thought, never regard with anything but contempt
acted weakly   twofold
a woman who had ⟨ given way ⟩ even under the ⟨ extremest ⟩
affectation
pressure(s) of physical mastery & the ⟨ mark of cozenship [?] ⟩ of
cousinship.[8]

Tess's acting 'weakly', or giving way, suggests seduction, but
'heartless coercion' and 'physical mastery' indicate rape.

Given the ambiguity, Ian Gregor's view of the event as both a
seduction and a rape has a great deal to recommend it. He argues that
Tess's ambivalence toward Alec throughout the novel, her feeling
that she belongs to him at the same time that she feels he is ashes and
dust to her, makes the most sense if the first sexual encounter is taken

as 'calculatedly ambiguous': 'We could say that as a woman, Tess feels it to be a seduction in the way the strawberry scene hints at; as an individual person, she knows it was rape.'[9] Appealing as this view is, however, a necessary implication of it seems to be that a reader must become resigned to a fundamental uncertainty about the decisive event in Tess's life. In fact this is what a reader must do. The text does not permit certainty.

Another example of an ambiguity that challenges the idea of inevitability may be observed in Tess's behaviour after Angel's proposal. As with the event in The Chase, one is uncertain if Hardy imagines her as willing her fate or surrendering to it. It is possible to take the view that at each opportunity to tell Angel she makes less than a conscientious effort. She always seems relieved when he fails to pursue the matter. When she writes her mother shortly after accepting Angel's proposal, she is more pleased than distressed by the predictable advice Joan Durbeyfield gives her. At this point we are told, 'The responsibility was shifted, and her heart was lighter than it had been for weeks' (XXXI; p. 246). The point of such a statement, however, is that the responsibility has not shifted. Of course, after Angel tells her that he has had a dream of 'fighting that fellow again who insulted you', she resolves to tell him, writes the four-page narrative of 'those events of three or four years ago', and slips the note under the door (XXXIII; p. 266). The note, though late in coming, is good evidence of her determination not to deceive Angel. But it was written and delivered on Christmas Eve. Six days go by. 'Had he really received her note? She glanced into his room, and could see nothing of it. It might be that he forgave her. But even if he had not received it she had a sudden enthusiastic trust that he surely would forgive her' (XXXIII; p. 267). Once again the responsibility has not shifted. The narrator seems unmistakable on this point. On the day of the wedding, after Tess discovers the letter under the carpet, he states that 'The incident of the misplaced letter she had jumped at as if it prevented a confession; but she knew in her conscience that it need not; there was still time' (XXXIII; p. 269). She makes one final attempt, which, as we learn later, Angel has his own reasons for discouraging. On the basis of her behaviour and the narrator's commentary, it seems that she is to be thought largely responsible for the consequences of not telling Angel. In other words, to a certain extent she wills her fate.

On the other hand, it is equally possible to take the view that she cannot be held responsible. If she has not met all the demands of conscience, she has gone further in that direction than Angel. If nothing else absolves her of responsibility, certainly his belated confession of a relationship with a stranger in London should, unless the reader is disposed to employ a double standard, as Angel does. More important, when the narrator invokes Nature as one of the determinants of Tess's fate, it becomes clear that instinct was all along to prevail over every other consideration. 'She might as well have agreed at first', we are told. 'The "appetite for joy" which pervades all creation, that tremendous force which sways humanity to its purpose, as the tide sways the helpless weed, was not to be controlled by vague lucubrations over the social rubric' (XXX; p. 244). Given such a statement, what kind of responsibility can she be thought to bear?

One might go on to examine other occasions when there seems to be a possibility of determining whether Tess wills or succumbs to her fate – for example, the visit to Emminster, when she might have been more persistent and when the narrator comments that 'the greatest misfortune of her life was this feminine loss of courage at the last and critical moment through her estimating her father-in-law by his sons' (XLIV; p. 384), or the final return of Alec, when she might have resisted for a few more days. But the result would be the same. Such occasions tantalise us with the possibility of resolving the ambiguity. There is no certainty to be found in any of them.

In defence of the uncertainty one could argue that perhaps nothing evokes a sense of the inevitability of fate so well as the repeated suggestion of a mysterious convergence of character and circumstance. The workings of fate are enigmatic. An individual often seems to co-operate with, or perhaps unconsciously to will, the fate that is prophesied or foreshadowed for him. A writer's deference to the mystery in human history is likely to strengthen rather than diminish a reader's sense of a determinism at work in the lives of his characters. Much of the power of *Tess of the d'Urbervilles*, it could be said, derives from Hardy's subtle and uncompromising intuition that the elements of tragedy cannot be reduced to a neat little certainty.

After every allowance has been made, however, the uncertainty remains an interpretive problem. Where, we cannot help but ask, is the tragic inevitability in Tess's character? What natural, social, or other determinants are we to understand most clearly dictate her fate? The truth is that what we are given is a multiplication of determinants that leaves the question of inevitability paradoxically open: her d'Urberville blood, her passionate nature, a tendency toward passivity, a degree of pride, unfortunate circumstances, unpredictable but never wholly improbable mishaps, and a world resonant with a vaguely threatening and casual determinism, the sport of the gods. While such a large number of determinants is not necessarily inconsistent with the idea of inevitability, it suggests that no one of them can be taken as decisive. Perhaps Hardy was unable to find a rationally consistent basis for the end designed for his heroine. The notion of heredity often seems to be the crucial determinant. Hardy emphasised it in an interview published in *Black and White* not long after the novel appeared: 'The murder that Tess commits is the hereditary quality, to which I more than once allude, working out in this impoverished descendant of a once noble family.'[10] But the notion is far-fetched. It is little more than a Gothic and Romantic borrowing, an imagined principle of motivation not really consistent with the more convincing strains of naturalism in the characterisation of Tess, or of realism in the depiction of her circumstances. The same might be said of the other notions of determinism appealed to throughout the novel. They create the rhetoric and atmosphere of inevitability, but not the logic. They appear to be screens for a sense of inevitability that Hardy felt was at work in his heroine's fate – one, indeed, that he was determined to impose upon it – but did not make explicit.

In going to some length to argue that there is an unresolved tension between the narrator's editorial insistence on inevitability and the ambiguity in his depiction of what happens to Tess, and why, my aim has been to call attention to a pattern of splitting in the novel. It is perhaps most evident in the characterisation, where essential feelings and attitudes are split into certain types of characters. I take the pattern to be a significant clue to the inevitability of Tess's fate. It is also a clue to the idea of tragedy in the novel. To anticipate and briefly summarise the rest of my argument, the decisive determinant of Tess's fate is a tendency in the fictional world in which she exists for men to have either sensual or spiritual feelings toward woman, but not both at the same time. The tendency is reflected not only in Alec and Angel, but in numerous characters in Hardy's other novels. Ultimately Tess is a victim of an ambivalent attitude towards woman that is traceable both to Hardy and to the culture in which he lived. The crucial determinism in the novel is therefore psychological, but the heroine's mind or character is not the place to look for it. It is rather to be sought in the nature of the imaginary world in which she and the other characters exist. Perhaps only because Tess is so sympathetically and convincingly drawn do we require a reminder that it is Hardy, not an indifferent Olympian, who presides over the fates of the mortals in this novel. The inevitability in the heroine's fate is not to be found in the various forms of determinism alluded to throughout the novel, but in the psychological nature of the existence that she and the other characters are imagined to have.

Numerous Hardy critics, among them some of the earliest, have attempted to identify the special features of Hardy's fictive world.[11] One of the features noted most often, and one that throws some light on the psychology in *Tess of the d'Urbervilles*, is the idea of love at first sight. It recurs with sufficient frequency to seem at times a virtual prerequisite of romance. In *A Pair of Blue Eyes*, an early novel that seems to prefigure some of the psychological issues in *Tess of the d'Urbervilles* more clearly than any other, Stephen Smith falls in love with Elfride the first time he sees her: 'It comes to this sole simple thing: That at one time I had never seen you, and I didn't love you; that then I saw you, and I did love you' (VII; p. 66). Angel and Tess do not fall in love when they first lay eyes on each other at the May-Day dance in Marlott, but Angel's memory of this first sight of Tess is used later as a basis for choosing her when they meet again at Talbothays Dairy: 'He concluded that he had beheld her before; where he could not tell. A casual encounter during some country ramble it certainly had been, and he was not greatly curious about it. But the circumstance was sufficient to lead him to select Tess in preference to the other pretty milkmaids when he wished to contemplate contiguous womankind' (XVIII; p. 155). Love at first sight, or a retrospective appeal to the idea, as in *Tess of the d'Urbervilles*, usually suggests that the two lovers, sometimes against their will, are fated for each other. The psychological basis of the idea is that the lover has in mind a prior, idealised image that the suddenly encountered object appears to match. As in *The Well-Beloved*, where the hero is not insignificantly a sculptor, or, as one of the characters remarks, an 'image-carver' (I, III; p. 16), Angel is in love with an image of his own making. The image is one of rustic innocence and virgin purity. His first comment to himself about Tess is, 'What a fresh and virginal daughter of Nature that milkmaid is!' (XVIII; p. 155). When walking together in the midsummer dawn to do the milking, 'She was no longer the milkmaid, but a visionary essence of woman – a whole sex condensed into one typical form. He called her Artemis, Demeter, and other fanciful names' (XX; p. 167). When she says 'Call me Tess', he does, but he persists in idealising her. At the heart of his image of her is an expectation of virginity so strong as to be virtually a demand. After Tess's confession, he holds on to the image: 'Nothing so pure, so sweet, so virginal as Tess had seemed possible all the long while that he adored her, up to an hour ago' (XXXV; p. 301). The discovery of what is later referred to as Tess's 'un-intact state' (XLIX; p. 435) so alters her appearance in his eyes that she seems to be a different person: 'You were one person; now you are another' (XXXV; p. 292). Tess, in desperation, asks if he has stopped loving her. He answers that 'the woman I have been loving is not you.' 'But who?' she asks. 'Another woman in your shape' (XXXV; p. 293).

Notwithstanding the various appeals to the forms of determinism we have already discussed, Angel's obsession with purity may be taken as a uniquely important determinant of Tess's fate. It is not going too far to say that without it there would have been no tragedy, especially of a 'pure' woman. Purity would not have been an issue. The conflict of his image of woman with the real woman Tess is becomes the turning-point in the novel. The characterisation of Angel is sufficiently plausible, in spite of a certain flatness, to make his attitude seem natural both to him and to the mental landscape of the novel. Although Joan Durbeyfield's letter to Tess suggests that many women approach marriage in Tess's state, her advice not to tell Angel may be interpreted as her awareness of the importance that the image (or illusion) of purity has. Farmer Groby's offhand but provocative comment is a similar indication that Angel's attitude is not thought to be an aberration.

With minor variations, it is an attitude that is a recurrent feature of the psychological world in which Hardy's characters are imagined to exist, and one which seems to increase in importance in the later novels. In *Desperate Remedies*, Miss Aldclyffe, on her deathbed, remains convinced that had Ambrose Graye known of the affair with her cousin and of the baby, 'he would have cast her out'. For that reason, she says of herself, she 'withdrew from him by an effort, and pined' (XXI; p. 442). Henry Knight in *A Pair of Blue Eyes* seems to prefigure Angel Clare in his obsession with purity. 'Inbred in him', the narrator points out, 'was an invincible objection to be any but the first comer in a woman's heart. He had discovered within himself the condition that if ever he did make up his mind to marry, it must be on the certainty that no cropping out of inconvenient old letters, no bows or blushes to a mysterious stranger casually met, should be a possible source of discomposure' (XX; p. 213). In *The Trumpet-Major* Captain Robert Loveday is willing, even eager, to marry Matilda in spite of her reputation, but his brother John, who is the hero named in the title and the moral centre of the novel, prevents it. In *The Woodlanders*, Fitzpiers, in spite of his claim in his letter to Grace that he could never feel estranged from her, even if she had slept with Giles, experiences 'mental sufferings and suspense' (XLIV; p. 401) and does not ask her to take him back until he learns from Marty South that Grace, contrary to her representation, had remained faithful.

In these and other instances where a woman's purity is in question, it is not difficult to distinguish Hardy's attitude from that of his characters. On the other hand, it may be doubted if his attitude is ever entirely out of sympathy with those of his characters, men and women, who are concerned about such matters. Most telling in this regard is the fact that the women in the novels are so often divided up into the two categories, pure and impure, that Angel invokes. 'Of the two classes into which gentle young women naturally divide', the narrator of *The Hand of Ethelberta* tells us, there are 'those who grow red at their weddings, and those who grow pale' (II; p. 24). On the morning of Tess's wedding, after she has discovered that Angel has not read her letter, 'She was so pale when he saw her again that he felt quite anxious' (XXXIII; p. 269). In the category of the so-called pure woman, who does not consummate a sexual relationship with a man prior to or outside of marriage, one finds major characters such as Cytherea Graye, Fancy Day, Elfride Swancourt, Bathsheba Everdene, Ethelberta and Picotee Chickerel, Thomasin Yeobright, Anne Garland, Paula Power, Elizabeth-Jane Newson, Marty South, and Grace Melbury, almost all of them heroines of one of the novels. With the exception of Marty South and Grace Melbury, all may be thought to find eventually a measure of happiness in marriage, though a marriage, it is worth noting, that is usually imagined as less a matter of passion than of some other feeling. One recalls that Bathsheba, quite practically, needs Gabriel Oak.

In the category of the so-called impure woman, whose reputation is in serious doubt or who consummates a sexual relationship prior to or outside of marriage, one finds major and minor characters such as Cytherea Aldclyffe, Fanny Robin, Eustacia Vye, Captain de Stancy's first love (and the mother of William Dare), Matilda Johnson, Lucetta Le Sueur, Suke Damson, Felice Charmond, and Tess. All but Suke and Matilda die. Suke marries Tim Tangs, but a cloud hangs over the marriage because of her past. Matilda, for better or worse, marries Festus Derriman. Certain characters are difficult to categorise. Viviette Constantine in *Two on a Tower* marries Swithin St. Cleeve prior to any consummation, but this second marriage is in fact illegal because the announcement that she was a widow was premature. At the time of her second marriage her husband is all too alive in Africa, living with a native princess. (His suicide, incidentally, seems to be a novelist's desperate remedy, suggesting that madness results from total sexual freedom, but it has some interest as an anticipation of Kurtz's cry 'The horror! The horror!' in *Heart of Darkness*.) Viviette dies on the last page. Two principal exceptions are Sue Bridehead and Arabella Donn. Yet it is clear that they are the two female characters most obviously conceived as pure and impure, Sue remaining spiritual even in marriage, Arabella remaining promiscuous in nature in spite of marriage.

Without attempting to devise a typology for Hardy's characters based on sexual behaviour one can observe that an important consideration in the conception of the female characters, and apparently crucial in the design of their fates, is the degree of sexuality attributed to them. Female characters with sexual experience prior to or outside of marriage usually do not survive, or do not fare well. In this tendency in Hardy's novels to divide the female characters in this way one can recognise a familiar theme in Western literature, the opposition between the fair maid and the *femme fatale*, represented by Una and Duessa in *The Faerie Queene*, Cynthia and Circe in *Endymion*, Jane Eyre and Bertha Mason, Rowena and Ligeia, and so on. One does not ordinarily encounter such glaring opposites in Hardy, although Grace and Felice in *The Woodlanders* and Sue and Arabella in *Jude the Obscure* may be thought to compare favourably enough.

The practice of splitting characters in this way is familiar to us as a form of doubling, the technical term for it being 'decomposition'. It is not the kind of manifest doubling one finds in Poe's *William Wilson* or Dostoevsky's *The Double*. In Hardy neither the author nor the characters show a conscious awareness of the idea of doubling, although at times in *The Well-Beloved* there almost seems to be a consciously playful exploration of the fictional delights of multiple decomposition. The doubling in Hardy is perhaps best thought of, following a psychoanalytic view of the subject, as latent doubling.[12] The two figures that are thought to be projected in the work of art are assumed to represent a conflicted unity in the mind of the author. The author's feelings toward a particular person, image, or subject – in this instance, woman – are assumed to be deeply ambivalent. There are two important ways an author is thought to be able to represent ambivalence in characterisation through doubling. One is to split a single image into two characters – for example, Sue and Arabella. The other is to split the attitudes towards the image – for example, the attitudes toward woman of a rake like Sergeant Troy and, on the other hand, of an aggressive innocent like Farmer Boldwood.

In *Tess of the d'Urbervilles* it is not the image of woman that is split into two characters, although the tendency is represented in Angel's prolonged inability to reconcile his image of the innocent milkmaid with the reality of a sexually experienced woman. His remark to Tess that 'You were one person; now you are another'(XXXV; p. 292) might be interpreted as an attempt to deny or defend against the possibility that he might love her in spite of her experience. The double standard that he employs in judging Tess and not himself is both a curious and characteristic example of the kind of doubling one finds in the attitude toward woman in a great deal of fiction. The sleep-walking scene at Wellbridge, for example, when Angel attempts to bury Tess, might be interpreted as an extension of the doubling, an attempt to deny the sexual nature of woman. It is rather the attitude toward woman in *Tess of the d'Urbervilles* that is split into two characters, Alec and Angel, one taking an attitude that woman is primarily a sexual object, the other an attitude that denies her sexual nature through idealisation. The approximate representation of these two attitudes may be seen in an apparent doubling of male characters similar to the one of female characters, at least to the extent that the heroes or other principal male characters are frequently to be found in rivalry with a rake or other figure who has had a wider and often socially unacceptable sexual relationship with a woman, or whose relationship with women seems to be primarily sexual. Examples are not hard to find: Edward Springrove and Aeneas Manston, Gabriel Oak (or Farmer Boldwood) and Sergeant Troy, Christopher Julian and Lord Mountclere, Clym Yeobright and Damon Wildeve, George Somerset and William de Stancy, and Giles Winterborne and Edred Fitzpiers.

Whatever else one might wish to say about the various thematic concerns and structural principles reflected in a recurrent opposition of such characters, it would seem clear that an irreconcilable conflict in the imaginary world of Hardy's novels is between the sexual and other (spiritual, intellectual, affectionate) feelings. The conflict functions throughout Hardy's novels as a virtual psychological law. It is an obvious determinant of the destinies of the characters in Hardy's last three novels. In each there is a central character created in a Shelleyan mould and unable to achieve in a relationship with a beloved a reconciliation of sexual and spiritual feelings. Although in *Tess of the d'Urbervilles* Angel appears to overcome the difficulty of Tess's sexual impurity after the conversation with his travelling companion and confidant in Brazil, and after the death of Alec (something he had earlier insisted was a virtual precondition of any reunion: 'How can we live together while that man lives? . . . If he were dead it might be different'[XXXVI; p. 310: ellipsis mine]), it is doubtful if such a reunion is possible in the psychological world of Hardy's novels. There is no precedent for it in the earlier novels. None of Hardy's major female characters is allowed to have premarital or extramarital sexual experience and survive. This is not the case with male characters. Lord Mountclere and Fitzpiers are both imagined as sexually promiscuous before marriage. Fitzpiers is a conspicuous example of the double standard, for even after he is reunited with Grace he will not remain faithful to her. Hardy, it will be recalled, remarked that 'the heroine is doomed to an unhappy life with an inconstant husband.'[13]

The prospects for a successful union between Tess and Angel were in fact never bright. Hardy revealed why in the interview published in *Black and White*:

> You ask why Tess should not have gone off with Clare, and 'lived happily ever after.' Do you not see that under *any* circumstances they were doomed to unhappiness? A sensitive man like Angel Clare could never have been happy with her. After the first few months he would inevitably have thrown her failings in her face. He did not recoil from her after the murder it is true. He was in love with her failings then I suppose; he had not seen her for a long time; with the inconsistency of human nature he forgave the greater sin when he could not pardon the lesser.[14]

If this comment may be trusted, contrary to Lawrence's injunction not to trust the teller, only the tale, then the phrase 'under *any* circumstances' may be taken to mean that circumstances such as the misdirected letter or the chance reappearance of Alec were never to be taken as crucial determinants of Tess's fate. The decisive determinant was all along an attitude held by Angel. Here is the inevitability that encompasses Tess in tragedy: 'he would *inevitably* have thrown her failings in her face.' One may go on to doubt if all those coincidences, circumstances, and mishaps with which Hardy's novels are so replete, or the symbolic shape of them as a divine Crass Casualty, are as relevant for the fates of his characters as one is made to feel while reading. In any case, an important form of determinism in Hardy's fiction is psychological, one that structures the characters and plots of several major novels around the following question: Can one's sensuous and affectionate feelings be successfully united in a permanent relationship with another person? The answer implicit in the last three novels leaves little doubt as to the conclusion Hardy reached.

The question is one that Freud thought haunted the love life of men and women, but particularly men. In one of his papers on the psychology of love, written at the time Hardy was preparing the Wessex Edition, Freud discussed what he said was one of the most common disorders a practising analyst was likely to encounter, psychical impotence. In his discussion of the disorder, he expressed the view that 'Two currents whose union is necessary to ensure a completely normal attitude in love have, in the cases we are considering, failed to combine. These two may be distinguished as the *affectionate* and the *sensual* current.'[15] Freud traced the affectionate current to a man's primary object-choice and argued that in cases of psychical impotence the loved and idealised object in adult experience is modelled too closely on a maternal image. An unconscious conflict over incest prevents the man from approaching sexually a woman for whom the current of feeling is too profoundly associated with a maternal image, or a woman who seems in some way an embodiment of it. The tendency to split the feelings in this way exists in every man, as Freud discusses it, but becomes a problem only for some. 'The whole sphere of love in such people', he writes, 'remains divided in the two directions personified in art as sacred and profane (or animal) love. Where they love they do not desire and where they desire they cannot love.'[16] They may love many women, and desire many, but they cannot unite their sensuous and affectionate feelings in the love of one. Such a one would be too dear for possessing.

In *The Hand of Ethelberta* Faith describes to her brother a painting she has just seen on a visit to the Royal Academy. It had been painted by Mr Ladywell and modelled by Ethelberta. The subject is an Elizabethan knight's farewell to a lady. The first two lines of Shakespeare's eighty-seventh sonnet serve as an inscription for the painting: 'Farewell! thou art too dear for my possessing, / And like enough thou know'st thy estimate' (XXIV; p. 190). In the novel the painting is symbolic of Christopher's relationship with Ethelberta; he will never possess her. Yet it may be taken as an emblem of the relationship that many of Hardy's male characters have to a particular woman or image. Stephen Smith, Christopher Julian, John Loveday, and Giles Winterborne love women who, for them, are too dear to be possessed. Henry Knight, Angel Clare, and Jocelyn Pierston love an image of woman more than any particular embodiment. Where these men love, they have no desire. For them, as Hardy once remarked, 'Love lives on propinquity, but dies of contact.'[17] The image is too well beloved, the woman not well enough. A reversal of this attitude is given expression when several women too dear to be possessed are finally desired and possessed by men who do not hold woman in such high esteem. One thinks of Lord Mountclere, Fitzpiers, and Alec.

When *Tess of the d'Urbervilles* is considered in the larger context of the world of Hardy's novels, with particular attention to the conditions that determine the course of love and marriage, it is clear that Tess's fate is to a large extent the result of a fierce psychological determinism at work in the imaginary world in which she exists. The psychological conditions of this imaginary world are as harsh and punishing as the physical conditions of Flintcomb-Ash or Egdon Heath. The men Tess knows represent totally opposing attitudes toward women. One sees her as a sexual object, the other as an idealised image of pastoral innocence and purity. While each is characterised as given to extremes, each experiences within himself the very division of attitudes represented as an irreconcilable conflict in the novel. Alec's religious conversion and Angel's 'eight-and-forty hours' dissipation with a stranger' (xxxiv; p. 286) reveal the other sides of these two characters and suggest that the process of doubling extends into each character. In a sense, Alec, Angel, and Tess are all victims of the conflict between the sensuous and affectionate feelings, but it is really the woman who pays. Ultimately, the novel reflects a conflict between a rational rejection of the unfair and sexist obsession with purity on Angel's part, a conscious meaning in the novel suggested by the subtitle, and Hardy's own irrational and unconscious sharing in that obsession in the design of his heroine's fate. This is in no way to deny Hardy's genuine and compelling sympathy with Tess, but it is to recognise that the sympathy was – inevitably – ambivalent.

Although Hardy was irritated by any suggestion of autobiography in his fiction, there seems to be wide agreement that certain novels are autobiographical. *A Pair of Blue Eyes*, for example, is usually thought to be partly based on Hardy's experience during his courtship of

Emma. Like the young Hardy, the hero is an architect sent to plan and supervise the restoration of a village church. Another autobiographical element may be present in the striking similarity between the worsening domestic scene at Max Gate and the increasingly dark view of marital relations in the last novels – particularly *Jude the Obscure*, which seemed so offensive to Emma. In a more speculative vein one might attempt to relate the various heroines to the kind of woman to which Hardy was attracted and, ultimately, to Jemima Hand, his mother.

In his chapter on Tryphena and Hardy's relationship with her, Robert Gittings observes: 'He was attracted again and again by the same type of woman, a replica of his own mother, with the striking features shared by all women of the Hand family.'[18] Gittings' emphasis is on physical characteristics, but the important implications are psychological. One has been recently developed by John Fowles in a brilliant essay which attempts to relate Jocelyn Pierston's pursuit of the Well-Beloved to an unending, doomed attempt by Hardy to recover imaginatively the lost mother of infancy. Fowles writes: 'The vanished young mother of infancy is quite as elusive as the Well-Beloved – indeed, she *is* the Well-Beloved, although the adult writer transmogrifies her according to the pleasures and fancies that have in the older man superseded the nameless ones of the child – most commonly into a young female sexual ideal of some kind, to be attained or pursued (or denied) by hiding himself behind some male character.'[19] The idea of an unending effort to restore or reinstate an image that is felt as lost has been thought in psychoanalytic theory to be a principal motive of creativity.[20] It could very well have been one for Hardy. Much of the poetry he wrote after Emma's death could be interpreted as a final effort to reinstate an image of the woman who, for the longest time, seemed an embodiment of the Well-Beloved.

The salient point for a reader of the fiction, however, remains the conflict between the sensuous and affectionate feelings in Hardy's imaginary world. Equally important to note is that a proper interpretation of the origin and significance of the conflict will not allow it to be seen in exclusively biographical terms. Although Tess is a creation of Hardy's imagination, she is also representative in certain ways of an imago of the culture in which Hardy lived. While his imagination may be thought to have been first nurtured in a matrix of primal relationships, the most formative of which would have been with his mother, it was later weaned from its personal and provincial origins by a cultural matrix that conceived of the human being as a double, body and soul, split between earthly origins and high aspirations. Shelley, from the beginning a figure of sympathy and influence in Hardy's development, and of importance in the conception of Angel (who is 'less Byronic than Shelleyan' [XXXI; p. 247]), was an eloquent exponent of the ancient but still cherished opposition between body and soul. One recalls Sue Bridehead's fondness for 'Epipsychidion' and the image of woman in it. In fact, the male demand for purity in woman and the use of the double standard in sexual matters were essential features of the social life of the nineteenth century.

At the time Freud attempted to analyse the tendency to split the sensuous and affectionate feelings, he laid the responsibility for this condition of the erotic life of civilised man on the incestuous tendencies of childhood and the frustration of the sexual instinct during adolescence. But he went on to speculate that 'we may perhaps be forced to become reconciled to the idea that it is quite impossible to adjust the claims of the sexual instinct to the demands of civiliz-ation.'[21] It was this kind of bold speculation that would lead eventually to discoveries beyond the pleasure principle. Whatever value may be finally placed on the speculation, it gives recognition to a psychological condition, part of the ache of modernism, intuited by Hardy and thought by Freud to be a principal determinant in the fate of romance and marriage in the culture in which they both lived. The psychological determinism that Freud sees is certainly no darker than anything in *Tess of the d'Urbervilles* or *Jude the Obscure*, or that 'mutually destructive interdependence of flesh and spirit' one finds in *The Return of the Native* (II, VI; p. 162). Perhaps only a determinism as dark as the one Freud posits does justice to the conception of Tess and the tragedy imagined for her.

NOTES

1. Florence Emily Hardy, *The Later Years of Thomas Hardy, 1892–1928* (London and New York: Macmillan, 1930) p. 14.
2. Lionel Johnson, *The Art of Thomas Hardy* (London: John Lane, The Bodley Head, 1923) pp. 231–49. Two perceptive discussions of the issue of responsibility are by Bernard J. Paris: '"A Confusion of Many Standards": Conflicting Value Systems in *Tess of the d'Urbervilles*', *NCF*, XXIV (1969) 57–9; and 'Experiences of Thomas Hardy', *The Victorian Experience: The Novelists*, ed. Richard A. Levine (Athens: Ohio University Press, 1976) pp. 203–37.
3. Florence Emily Hardy, *The Early Life of Thomas Hardy, 1840–1891* (London and New York: Macmillan, 1928) p. 157.

4. For a discussion of the evidence, although in a context of an argument for rape, see F. B. Pinion, *Thomas Hardy: Art and Thought* (London: Macmillan; Totowa, N. J.: Rowman & Littlefield, 1977) pp. 119–35.

5. The manuscript of *Tess of the d'Urbervilles* (British Library Additional Manuscript 38182), fol. 84 (microfilm), quoted by permission of the British Library, the Trustees of the Thomas Hardy Estate and the Trustees of the Estate of the late Miss E. A. Dugdale.

6. The manuscript of *Tess*, fol. 85.

7. Pinion, p. 121.

8. The manuscript of *Tess*, fol. 204ᵛ.

9. Ian Gregor, *The Great Web: The Form of Hardy's Major Fiction* (London: Faber & Faber; Totowa, N. J.: Rowman & Littlefield, 1974) p. 182.

10. Hardy, quoted by Raymond Blathwayt, 'A Chat with the Author of "Tess"', *Black and White*, IV (27 August 1892) 238.

11. See, e.g., Pierre d'Exideuil, *The Human Pair in the Works of Thomas Hardy*, trans. F. W. Crosse (London: H. Toulmin, 1930); Albert J. Guerard, *Thomas Hardy: The Novels and Stories* (Cambridge, Mass.: Harvard University Press, 1949); and, especially, J. Hillis Miller, *Thomas Hardy: Distance and Desire* (London: Oxford University Press; Cambridge, Mass.: Harvard University Press, 1970).

12. My discussion of doubling is generally indebted to Robert Rogers' authoritative *A Psychoanalytic Study of the Double in Literature* (Detroit: Wayne State University Press, 1970).

13. *Early Life*, p. 289.

14. *Black and White*, p. 238.

15. 'On the Universal Tendency to Debasement in the Sphere of Love' (1912); in *The Standard Edition of the Complete Psychological Works of Sigmund Freud*, trans. and ed. James Strachey (London: The Hogarth Press, 1953–66) XI (1957) p. 180.

16. *The Standard Edition*, XI, p. 183.

17. *Early Life*, p. 288.

18. Robert Gittings, *Young Thomas Hardy* (London: Heinemann; Boston: Little, Brown, 1975) p. 114.

19. John Fowles, 'Hardy and the Hag', *Thomas Hardy after Fifty Years*, ed. Lance St. John Butler (London: Macmillan; Totowa, N. J.: Rowman & Littlefield, 1976) p. 33. The psychiatrist Charles K. Hofling, in an earlier consideration of Hardy from a psychoanalytic point of view ('Thomas Hardy and the Mayor of Casterbridge', *Comprehensive Psychiatry*, IX [1968] 428–39), has argued persuasively that Michael Henchard represents certain aspects of Hardy's psychological nature. Of particular relevance is his speculation 'that Hardy, like Henchard, was prevented by an unconscious inner force . . . from effecting a satisfactory union with the principal woman-figure of his adult life' (p. 439). I interpret this statement as consistent with my argument for splitting. While Hofling does not mention Freud's paper, the theoretical basis for his speculation derives from Freud's analysis of the tendency to split the sensuous and affectionate feelings. Less persuasive for me is Robert Gittings' suggestion that 'delayed or imperfect physical development' may have left Hardy with 'an attraction to the idea of love without the power to fulfil it' (Gittings, p. 29). On the basis of evidence that is acknowledged to be 'fragmentary', Gittings offers a conjecture about Hardy's physical development when a psychological explanation seems called for.

20. Melanie Klein, 'Mourning and Its Relation to Manic Depressive States',

Contributions to Psycho-Analysis, 1921–45 (London: The Hogarth Press, 1948) pp. 311–38; W. R. D. Fairbairn, 'The Ultimate Basis of Aesthetic Experience', *British Journal of Psychology*, XXIX (1938) 167–81; and Hanna Segal, 'A Psycho-Analytical Approach to Aesthetics', *International Journal of Psycho-Analysis*, XXXIII (1952) 196–207.

21. *The Standard Edition*, XI, p. 190.

9 How to Read *A Few Crusted Characters*

RICHARD C. CARPENTER

Among Hardy's less-remarked accomplishments is his ability to create cryptic or ambiguous titles for some of his works: *Far from the Madding Crowd, A Laodicean, A Group of Noble Dames, Jude the Obscure*. Despite an oblique relationship to the works they designate, such titles are hardly exact descriptions. *Far from the Madding Crowd*, while pastoral in setting, is not really about a world removed from ignoble strife but is concerned with the tragic concatenations of love affairs; *A Laodicean* is only marginally interested in religious attitudes; and Jude's obscurity is a complex pun on his nature, obscure to himself as well as others, and on his social situation. Similarly, *A Few Crusted Characters*, which we would expect to be a series of sketches of quaint personalities valued for their well-aged eccentricities, like a fine old crusted port, turns out to be instead of group of short tales, an interlinked 'frame-story' principally built around the ironic mischances of love and ranging from pastoral farce to grim psychological tragedy.

The critics who have occasionally glanced at *A Few Crusted Characters*[1] have perhaps allowed their attention to be diverted by expectations derived from the title. Although they have been in general agreement that the work is among Hardy's best shorter pieces, with Irving Howe enthusiastically terming it a 'minor masterpiece' that is 'buoyant with delight' and 'utterly winning', they have not been moved to do any more than glance, and then only at the frame-story, which has been the sole subject for any critical comment, a procedure roughly equivalent to focusing on the picture-frame of one of Hardy's favourite Dutch masters like Douw or Terborch.

Even Howe, who certainly wants to give *A Few Crusted Characters* a square deal, looks only at the frame-story, characterising the rest of the work in a few words as 'a string of anecdotes, set pieces, and miniature portraits', and dismissing the powerfully morbid tale of 'The Winters and the Palmleys' as a 'sketch of obsessional vengeance'. Howe is an admirably astute critic, but, like John Wain, Samuel Hynes, and J. Hillis Miller, he has not seen fit to pay any close attention to the tales of *A Few Crusted Characters* to see whether or not there might be more to them than merely a string of anecdotes.

Expectations influenced by the title may be at work here, but I suspect there is a more general tendency which may account for the casual treatment of a work that is considered by all its recent interpreters as excellent of its kind. Busy critics have more important fish to fry than minnows like *A Few Crusted Characters*. Literary works which are serious, complex, and fairly large ('of a certain magnitude') get the bulk of critical attention; works which are light and amusing, simple, and brief are by definition 'minor' and are treated in the critic's spare time. A kind of Aristotelian squint often prevents even the best critics from seeing some small things distinctly, blurring the image of short story writers, familiar essayists, writers of light verse, and dramatists who specialise in one-acts. With major writers who also have on occasion turned to 'minor' forms, the situation is aggravated. We then have a body of 'serious' work and some minor productions done when the writer was in a relaxed mood, on an artistic vacation from his weightier accomplishments. The result, critically, is that this minor work is either completely ignored – the case for many years with *A Few Crusted Characters* – or given an appreciative nod but not really recognised as worthy of thoughtful consideration.

Further reinforcing this tendency are certain critical assumptions and methods which make it difficult to find anything very interesting to say about minor works. Briefly, the assumptions are that works are somehow arranged in a hierarchy of value, that they are best understood by comparing them with other works by the same author or other authors, and that the more complex and problem-laden they are the more rewarding they become for critical investigation. The methods which complement these assumptions are those of formal or structural analysis, broadly considered: the discussion of themes, comparison of characters, analysis of imagery and symbolism, patterns of myth, delineation of structural design. The work of Hardy critics from Lionel Johnson to Michael Millgate can generally be regarded as based on such assumptions and following such methods.

Now I do not want to be misunderstood as implying that these assumptions and methods are not valid or that works should not be assigned values and treated accordingly. I simply wish to suggest that quite possibly the standard approaches may not work as well as they might with certain kinds of literary productions, that there may be alternative ways of going about the task which can give a different perspective on minor works and enable us to assess them more adequately according to their intrinsic qualities. The point is that the assumptions with which we begin and the methods which support them predetermine what we can come up with. However we proceed we cannot hope to do everything with any one procedure; inevitably certain questions will not be asked and certain answers will consequently not be forthcoming. If we shift the assumptions and methods, new vistas open up, matters which seemed trivial before become important, questions which seemed settled become questions again. As Morse Peckham has made clear, [2] works of art are almost infinite in 'interpretation variability'; it all depends on how you go about the interpretation.

The alternative assumptions I would like to adopt in considering *A Few Crusted Characters* are simply the opposite of the usual: that works should be treated as even-handedly as possible without seeing some as more equal than others; that each work should be examined with the objective of bringing out its own uniqueness, its intrinsic *gestalt*; that complexity and weight are relative matters to be determined in regard to the work at hand and that other values may be just as worthy of consideration – simplicity and grace, for example. The method I would like to use is an adaptation of the kind of sequential analysis advocated by Stanley Fish, complemented by a phenomenological treatment in the manner of Wolfgang Iser: an examination of how the work *moves* as the reader encounters it, what *happens* in the process of reading. [3] And since the process of reading is a synergistic one, in which new experiences are interacting with prior ones in a continually unfolding development, this method involves looking both backward and forward, noting what a new story does to the reader's feelings and perceptions *vis-à-vis* the old stories already encountered. What should begin to appear as we examine this process is a picture of the 'virtual' work, the work as it takes place in a reader's consciousness. (In this case, the 'reader' is, of course, myself, with the hope that what happens in my consciousness will be reasonably similar to what would happen to any typical reader of Hardy.) When we finally conclude our examination of the ongoing nature of the work, we should also have a grasp of its unique *gestalt*, its quiddity, the particular configuration of elements which results in its being that thing which it is and no other thing, as Stephen Dedalus once put it.

Probably the first thing that strikes the reader's perception in beginning *A Few Crusted Characters* is the tone and atmosphere, a pastoral-rural ambience with pleasant scenes, quaint and old-fashioned details, a sense of long-established habit and custom, peace and serenity. It is a 'Saturday afternoon of blue and yellow autumntime', the place an inn-yard, the event the eminently simple one of passengers arriving for a journey in an old-fashioned, horse-drawn carrier's van going to 'Longpuddle'. The activity is exceedingly leisurely as one after another of the passengers come slowly into view and mount into the van, still without its horse or driver – the aged groceress of Longpuddle, the postmistress, the registrar's wife. There is no sense of urgency, or of any untoward occurrences; all this has been done a hundred times before in exactly the same way. Although we do not know for sure at this point, we suspect that we are going to be treated to some kind of tale in the rural tradition, something of long standing, but as unexciting as the preparations for going to the village on this pleasant afternoon. The appearance of the schoolmaster, the master-thatcher, and Christopher Day, the unknown landscape painter, unknown, that is, anywhere outside Longpuddle but much appreciated there, reinforces these impressions, since it is increasingly evident that these worthies are all known to one another, down to the last detail of their lives. The reader, having picked up these clues, begins figuratively to settle back into a feeling of quiet anticipation, expecting something in the nature of a familiar essay, with small events and mild pleasures.

This expectation is increased with two minor happenings of a rather similar nature: as the van starts off, it is realised that the curate is not with them and there is a mild flurry of concern until he approaches, a sign that even minute deviations from custom are notable. Then this aspect is furthered with the later appearance of a stranger, of all things, hailing a ride, and we become aware that a totally new element has been brought into the situation. At first it is hard for the carrier to believe that the man can really be what he claims to be – 'one of these parts' – since absolutely everyone in Upper Longpuddle is known to the carrier, but it turns out that the aged groceress soon recognises the stranger as John Lackland, who had left the village thirty-five years ago, sufficient proof of the long memories and intimate acquaintance with the inhabitants of the village possessed by these passengers in the van. Why John Lackland went away, and why he has returned are soon settled, because we learn that he is looking for news of what has happened to those he knew and to the townspeople in general. He is trying to find out whether or not he 'can come home again'. The preamble has been established, and now we are sure what the main subject is going to be: news of the inhabitants of Longpuddle and what their lives have been like.

Lackland is interested in anything that may have happened to Tony Kytes, who had taken him in Tony's father's 'waggon' to Caster-bridge that day thirty-five years ago; and we are launched into the story, told by the carrier, of 'Tony Kytes, the Arch-Deceiver'. There is, at this point, a most skilful transition of the sense of space for the reader, who has been imaginatively located in the carrier's van along with the passengers; for most of the story of Tony takes place in the same wagon in which Lackland had gone to Casterbridge, traversing the identical country roads on which we are travelling. There is the same sense of leisurely progression in the one as in the other, but an essential difference in the situation.

Tony, a Longpuddle Lothario, has recently been courting three different girls, and by being unwilling to say 'no' to any of them, has managed by various mischances to get all three into the wagon simultaneously: Unity Sallett hiding from Milly Richards under the tarpaulin in the back, Milly hiding from Hannah Jolliver under the empty sacks in front, and Hannah on the seat beside Tony, snuggling up to him and inveigling him into saying that he prefers her to her rivals. A classic bedroom farce has been transported to the country lanes of Wessex; the reader's anticipation from the introduction is deftly realised, shifted only slightly in that the 'nunnywatch' into which Tony has fallen is more rollicking and farcical than we might have expected.

The nunnywatch comes to its conclusion when Tony stops to ask advice of his father, who sagely advises him to marry the girl who has not asked for a ride, and the horse runs away, spilling the girls into the hedge. Tony, his cover completely blown, proposes to all three in turn, being refused by both Hannah and Unity, who will not take another's 'leavings'. The gentle, and practical, Milly is femininely wise enough to accept Tony's explanations that he did not mean a word he had spoken to Hannah, and forgives him, bringing this miniature folk comedy to a close.

The pleasure the reader derives from the tale comes from being caught up with Tony in his difficulty, watching this village lover entangling himself ever more inextricably in a romantic web and wondering how he will get out. His problem is, of course, brought about solely by his essential character as an indiscriminate appreciator of girls, especially the one he happens to be with at the moment. We are amused by the tactics he employs in his desperation as each of the maidens appears, and nicely satisfied with the sly irony at the end when the least demanding girl gets what they all want. There are delightful touches of comedy in the situation with Hannah on the seat beside Tony and the other two under the coverings, neither one daring to admit she is there. And Tony's successive proposals demonstrate as nothing else could how direct marriage customs were in the Wessex of that long-ago time.

Despite the triviality of the tale of Tony Kytes, however, the curious reader may detect just beneath its smiling surface a motif of different import. Tony manages to emerge from the entanglements of desire without too much damage, except to his ego, but such complicated and baffling love affairs could also, obviously, lead to disaster with just as much ease. Such is the case with the following tale, which begins with a slight romantic contretemps but soon slides into a more melancholy mood, a definite shift in tone from the farcical adventures of Tony. Whatever expectations we may have formed from the former tale are necessarily altered a good deal as we read 'The History of the Hardcomes'.

The parish clerk begins the story of the Hardcomes, in fact, with Tony's 'wedding-randy', described with appropriate gusto, a randy to beat all, with more guests and dancing than had been seen in many a year. At first we are sure that we are going to be regaled with another farce, but a subtle change soon takes place, although its implications take quite a while to be realised. The Hardcomes are two cousins who are both compatibly engaged to girls like themselves, quiet James to Emily, a 'gentle, nice-minded, in-door' person, and Steve to Olive, both of them 'of a more bustling nature, fond of racketing about'. During the dancing, each of the partners discovers that they have become fond of the other's betrothed: gentle Emily with bustling Steve, racketing Olive with nice-minded, in-door James, so much so that they agree to swap, an action that arouses in the reader misgivings almost as soon as it occurs, for such sudden impulses are not really the stuff out of which Hardy makes humour. The implications of the situation have turned around from those of Tony's, while we concurrently realise that the same motif of entangled love relations is concerned.

It is not long after they are married, James to Olive, Steve to Emily, that the cousins realise that they had both been foolish 'in upsetting a well-considered choice on the strength of an hour's fancy in the whirl and wildness of a dance'. Being 'sensible and honest', however, they feel that there is nothing that will change the situation and resolve to abide by it – that is, until they take their annual holiday at Budmouth-Regis. There, after they have walked on the sands and eaten at an inn and walked on the sands again, Olive and Steve decide that they would like a row on the water, while their respective spouses, who don't care for the water, remain on shore watching them. While James and Emily sit on the Esplanade the two row out into the bay, but in a most peculiar fashion. They look back only once, while Olive waves, then go straight out to sea. It is later reported that they 'had sat looking in each other's faces as if they were in a dream, with no consciousness of what they were doing, or whither they were steering.'

Aha! we think, they have recognised their intolerable dilemma and have eloped. James and Emily have this passing thought, too, but also wonder if perhaps they have simply put in farther down the coast. But, of course, such a thing is not to happen. When James and Emily, after having gone home to Longpuddle for the night, return to Budmouth, the news comes to them: the boat has been found drifting bottom up and then later the bodies of the missing pair are cast ashore in Lullwind Cove, and 'It was said that they had been found tightly locked in each other's arms, his lips upon hers, their features still wrapt in the same calm and dream-like repose which had been observed in their demeanour as they had glided along.'

Now this is something else again. If we have been relaxing in the notion that all the tales are to be like that of Tony Kytes, we certainly have to revise our opinion. Despite the fact that, after a suitable interval, James and Emily are married, the tale that has been told is not funny in the slightest, not even a comedy, but a sad and eerie tale of erotic possession. What is happening in the reader's consciousness is, in fact, more than a mere revision or alteration of perspective. It is here that Stanley Fish's term 'subversion' may be seen as more applicable, for the casual amusement aroused by Tony Kytes' misadventures is a totally inappropriate response to the tale of the Hardcomes, and it is necessary to turn our attitude right around in order to enjoy what is occurring as the tale moves on. It is especially noteworthy that Hardy leads us on at the beginning of the tale to expect another farce, since he expends so much good nature and

energy in describing the wedding-randy, with the dance having so
many couples that some of them were 'among the faggots and
brushwood in the out-house', and the ancient fiddler, 'very weak in
the wrist', who kept up 'a faltering tweedle-dee'. The gradual shift to
the impressive scene of the little yellow skiff going out farther and
farther on the glass-smooth sea while the other couple watch from the
shore may at first not quite penetrate the reader's imagination, but as
the incident unfolds, a whole new area of feeling toward the tale
unfolds with it.

Moreover, the trance-like uncanniness of this crucial part of the
Hardcomes' story reflects back on our responses to the story of Tony
Kytes, by contrast emphasising the humour of that concatenation of
lovers, as Hardy would have termed it, as opposed to this romantic
and faintly sinister scene. With the two tales now brought into
relationship, the reader finds the comedy of the first made ambiguous
by the melancholy of the second, an effect I call synergistic, since it
achieves more than the two stories could simply by adding the effect
of one to that of the other. We no longer have a funny tale followed
by one of romantic melancholy but two tales interfusing each other
with feeling.

As we begin the third tale of *A Few Crusted Characters*, this
uncanniness is used as the starting point. 'The Superstitious Man's
Story' is a slight sketch, less than four pages long, about the omens
that announced the approaching death of William Privett, a rather
morbid tale that apparently makes no point about ironic mischances
of life, implying rather the inevitability of fated circumstance.
William is in himself something of an uncanny individual, making
you feel clammy when he approaches close behind you, and having a
most serious and silent mien. A string of macabre portents attaches to
him as the sketch develops: the church bell goes "heavy" in the
sexton's hand, meaning someone in the parish is going to die; William
is seen by his wife going out in the evening, when he is really asleep
upstairs; the village girls, waiting for ghostly apparitions at the church
on Midsummer Eve, see him go into the porch but not come out
again; a miller's moth flies from his mouth while he is asleep after
mowing in Mr Hardcome's meadow; and finally he is seen at the
spring where his little son had drowned when he is actually lying dead
in the meadow.

'A rather melancholy story', John Lackland observes, and we
would have to agree, wondering what purpose it serves. But it does
have a place in the work because of its tone and the consequent

manipulation of our feelings. The romantic melancholy of the
Hardcomes' story here becomes darker, a sense that death is as much a
part of the Longpuddle world as life and love. We are prepared by
'The Superstitious Man's Story' for further developments of the
melancholy, grim, or inescapable realities of rural existence. The very
brevity of the tale and its apparent lack of more than anecdotal
significance make its position in the developing sequence important,
in much the same way that the isolated statement of a motif in music
which has been previously announced, but only in conjunction with a
more dominant initial motif, brings it out more forcibly for later
treatment. The tale, insignificant in itself, becomes significant because
of its relationship with the tales preceding and following it.

This becomes more readily apparent with the following story, a
more full-fledged tale with plot and characters, recited by the master-
thatcher, which returns us in certain ways to the world of Tony
Kytes. Once again a subversion of feeling takes place; for, although
we are now prepared for radical alterations in tone and subject-
matter, we still have to turn our responses in another direction. *A Few
Crusted Characters* calls for a degree of lightness and flexibility of
feeling in order for appreciation to take place: 'Andrey Satchel and
the Parson and the Clerk' is certainly one of the funniest stories in the
collection, but the situation trembles on the edge of pathos at least,
and fun is achieved at the cost of suffering on the part of one of the
characters.

Parson Toogood (whose name implies the traditional nature of one
aspect of the tale) has been called upon to wed, early one morning,
Andrey Satchel to a very pregnant Jane, who is understandably
anxious to 'get the thing done'. But Andrey, wanting to celebrate the
occasion of being a 'godfather one day, and a husband the next, and
perhaps a father the next', had been drinking all night and is in no
condition for marriage, according to the parson. Jane, however,
prevails upon him to lock the to-be-happy couple in the church tower
for an hour or two until Andrey can sober up, because she knows she
may not get another chance. Parson Toogood agrees, the immure-
ment takes place, and he and the clerk set off homeward, only to
forget almost immediately about the wedding in the excitement of a
fox hunt. The parson and clerk are 'frantical' pursuers of foxes who
joyfully rationalise their unclerical behaviour as a means of giving
their horses needed exercise. Exhausted after the hunt, they do not
recall the prisoners until the next morning and hope they have
escaped. But the famished and weary couple are still in the tower,

shame having prevented them from calling for help. The wedding duly transpires and Jane has her man, though he is no prize, as the narrator wrily observes.

Apparently we are at this point right back in the world of Tony Kytes, especially in terms of structure and tone. There is the introduction of the problem of getting married, the awkward contretemps, the development of certain delaying tactics to increase the suspense, the amusing reversal and the dénouement in the form of a wedding. Both stories are light and farcical, told with broad strokes of humour, particularly in the middle part, where the plot is complicated by the fox hunt. But even with all these similarities, some alterations are taking place. The story repeats the design of the first tale and recalls us to the realisation that rural happenings may be seen as funny, yet the centre of the story is not what must have gone on in the church tower during the day and night, but the side-issue of the parson who seems to be more out of Fielding or Smollett than Hardy, an archetypal fox-hunter, and his clerk not quite a Sancho Panza, but in that generic category. The comedy here is very broad and traditional, showing how the cloth cannot change the obsessions of men, although it may provide them with the right cant to hide their real motives a trifle from themselves, though not quite, since there is a twinkle in the eye of both parson and clerk as they persist in calling the hunt a beneficial act of exercise for the horses. This is really literary rather than folk-comedy, and makes the parson and clerk kin to other genial hypocrites, from the Prioress to W. C. Fields. Recognising this shift from one genre to another, we find the humour of *A Few Crusted Characters* enriched and deepened by its connection with literary tradition.

Hardy adroitly pursues this tack in the next sketch, the tale of the elder Andrey Satchel and his attempt to fob himself off as a musician in order to get a free Christmas dinner at the Squire's, a situation which combines the ancient motif of the penetrated disguise and the typical country story of the hungriest man in town. Within the development of *A Few Crusted Characters* it also serves another purpose; in fact, it might be said to be 'musical' in more than one sense, since it is the third tale where a country celebration is the setting or occasion for an untoward and ironic mischance. (Without wedding-randies and holiday gatherings, life in Longpuddle would have gone along on a much more even keel.) Hardy is skilfully weaving together not only his major themes but also minor motifs which provide structural echoes and overtones as the work proceeds.

As a matter of fact, if the reader is not only responsive to Hardy's manipulation of his feelings but also curious as to what the overall purpose or direction of the work is supposed to be, it is about at this point that he might ask himself whether or not there is any unifying principle to these miscellaneous tales or if they are merely a pastiche of old country stories cobbled together to make a collection. The final answer would properly have to wait until the end, to be sure, but it would still be possible to hazard a guess based on the evidence to this point. From the nature both of the frame and the tales thus far, it appears that there may be two unifying principles at work, a structural and a thematic. Structurally it is evident that Hardy is employing a patterning analogous to a musical composition. He establishes different 'voices' – the farcial, the melancholy, the morbid – and alternates their speaking, playing one off against another, resolving the tone of farce into that of melancholy through transitional passages and then moving back again to farce, introducing combinations of the voices to bring about new harmonies. At the same time he introduces various motifs such as criss-crossed sexual relationships, love and death, even country celebrations, and also alternates and counterpoints these against one another as the tales move on. Structurally, then, the tales are much more organised than it might at first appear.

Similarly, the themes which might be abstracted from the tales are no hodgepodge, either, for it is clear that all of them (with the possible exception of William Privett's) are concerned with ironic mischance in one form or another. Through the co-operation of human frailty and the inscrutability of happenstance, people fall into various difficulties, ranging from the merely embarrassing to the life-destroying. Even the death of William Privett is ironic in a way, because, although everyone, including his wife, is certain that he is the one in the parish who is going to die, nothing can be done about it and no reason for his sudden passing is given. Unexplained and inevitable occurrences are ironic means of emphasising that human beings are at the mercy of time and chance. Despite the laughable nature of several of the tales, the contretemps into which their protagonists fall also underline the ways in which people are hostages to outrageous fortune, in the same fashion as in the more serious stories.

These impressions created in the reader up until the story of Andrey, Jane, and the Parson are strengthened with the last four tales. 'Absent-Mindedness in a Parish Choir', the first of these, is a very funny story, but at the same time it picks up a motif which has been present but not emphasised and which will be the main point of the conclusion of the frame-story: the fact that all the incidents being recounted are far in the past, their principals mostly dead or their fortunes changed for the worse or simply no longer known — 'where are the snows of yesteryear?' The choir was replaced 'twenty year' ago and their place taken by a 'young teetotaller' who plays the organ, mostly as a result of the ironic mischance into which they fell. The 'absent-mindedness' came about because the choir was very weary from playing at 'one rattling randy after another' during the Christmas season and took along a gallon of hot brandy and beer to keep up their spirits and keep them warmed during the service while they sat in the 'mortal cold' of the gallery. They all took a 'thimbleful in the Absolution, and another after the Creed, and the remainder at the beginning 'o the sermon', and promptly fell asleep, every one. When it came time for the final hymn and they were nudged awake by a boy in the gallery who said 'Begin! Begin!' they became confused in the darkness and struck up 'The Devil Among the Tailors' for all they were worth. They kept on to the end of the tune, oblivious to the horror of the congregation, particularly the Squire and the parson, who soon descended on them. Although the parson eventually forgave them, as a parson should, the Squire did not and they never played in the church again.

This is humorous irony, tinged with the lightest touch of pathos and nostalgia, but the next tale, 'The Winters and the Palmleys', is in utter contrast to such amusing misadventures, a grim story of pitiless vengeance, by far the most sombre in the collection. If we had not been previously forewarned by the stories of the Hardcomes and William Privett, the gloomy chronicle of the hatred of Mrs Winter and Mrs Palmley would no doubt strike us as an unreasonable excrescence in this group of comic folk tales. Even so, it is rather a bitter pill, which shows the extremities to which people could be driven in the quiet backwaters of Wessex.

Furthermore, in this tale Hardy is more complex in the development of plot and character than he is in any of the other stories. The antipathy between Mrs Winter and Mrs Palmley harks back many years: a stolen lover, the prosperity of the temptress and the misfortunes of the jilted, the later death of the second woman's little son because of the first woman's carelessness — a sorry tale of jealousy and hate. It comes to a head when Mrs Winter's son, Jack, falls in love with Mrs Palmley's niece, Harriet, a city girl with rather elevated tastes for Longpuddle. Hobbledehoy Jack, at first encouraged by

Harriet, loses her regard when he writes illiterate letters to her, letters which she refuses to return to him, however, so that he desperately breaks into Mrs Palmley's house one night and steals them, unwittingly taking some money at the same time. Caught red-handed the next morning, he is sent to the assizes and sentenced to execution under the savage criminal code of the time. Harriet could save him by explaining the real situation, but under her aunt's influence she does not appear at the trial, and Mrs Palmley has her revenge at last.

The final scene of the tale, as Jack's body is brought home to Longpuddle, is Hardy at his sombre best, with a tone and atmosphere reminiscent of the funeral journey of Fanny Robin: 'About eight o'clock, as we hearkened on our door-stones in the cold bright starlight, we could hear the faint crackle of a waggon from the direction of the turnpike-road. The noise was lost as the waggon dropped into a hollow, then it was plain again as it lumbered down the next long incline, and presently it entered Longpuddle.' The pathos of this whole series of events, the multiplied ironies — from the disasters that overtook Mrs Palmley to Jack's rejection because he could not spell, to the attempt to recover his pitiful letters being construed as burglary in the night, to the implacability that led to his death — is communicated with single-minded intensity, no light touches of folk ways, no quaint observations on the part of the narrator, the aged groceress who was the first to recognise John Lackland. The reader, conditioned by now to expect a blend of motifs and tones, is sharply brought up to the realisation of the grim potentialities in Longpuddle life, as if Hardy had been subtly preparing him for this sudden shock of recognition, providing hints that such things might be but softening the implications until this point. This is the final 'subversion' of the mild and pleasing anticipations with which we began the stories, the nadir of their melancholy and the zenith of their art.

With great artistry, Hardy has placed this tale at the ante-penultimate position in the collection, so that we can be brought back part way to the attitudes with which we started. It would never do to end the stories on this note, yet it would be too insipid to return all the way to farce. The final two tales reiterate instead the motifs of the clever fellow to be seen in Tony Kytes and the girl who refuses to be denied her rights, like Andrey's Jane; but the first is only a mildly amusing anecdote of the cheater cheated, while the second has more bemused astonishment at the will of a maid than it does humour.

George Crookhill, a would-be con man, is 'stung' when he changes clothes with a chance acquaintance and steals his horse while the latter is supposedly asleep. But the apparently prosperous farmer is really an army deserter, and Georgy is soon taken up by the constables since he fits the description. Fortunately for him the soldiers come by and say that he is not their man, so that he gets off with a light sentence instead of execution. And the sly deserter is never caught.

A slight sketch with no great point except its ironic connection with the other stories, although it does add one more type to a gallery of Longpuddle folk: the village petty criminal who is both a source of concern and an object of curiosity to the other folk. It also serves to soften the harshness of the preceding tale and modulates the theme of ironic mischance into another phase, this time the mischief that may lie in the desire for property, as contrasted with the prevailing sexual and social motifs of the other tales. 'Netty Sargent's Copyhold' similarly focuses on this motif, with Netty wanting to hang on to her property, however, so that she may get a husband. The plot is complicated for so brief a story, depending on Netty's possibly being deprived of her inheritance of a house because her uncle has not signed a renewal of the copyhold. He finally gets around to making the arrangements, but dies in his chair just before the agent comes with the papers. Netty puts the agent off by saying that her uncle is nervous about such legal affairs and asking the agent to look in the window while she guides her uncle's hand, so that the deed will be properly witnessed. With the chair back to the window she succeeds in deceiving the agent, gets her inheritance, and later her husband.

The reader's reaction to this story is a mingled one of admiration for such an exercise of cool nerve, and realisation that this trickery belongs in somewhat the same category as that of George, although now the motive is much more justifiable: the property should by rights go to Netty and only her uncle's dilatoriness and the irony of chance have intervened. But as we also might now anticipate, the eventual outcome is neither triumph nor disaster, because Netty's marriage did not turn out too well and the story of how she gained the house and husband got around. When the young Squire, heir to the old Squire who coveted the copyhold, heard about it, however, he took no proceedings against Netty. The narrator, who is Mr Day, the world-ignored painter, concludes with appropriately worldly observation that nothing happened to Netty because she 'was a pretty young woman, and the Squire's son was a pretty young man at that time'.

And similarly the ending of the whole series of tales concludes on a dying fall. The van comes down the hill into Longpuddle, the passengers drop off one by one, and Lackland wanders through the village, coming finally to the graveyard. Here he recognises that time has passed him by as it has the people about whom he has been hearing, the Sallets, the Privetts, the Sargents, whose stones are in the graveyard. All have been gone these many years, and there is no place prepared for him to come home to. 'Time had not condescended to wait his pleasure, nor local life his greeting.' He lingers for a few days, then disappears, and 'it is now a dozen or fifteen years since his visit was paid, and his face has not again been seen.'

A Few Crusted Characters has come to an end, and as the reader looks back he realises how much there really has been to this apparently slight and insignificant work. With great skill and artistry Hardy has controlled our responses from tale to tale, moving us from hearty enjoyment of broad country farce to romantic melancholy to feelings of uncanniness back to farce again and then to pathos, weaving his effects with immensely adroit precision. Varying in length, pace, complexity, thematic import, and tone, the tales provide a panorama of life in Longpuddle many years ago; yet with all their variety they are no mere ragbag of rural stories loosely wrapped in the package of the frame-story. Knitting them tightly together are both structure and theme, functioning sequentially to produce a rich succession of affective and perceptual experiences in the reader's consciousness. Both the structures and the themes echo and counter-point from tale to tale, progressively adding to the reader's comprehension of the possible range of ironic interrelationships which Hardy is treating.

The quiddity of the work would seem to be, then, this progressive presentation of the different voices of irony — theme and variations, to use a musical analogy once again. An interlinked continuum is established along which the tales are arranged like a series of pieces in a suite, each having to do with the unifying idea or 'argument' that infuses the whole composition. Although the bulk of these tales are comic in mode, the most important are serious, melancholy, almost tragic, so that in terms of our response as readers, both while we are reading and as we look back, the quantity of humorous material is balanced by the quality of the serious. The particular pleasure in reading *A Few Crusted Characters* is not that with which we began the process — the mild and relaxing pleasures of reminiscence and quaintness — but the alternations and variations of humour and pathos, blended in an unfolding sequence of impressions. Hardy successively, and successfully, subverts our easily formed expectations with new insights, bringing us closer and closer to an overall perception of the manifold possibilities of Life's Little Ironies melded together in an objective correlative.

Does this mean, then, that *A Few Crusted Characters* should be given a revised standing in the hierarchy of Hardy's works? I do not really think so. What the type of analysis we have been performing indicates, rather, is that *any* work may be found to be both 'self-intelligible' and 'self-significant', as Ralph Radar has helpfully said,[4] provided we go about reading it in ways suited to its nature. It is possible that a similar method, focusing on larger sequences, might show that *The Mayor of Casterbridge* or *Jude the Obscure* are as much greater masterpieces than *A Few Crusted Characters* as has usually been thought. Yet the converse, in a way, can also be true: that 'minor' works, properly interpreted with the tools suited to them, may demonstrate hitherto unsuspected qualities. If the instruments applied in the interpretation of literary works are too blunt or too powerful, they may simply be unable to discern the distinctive attributes that make those works that which they are and no other thing. Irving Howe says of *A Few Crusted Characters* that it takes a good deal of 'literary tact' to appreciate a work of its sort, more than 'to play with the symbols of *Moby-Dick*', a sentiment with which I agree. But I would add that literary tact is not enough if the critical assumptions and methods do not fit the work under consideration. What serves well for *Moby-Dick* is, I feel quite sure, not likely to serve well for *Typee* or *The Encantadas*, and the fact that these works are sometimes wrenched into conformity with weighty symbol-playing may mean either that the critic lacks tact or the appropriate method and assumptions. The comparative neglect of Hardy's minor works, especially those which are light, amusing, or brief – *The Romantic Adventures of a Milkmaid*, *The Distracted Preacher*, ballad poems, and even *A Few Crusted Characters* – is probably due to reasons of this sort. If we were to employ a greater variety of critical approaches, making sure in each case that they fit the work at hand, we might well give these 'minor masterpieces' the justice they deserve.

NOTES

1. See, for example, Irving Howe (ed.), *The Selected Writings of Thomas Hardy*

(Greenwich, Conn.: Fawcett Publications, 1966) p. 15; Samuel Hynes (ed.), *Great Short Works of Thomas Hardy* (New York: Harper & Row, 1967) p. xxiv; and J. Hillis Miller, *Thomas Hardy: Distance and Desire* (London: Oxford University Press; Cambridge, Mass.: Harvard University Press, 1970) pp. 49, 107. All these comments together total about a page, and only Hynes mentions the stories at all, his comments being brief observations on Tony Kytes and Netty Sargent. Comment by other critics is similarly notable for its brevity and its focus on the frame-story.

2. Morse Peckham, *Man's Rage for Chaos: Biology, Behavior, and the Arts* (New York: Schocken, 1967) *passim*.

3. Stanley E. Fish, 'Literature in the Reader: Affective Stylistics', in *Self-Consuming Artifacts: The Experience of Seventeenth-Century Literature* (Berkeley, Los Angeles, London: University of California Press, 1972), Appendix, pp. 381-427 – first published in *NLH*, II (1970) 122–61, in slightly different form; Wolfgang Iser, 'The Reading Process: A Phenomenological Approach', in *The Implied Reader: Patterns of Communication in Prose Fiction from Bunyan to Beckett* (1972; trans. Baltimore and London: The Johns Hopkins University Press, 1974), pp. 274–94 – also published in *NLH*, III (1971) 279–99.

4. Ralph W. Rader, 'Fact, Theory and Literary Explanation', *CI*, I (1974) 245–72. The fact that Rader disagrees pointedly with Fish does not invalidate the use of his concept at this point in any essay that bears some resemblance to Fish's method.

10 One Name of Many Shapes: *The Well-Beloved*

MICHAEL RYAN

The Well-Beloved occupies a place of dubious privilege in the Hardy canon. The first version, serialised in late 1892, was written in reaction to the rejection of *Tess of the d'Urbervilles* for moral reasons by Tillotson & Son. The revised version appeared as a book in 1897, thus making it Hardy's last novel before he gave up novel-writing altogether. That he chose to make this novel his parting salute to the genre suggests that the spirit with which he bade farewell to prudent publishers and unrelenting reviewers relates in some way to his feelings concerning the rejection of *Tess of the d'Urbervilles*. His feelings at that time seem best reflected in a short essay, 'Candour in English Fiction', published in the *New Review* in 1890, in which he calls 'our popular fiction' 'a literature of quackery'.[1] I shall argue that the bitterness one finds in this essay also informs *The Well-Beloved*.

Between 1889 and 1892, the time of the conception and writing of *The Well-Beloved*, Hardy wrote most of the stories that were later collected as *Life's Little Ironies*. One of those stories, 'An Imaginative Woman' (1893), which originally did not belong to the collection but which was later included because, like the others, it turned upon 'a trick of Nature',[2] resembles the novel in its joining of the themes of unfulfilled desire and artistic creation. The irony of the story, like that of the novel, turns upon a trick of genealogical resemblance. Mr Marchmill rejects his own son because, by accident, he resembles Robert Trewe, the poet who Marchmill suspects had been his wife's lover. Mrs Marchmill had loved Trewe, but she never let him know this – in fact, they never met. Trewe, like Jocelyn Pierston, the hero of *The Well-Beloved*, had desired an ideal Beloved, but, unable to find her, committed suicide. (In the first version of the novel, Pierston attempts suicide, but fails.) Clearly, Hardy's treatment of the artist in the short story is ironic, if not mocking. Here is part of Trewe's suicide note, written to a friend: 'I have long dreamt of such an unattainable creature, as you know; and she, this undiscoverable, elusive one, inspired my last volume; the imaginary woman alone, for, in spite of what has been said in some quarters, there is no real woman behind the title. She has continued to the last unrevealed, unmet, unwon. I think it desirable to mention this in order that no blame may attach to any real woman as having been the cause of my decease by cruel or cavalier treatment of me.'[3] 'Imaginary woman', of course, plays off the 'Imaginative Woman' of the title. In a certain sense, Ella Marchmill is both. By remaining 'unrevealed', she causes his death, and ironically, his attempt to excuse 'any real woman' only places the blame on her.

I suggest that *The Well-Beloved* also should be read in this mocking, ironic light.[4] If it is a fable[5] of the artistic temperament, it is also at the same time a mockery of aestheticism. It shares the bitter-sweetness of 'An Imaginative Woman' by pretending to present a straightforward account of a Shelleyan, Platonic 'aesthetic temper', while simultaneously mocking and undermining that very notion. Hardy's choice of aestheticism as the butt of his irony should not be surprising. That movement's ideals of narcissistic and Platonic love were antithetical to Hardy's own demand that the novel reflect, reveal, and criticise life as a 'physiological fact' and that 'its honest portrayal must be largely concerned with, for one thing, the relations of the sexes.'[6]

Even as Hardy was launching this polemic, Oscar Wilde was stealing popular attention away from Hardy with *The Portrait of Dorian Grey* (serial version 1890). Walter Pater had already done so five years earlier with *Marius the Epicurean* (1885). Both of these novels are implicitly mocked in *The Well-Beloved*, and one cannot help but suspect that jealousy is at least in part the motive.

Along with aestheticism, Hardy singles out Pater's version of Platonism as an object of mockery. In the *Life*, Hardy himself admits that the idea for the novel came from his fascination with the 'Platonic Idea'.[7] In the Preface (written in 1897), he writes that the novel deals with ' a delicate dream . . . by no means new to Platonic philosophers', and the epigraph from Shelley – 'One shape of many names' – recalls Pater's discussion of the relationship between the one and the many in *Plato and Platonism* (1894) as well as Plato's *Cratylus*, to which Pater refers directly in his first lecture and which Hardy read shortly before writing the novel.[8] Pater's lectures on Plato were originally delivered in 1891 – 92, a time when he was known to be a visitor at the Hardys' house in Kensington. It is conceivable, therefore, that Hardy was aware of Pater's work even at the time of the writing of the first version of the novel. Pater portrays Plato as an artist who seeks the Ideal as 'vision' above all. He stresses Plato's aesthetic temper which compels him to worship Beauty as a lover. Already in the first title of the novel – *The Pursuit of the Well-Beloved: A Sketch of a Temperament* – one can detect a connection with Pater's Platonism.

The aesthete desiring an ideal Beloved – the Rossetti who paints a picture entitled 'The Beloved', or Pater's Marius – is not the only victim of Hardy's humour.[9] After going back on the agreement to publish *Tess of the d'Urbervilles*, Tillotson asked Hardy to write 'something light' in its place, something un-obscure. Hardy responded with a novel which is not just transparent, but also aggressively systematic and obvious. *The Well-Beloved* is a resolutely un-obscure book which mocks its own lack of obscurity. This becomes evident when one compares the prospectus Hardy wrote for Tillotson in 1889 with the essay on 'Candour' of a year later. At first, the prospectus seems innocent enough:

> The novel is entirely modern in date and subject, and, though comparatively short, embraces both extremes of society, from peers, peeresses, and other persons of rank and culture, to villagers. . . .
>
> The story, though it deals with some highly emotional situations, is not a tragedy in the ordinary sense. The scenes shift backwards and forwards from London studios and drawing-rooms of fashion to the cottages and cliffs of a remote isle in the English Channel, and a little town on the same.
>
> There is not a word or scene in the tale which can offend the most fastidious taste; and it is equally suited for the reading of young people, and for that of persons of maturer years.[10]

The unmistakable irony of the final paragraph undermines the apparent simplicity of what has gone before.

Hardy makes even more vicious fun of 'the most fastidious taste' in his polemical essay on English fiction. Ostensibly an attack on 'the magazine in particular and the circulating library in general', which 'do not foster the growth of the novel which reflects and reveals life', the essay, more importantly, makes mock of 'English prudery', with a seemingly direct reference to the rejection of *Tess of the d'Urbervilles*:

It is in the self-consciousness engendered by interference with spontaneity, and in aims at a compromise to square with circumstances, that the real secret lies of the charlatanry pervading so much of English fiction. It may be urged that abundance of great and profound novels might be written which should require no compromising, contain not an episode deemed questionable by prudes. This I venture to doubt. In a ramification of the profounder passions the treatment of which makes the great style, something 'unsuitable' is sure to arise; and then comes the struggle with literary conscience. . . . But, though pointing a fine moral, it is just one of those issues which are not to be mentioned in respectable magazines and select libraries.[11]

Hardy hypothesises about a story which 'may, in a rash moment, have been printed in some popular magazine before the remainder is written'. If the writer wants to describe the 'profounder passions', as did Hardy in *Tess of the d'Urbervilles*, he is confronted with a dilemma: 'he must either whip and scourge those characters into doing something contrary to their natures, to produce the spurious effect of their being in harmony with social forms and ordinances, or, by leaving them alone to act as they will, he must bring down the thunders of respectability upon his head, not to say ruin his editor, his publisher, and himself.' Clearly, the hypothetical writer is Hardy himself, and the novel, *Tess of the d'Urbervilles*. Hardy goes on to lament his readers' inability to distinguish 'a prurient treatment of the relations of the sexes' and a frank rendering of 'things which everybody is thinking but nobody is saying'. All writing, he argues, is for the triumph of good, 'But the writer may print the *not* of his broken commandment in capitals of flame; it makes no difference. A question which should be wholly a question of treatment is confusedly regarded as a question of subject.' The suggestion with which Hardy closes the essay recalls the final sentence of the prospectus for *The Well-Beloved*. Rather than demand that all fiction be suitable for young and old alike, there should 'be at least one magazine for the middle-aged and old', which would treat subjects otherwise deemed unfit for 'minors' and 'budding womanhood'. This, for Hardy, is the only way 'to circumvent the present lording of nonage over maturity, and permit the explicit novel to be more generally written'.[12]

The Well-Beloved is hardly the 'explicit novel' Hardy calls for. On the contrary, it goes out of its way to avoid anything that would offend conventional morality. By means of this systematic avoidance, however, it mocks the very notion of an unexplicit novel, one which would be suitable for all ages. Its transparent lack of candour makes it an ironic fictional version of Hardy's essay. I shall look at the novel, therefore, as a mock fable which makes fun of both the Platonic aestheticism of the latter part of the century and the innocuous, popular society novel which Hardy's publishers would have preferred he write.

'Temperament', in Hardy's subtitle, carries resonances of the term 'aesthetic temper', which was a commonplace of the eighties and nineties, as well as of the notion of Platonic 'temperance' and the 'temper' of the artist/lover as Pater describes him. In the Preface, Pierston's character is given in a recognisably Platonic language: 'Hence it is a spot apt to generate a *type* of personage like the character imperfectly sketched in these pages – *a native of natives* – whom some may choose to call a fantast . . . , but whom others may see only as one that gave objective continuity and a name to a delicate dream which in a vaguer form is more or less common to all men, and is by no means new to Platonic philosophers' (p. vii; italics mine). Pierston is not only a type or essence, but also an embodiment, 'objective continuity', of an ideal, 'dream'. He embodies an ideal Temperament, and he seeks an ideal Beloved. This sought-after ideal repeats the Platonic pattern. She is the 'idol', or *eidolon*, 'of his fancy', a 'spirit' which is embodied as 'a parting of the lips' or 'a light of the eye': 'To his Well-Beloved he had always been faithful; but she had had many embodiments. Each individuality known as Lucy, Jane, Flora, Evangeline, or what-not, had been merely a transient condition of her. . . . Essentially she was perhaps of no tangible substance' (I, II; pp. 10–11). Like the Platonic idea, she remains one despite assuming many shapes, and her ideality transcends its material embodiments. The arbitrariness of names – 'Flora, Evangeline, or what-not' – is associated with the mutability of her material shapes, and this seems to reinforce her ideal transcendence – 'she was perhaps of no tangible substance.'

Pierston's Beloved takes five important shapes. He first falls in love with Avice Caro. He jilts her for Marcia Bencomb, who in turn leaves him when her parents refuse to approve of their planned marriage. Several years later, the Beloved reappears as Nichola Pine-Avon. After hearing of the first Avice's death, Pierston returns home and falls in love with Avice's daughter, Ann Avice Caro, whom he nevertheless calls Avice. She turns out to be married already, so he leaves home once again. When the second Avice asks him to return and visit her twenty years later, he discovers the Beloved in her daughter, also called Avice. She jilts him for Marcia's stepson, and Pierston is left to marry Marcia. After an illness, he loses his desire for the Beloved as well as his aesthetic taste. He turns to business, and, finally, dies. Even in this sketch, one gets a sense of what Joseph Warren Beach calls 'the playful malice of Fate' in the novel.

A projected fantasy of Pierston's, the Beloved mirrors his temperament. If she is 'One shape of many names', he seems to remain the same despite change. This would appear to be the point of the section titles: 'A Young Man of Twenty', 'A Young Man of Forty', 'A Young Man of Sixty'. The repetition of the Phrase, 'A Young Man', seems to connote an eternal youthfulness. Pierston is the same young man throughout. Like the Platonic idea, he seems infinitely repeatable. However, the titles also record a change: 'Twenty', 'Forty', 'Sixty'. At the same time that Hardy presents Pierston as a perpetual youth, an unchanging Temperament, he mocks this very (Platonic) idea by showing how Pierston actually ages. If the novel is, as Hardy says it is, about 'the passage of Time', [13] then it is a passage which mocks the pretensions of Platonic idealism to transcend Time.

Like his Beloved, then, Pierston seems to be characterised by a oneness in multitude: 'His record moved on with the years, his sentiments stood still' (II, vi; p. 93). Not only his sentiments, but also his physical appearance seems unaltered with time. Upon his return to the island from London, Avice Caro remarks: 'O yes, and for the moment I forgot! He seemed just the same to me as he used to be' (I, i; p. 6). Curiously enough, her daughter, forty years later, uses the same words: 'The widow in mourning who received him in the front parlour was, alas! but the sorry shadow of Avice the Second. How could he have fancied otherwise after twenty years? Yet he had been led to fancy otherwise, almost without knowing it, by feeling himself unaltered. Indeed, curiously enough, nearly the first words she said to him were: "Why – you are just the same!" ' (III, i; p. 150). Repeatedly, Pierston's feelings and appearance are contrasted with his actual age: 'He felt as he had felt when standing beside her predecessor; but, alas! he was twenty years further on towards the shade' (II, vi; p. 95). The narrator's 'alas's often seem slightly insincere, especially here where it is followed by a premonition of future death which mocks the continuity Pierston seeks to establish between past and present. In fact, most of the narrator's remarks about Pierston's essential and apparent youth in contrast to his actual age seem to rest on an ironic double edge: 'Pierston was always regarded as a young man, though he was now about forty' (II, 1; p. 57). No one of Pierston's incarnations is more a figure of fun than the sixty-year-old man with the twenty-year-old heart who woos the granddaughter of his original love:

> He was subject to gigantic fantasies still. . . . In a crowd secretly, or in solitude boldly, he had often bowed the knee three times to this sisterly divinity on her first appearance monthly, and directed a kiss towards her shining shape. The curse of his qualities (if it were not a blessing) was far from having spent itself yet. . . . Whatever Pierston's years might have made him look by day, in the dusk of evening he was fairly presentable as a pleasing man of no marked antiquity, his outline differing but little from what it had been when he was half his years. He was well preserved, still upright, trimly shaven, agile in movement; wore a tightly buttoned suit which set off a naturally slight figure; in brief, he might have been of any age as he appeared to her at this moment. (III, II; pp. 158–60: ellipses mine)

The narrator's irony should be clear in such phrases as 'fairly presentable' and 'of no marked antiquity'. Even though Pierston here seems to elude, if not to transcend time – 'he might have been of any age' – it is still true that in order for his external appearance to be consonant with his unaltered Temperament, he has to do his courting in the dark. (If one recalls the proximity of *eidos*, or idea, to *helios*, or sun, in Greek, this is indeed ironic. In order to attain the timeless state of the idea, Pierston must avoid the sun, which *is* the idea.) The greatest moment of revelation in the novel is a moment of self-revelation due to sunlight:

> As he sat thus thinking, and *the daylight increased*, he discerned, a short distance before him, a movement of something ghostly. His position was facing the window, and he found that by chance the looking-glass had swung itself vertical, so that what he saw was his own shape. The recognition startled him. The person he appeared was too grievously far, chronologically, in advance of the person he felt himself to be. . . . Never had he seemed so aged by a score of years as he was represented in the glass. . . . While his soul was what it was, why should he have been encumbered with that

withering carcase, without the ability to shift it off for another, as his ideal Beloved had so frequently done? (III, IV; pp. 175–6: ellipses and italics mine)

What comes to light, what is revealed to the Platonist who believes that his idea of himself as an eternally youthful Temperament somehow overcomes the laws of time, is the pitifulness of a Platonism applied to the self. He slowly rots while his ideal flourishes, and a subjective idea of oneself is shown to be no guarantee against the inevitable objectification of death. Death mocks Pierston's feeling that he possesses an infinitely repeatable youthful Temperament. Similarly, the possibility of a past in which he did not exist serves to make fun of the seemingly endless displaceability of his desire along a genetic line. The third Avice asks, after he has confessed to being her grandmother's and her mother's lover: 'And were you my great-grandmother's too?' (III, IV; p. 177). Were Pierston as ageless as his Beloved, he would have been. Closet Platonism is mocked further when even the Beloved begins to show the effects of age: 'He was fully aware that since his earlier manhood a change had come over his regard of womankind. Once the individual had been nothing more to him than the temporary abiding-place of the typical or ideal; now his heart showed its bent to be a growing fidelity to the specimen, with all her pathetic flaws of detail' (III, I; p. 150). Hardy may be presenting Pierston as another version of Angel Clare and making a point about women as real and ideal objects of love, but he is also showing how Pierston's subjective idealism is undermined by time. For Hardy, something in the very nature of things mocks the Platonist's elevation of the material into the ideal.

As well as being a Platonist who reduces everything to the same idea, Pierston is also characterised as an aesthete of aesthetes: 'He would have gone on working with his chisel with just as much zest if his creations had been doomed to meet no mortal eye but his own. This indifference to the popular reception of his dream-figures lent him a curious artistic *aplomb* that carried him through the gusts of opinion.' Nevertheless, the narrator is careful to point out that he was a material success: 'He prospered without effort. He was A. R. A.' (I, IX; p. 49). Throughout the novel, the aesthetic and the commercial are juxtaposed ironically. At the beginning, Pierston is described as 'the sculptor of budding fame' while, in the same sentence, his father is presented as 'an inartistic man of trade and commerce merely, from whom, nevertheless, Jocelyn condescended to accept a yearly allowance pending the famous days to come' (I, I; p. 6). In the serial version, Pierston's aestheticism is more openly mocked by showing how it contains what it supposedly excludes. In the following passage, for example, Pierston burns the letters of former loves and realises that a lock of hair is included in one of the letters:

> He cut the string, loosened the letters, and kindled another match. The flames illuminated the handwriting, which sufficiently re-called to his knowledge her from whom that batch had come, and enabled him to read tender words and fragments of sentences addressed to him in his teens by the writer. Many of the sentiments, he was ashamed to think, he had availed himself of in some attempts at lyric verse, as having in them that living fire which no lucubration can reach. . . .
> 'Good heavens!' said the budding sculptor to himself. 'How can I be such a brute? I am burning *her* – part of her form – many of whose curves as remembered by me I have worked into statuettes and tried to sell. I cannot do it – at any rate, to-night.'[14]

Pierston may be an idealistic lover /artist, but, here at least, he is also presented as a materialistic and foolish charlatan.

Like Pierston himself, everything connected with him seems infected with an absurd reductiveness – his Beloved, his geography, his genealogy. In the Preface, he is characterised as a fantast whose peculiar Temperament is generated by the island. The same origin is attributed to his art: 'But one figure had never been seen on the Channel rock in the interval, the form of Pierston the sculptor, whose first use of the chisel that rock had instigated' (III, I; p. 145). The repetition of the word 'rock' is here not a case of stylistic clumsiness. Repeatedly, like Pierston's lugubrious and reductive model of the 'Well-Beloved', the island appears as a repetitively stony unity: 'The peninsula carved by Time out of a single stone. . . . the unity of the whole island as a solid and single block of limestone' (Preface [p. vii]; I, I [p. 4]). Not only Pierston's Temperament and art, but also his name seems generated by this rocky stone of reductive impoverish-ment. Literally, Pierston means Stonestone, and a variation of it would be Fatherstone. This playfulness should not be surprising, since at the same time, in *Life's Little Ironies*, Hardy was calling a poet Trewe, a factory-owner Marchmill, and a carrier Burthen. The humour of the name-play emerges more fully when one remembers that Pierston carves the same stone his father quarries from the island:

'While the son had been modelling and chipping his ephemeral fancies into perennial shapes, the father had been persistently chiselling for half a century at the crude original matter of those shapes, the stern, isolated rock in the Channel' (II, 1; p. 55). Value is given to the father here, and the narrator's attitude towards Pierston is clearly mocking. Even more mocking, however, is the formula that emerges from the anagrammatic pun at work in the name and the description of the island – Stonestone sculpts the same stone as Fatherstone cuts from the stony island. However exaggerated, this does not betray the spirit of mockery Hardy invests in his reductive manipulation of names and stones. This manipulation at once establishes the ground of Pierston's highly spiritual aestheticism as something extremely common and earthly, illuminates the absurdity of the unitary 'Platonic' model, and comically pulls the rug out from under the feet of his pretensions.

The narrator links the Beloved to geography and genealogy by means of Pierston's Temperament: 'Never much considering that [the Well-Beloved] was a subjective phenomenon vivified by the weird influences of *his descent and birthplace*, the discovery of her ghostliness, of her independence of physical laws and failings, had occasionally given him a sense of fear' (I, II; p. 11: italics mine). In each of the three – Beloved, geography, and genealogy – one finds the same pattern of continuity, repetition, and reduction as one finds in Pierston's Platonic Temperament. In each case, the present is reduced to something that precedes it, just as Pierston, no matter what age he is, seems always to be the same young man, and just as in the Platonic system, everything that exists is conceived as remembering an unchanging Idea. As Hardy mocks Pierston's agelessness, so also he makes fun of each one of these *soi-disant* versions of Platonism.

Mythological references in Victorian fiction, as J. Hillis Miller has pointed out, are often something more than mere decorations.[15] This is certainly the case in this novel where the Beloved's depiction as a Greek deity reinforces the Platonic thematic while also functioning within that thematic to establish a continuity between the past and the present: 'Sometimes at night he dreamt that she was "the wile-weaving Daughter of high Zeus" in person, bent on tormenting him for his sins against her beauty in his art – the implacable Aphrodite herself indeed' (I, II; p. 11). If the Beloved stands behind all of Pierston's loves, she too has something behind her: 'In this he was aware, however, that though it might be *now, as heretofore*, the Loved who danced before him, it was *the Goddess behind her* who pulled the string of that Jumping Jill. . . . He began to have misgivings as to some queer trick that his migratory Beloved was about to play him, or rather *the capricious Divinity behind that ideal lady*' (II, I [p. 64]; II, v [p. 88]: italics mine). Even with such impressive credentials, the Beloved is still subject to mockery. For one thing, her ideality is tinged with materiality. Pierston's relationship to each of the major embodiments of the Beloved is mediated in some way. In the case of Nichola, her dress catches his eye; laundry and sheets help further his relationship with Avice the Second; with the third Avice, it is the shoe jammed between the rocks when he saves her, which he subsequently pockets. The most ironic example is Marcia's wet clothes which he dries for her: 'Then Jocelyn opened proceedings, overhauling the robes and extending them one by one. As the steam went up he fell into a reverie. . . . The Well-Beloved was moving house – had gone over to the wearer of this attire. In the course of ten minutes he adored her' (I, v; p. 27). The last sentence betrays a certain irony on the narrator's part. This emerges more clearly in the way in which the narrator's terms contrast with the terms Pierston uses to characterise the Beloved. Pierston resorts to biblical language: 'As flesh she dies daily, like the Apostle's corporeal self' (I, IX; p. 52). The narrator's version is somewhat different: 'She would flit away, leaving the poor, empty carcase that had lodged her to mumm on as best it could without her' (I, IX; p. 50). The narrator repeatedly uses words like 'corpse' and 'carcase' to describe the Beloved's 'remains', and these clash with the solemn language Pierston uses in turning her into a mythological figure. This linguistic gesture summarises the narrator's entire attitude towards Pierston. Whereas Pierston tends to idealise the material, the narrator, in contrast, points toward what Hardy calls the 'physiological fact' of life. This, of course, implies pointing towards death, which most often interrupts and suspends the kinds of continuity Pierston tries to establish.

Like Pierston, the geography of the island has the peculiar characteristic of always seeming the same despite the passage of time:

> More than ever the spot *seemed what it was said once to have been*, the ancient Vindilia Island, and the Home of the Slingers. . . . All now stood dazzlingly unique and white against the tinted sea, and the sun flashed on *infinitely* stratified walls of oolite,

> > The melancholy ruins
> > Of cancelled cycles, . . .

. . . Jocelyn looked round the familiar premises, glanced across the Common at the great yards within which *eternal* saws were going to and fro upon *eternal* blocks of stone – the very *same* saws and the very *same* blocks that he had seen there when last in the island, so it seemed to him. . . .

Twenty years had spread their films over the events which wound up with the reunion of the second Avice and her husband; and the hoary *peninsula called an island* looked just the *same* as before. (I, 1 [pp. 3, 4, 6]; III, 1 [p. 145]: italics in the prose mine)

The island seems another version of Pierston's Temperament, a somewhat material *topos noetos*. As it is continuous with its own past, so also is it continuous with the mainland – 'the hoary peninsula called an island'. However, in this 'unique', 'white', and 'eternal' rural English version of the Greek philosopher's ideal place, Hardy seems once again to be undermining Platonism. The 'very same'-ness of the island seems somewhat exaggerated, and the narrator's 'so it seemed to him' stands out too pointedly. What this last qualification suggests is that the continuity and sameness he finds is only a matter of perception. This possibility also arises at one point where Pierston remembers the island: 'The unconscious habit, common to so many people, of *tracing likes in unlikes* had often led him to discern, or *to fancy he discerned*, in the Roman atmosphere . . . the atmosphere of his native promontory. Perhaps it was that *in each case the eye was mostly resting on stone* – that the quarries of ruins in the Eternal City reminded him of the quarries of maiden rock at home' (III, 1; p. 146: italics and ellipsis mine). Hardy gives the formula for the sameness Pierston finds in everything – 'tracing likes in unlikes'. The infinitely repeatable idea, whether in the form of Pierston's Temperament, the island, or the Beloved, is the work of the imagination, and hence as illusory as Pierston's agelessness: 'I thought that what you looked you were' (III, IV; p. 177). The Platonic idea, the Greek word *eidos*, also means vision, aspect, how something appears to sight. The identity of rock and ruin Pierston imagines depends on vision – 'in each case the *eye* was mostly resting on stone.' The application of the same word 'quarries' to both 'ruins' and 'maiden rock' marks the positing of identity. The ruins only apparently resemble the quarries; Pierston only appears to be eternally young; the island only looks the same; and, as I shall point out, the three Avices only *seem* to be one.

The island also serves as an ideal place for assuring historical continuity and genealogical repetition. Its self-enclosure promotes intermarriage and the perpetuation of a limited number of family names: 'He remembered who had used to live there – and probably lived there now – the Caro family; the "roan-mare" Caros, as they were called to distinguish them from other branches of the same pedigree, there being but half-a-dozen christian and surnames in the whole island' (I, I; p. 4). This peculiarity of the island accounts for the repetition of the name Avice through three generations. Just as the repetition of the names is aided by Pierston's changing of one of the women's names, so also his talent for tracing likes in unlikes aids genetic repetition: 'From his roomy castle and its grounds and the cliffs hard by he could command every move and aspect of her who was the rejuvenated Spirit of the Past to him – in the effulgence of whom *all sordid details were disregarded.* . . . He could not read her individual character, owing to the confusing effect of her likeness to a woman whom he had valued too late. He could not help seeing in her all that he knew of another, and *veiling in her all that did not harmonize with his sense of metempsychosis*' (II, VIII [p. 103]; II, VI [p. 92]). The 'continuity through three generations' of his 'genealogical passion' does have its basis in fact. The three Avices do resemble each other: 'The three Avices, the second something like the first, the third a glorification of the first, at all events externally, were the outcome of the immemorial island customs of intermarriage and of prenuptial union, under which conditions the type of feature was almost uniform from parent to child through generations' (III, II; p. 161). Where Pierston finds similarity he posits identity. Of the second Avice: 'She was in all respects the Avice he had lost. . . . Before she had receded a hundred yards he felt certain that it was Avice indeed; and his unifying mood of the afternoon was now so intense that the lost and the found Avice seemed essentially the same person. Their external likeness to each other – probably owing to the cousinship between the elder and her husband – went far to nourish the *fantasy.* . . . this perfect copy . . . her mother's image' (II, IV [p. 81]; II, V [p. 86]; II, VI [pp. 93, 95]: italics mine). Of the third: 'It was the very she, in all essential particulars . . . who had kissed him forty years before. . . . the thing itself in the guise of a lineal successor . . . this terribly belated edition of the Beloved . . . "Therefore I do not require to learn her; she was learnt by me in her previous existences"'(III, I [p. 154]; III, II [p. 161]; III, III [p. 163]). By reducing three different women to one woman, Pierston turns genealogy into yet another version of Platonic idealism. The lineal successor remembers the ancestor just as the embodiment remembers the ideal. As the ideal has priority over its representations, the genealogical predessor holds ascendancy over her descendants.

This version of Platonism is, like the others, mocked and undermined. The narrator's description of Avice Caro's idealisation is clearly ironic: 'He loved the woman dead and inaccessible as he had never loved her in life. . . . Now she was a corpse. . . . The flesh was absent altogether; it was love rarefied and refined to its highest attar. He had felt nothing like it before' (II, III; pp. 74 – 5: ellipses mine). As I shall later argue, this seems also to be an example of Hardy's mockery of the aesthete's cultivation of sensation. There is some doubt as to whether Avice really embodies the ideal: 'But did he see the Well-Beloved in Avice at all?' (I, II; p. 11). Like the Beloved's representations, Avice's descendants might not so much repeat her as constitute her. Avice also, like the Beloved, seems to embody an historical continuity, to have an origin behind her of which she is merely a repetition and a continuation:

> Avice, the departed one, though she had come short of inspiring a passion, had yet possessed a ground-quality absent from her rivals, without which it seemed that a fixed and full-rounded constancy to a woman could not flourish in him. Like his own, her family had been islanders for centuries -- from Norman, Anglian, Roman, Balearic-British times. Hence in her nature, as in his, was some mysterious ingredient sucked from the isle; otherwise a racial instinct necessary to the absolute unison of a pair. Thus, though he might never love a woman of the island race, for lack in her of the desired refinement, he could not love long a kimberlin – a woman other than of the island race, for her lack of this groundwork of character. (II, III; p. 76).

The narrator undercuts this racial version of the Platonic model by pointing out that Avice is, in fact, an aberration from the island race. She refuses to follow the ancient custom of 'prenuptial union', and she has been taught 'to forget all the experiences of her ancestors; to drown . . . the local vocabulary by a governess-tongue of no country at all' (I, II; p. 13: ellipsis mine). Significantly, in the end Pierston is undone by her granddaughter's marriage to a kimberlin.

The repetition of names,[16] as I suggested, reinforces the identity of the three women. Considered in terms of Plato's *Cratylus*, it might also be an attempt to turn a false, or arbitrary, name into a true, or motivated, one. The name Avice derives from *eidos*.[17] In this sense, the continuity of the name is the continuity of the idea; to repeat the name is to assure the repeatability of the idea. This aspect of Pierston's Platonism is undermined through a confusion of reference: ' "Well, Ann or otherwise, you are Avice to me." . . . He could not get further, and after a while Pierston left them, and went away thinking of Avice more than ever. . . . His appreciativeness was capable of exercising itself only on utilitarian matters, and recollection of Avice's good qualities alone had any effect on his mind; of her appearance none at all' (II, IV [p. 82]; II, V [p. 87]; III, VIII [p. 209]). The name seems to refer to one person in each case, but it could also refer to another, or to two others. Here, the tracing of likenesses in order to gain a unity produces a multiplicity. Instead of 'One shape of many names', 'One name of many shapes'.

Hardy's mockery of Platonism is inseparable from his mockery of aestheticism. For instance, it is possible to read into his ironic presentation of Pierston's agelessness a mockery of Oscar Wilde's *The Portrait of Dorian Grey*, the fanfare about which, during its serial publication in 1890, just after the rejection of *Tess of the d'Urbervilles*, might easily have influenced Hardy. At that same time, Hardy was asking, in his essay on English fiction, 'how best to circumvent the present lording of *nonage* over maturity'. In this sense, Pierston is an ironic version of the perfect fictional character, both young and old at the same time, who was undoubtedly meant to please the most fastidious taste. Hardy's mockery of Pierston's aestheticism in the novel seems also to have for its target a particular novel as well as a particular English attitude. That novel might be *Marius the Epicurean*, and the attitude what Hardy calls 'English prudery'. Like Pierston, Marius also seems ageless, and both end up going to that most ageless of cities, Rome. Especially in the beginning of the novel, Pierston's sensitive appreciation of things resembles that of Marius: 'He stretched out his hand upon the rock beside him. It felt warm. That was the island's personal temperature when in its afternoon sleep as now. He listened, and heard sounds: whirr-whirr, saw-saw-saw. Those were the island's snores – the noises of the quarrymen and stone-sawyers' (I, 1; p. 4). This offers a somewhat ironic version of the Epicure's gem-like flame. With Pierston's loss of creativity at the end of the novel comes a simultaneous loss of taste or appreciation: 'On another afternoon they went to the National Gallery, to test his taste in paintings, which had formerly been good. As she had expected, it was just the same with him there. He saw no more to move him, he declared, in the time-defying presentations of Perugino, Titian, Sebastiano, and other statuesque creators than in the work of the pavement artist they had passed on their way' (III, VIII; p. 213). The 'time-defying presentations' that Pater delighted in describing are here compared with one of the most short-lived forms of art. This also points out an ironic contrast between desired permanence and inevitable transcience, aesthetic appreciation and the commercial necessities of life. Like Marius, Pierston also seems asexual. When, in his essay, Hardy spoke out against a lack of candour concerning sex, he placed himself in opposition to the aesthetic idealisation of woman. Hardy's mock excuse for Pierston in the novel seems also directed against English prudery:

> The probable ridicule that would result to him from the events of the day he did not mind in itself at all. But he would fain have removed the misapprehensions on which it would be based. That, however, was impossible. Nobody would ever know the truth about him; *what* it was he had sought . . . and had at last, as he believed just now in the freshness of his loss, been discovered in the girl who had left him. It was not the flesh; he had never knelt low to that. Not a woman in the world had been wrecked by him, though he had been impassioned by so many. . . . His attraction to the third Avice would be regarded by the world as the selfish designs of an elderly man on a maid. (III, VII; p. 202)

Hardy does not simply mock the English reading public's demand for asexual fiction. He also accuses it of reading-in sex where only idealism can be found.[18] After the rejection of *Tess of the d'Urbervilles* for its explicit treatment of sex, Hardy here turns around and gives his publishers exactly what they wanted in a somewhat exaggerated, and indeed, caricatured, form. The spirit of his gesture is summed up in a comment in the *Life*: 'There is more fleshliness in *The Loves of the Triangles* than in this story.'[19]

To the list of Hardy's victims in the aesthetic movement can be added Rossetti. Pierston, in his habit of reducing all to the same idea of a Beloved and of tracing likes in unlikes, bears a great deal of similarity to Rossetti as Holman Hunt describes him: 'Rossetti's tendency . . . in sketching a face was to convert the features of his sitter to his favourite ideal type, and if he finished on these lines, the drawing was extremely charming, but you had to make believe a good deal to see the likeness, while if the sitter's features would not lend themselves to the pre-ordained form, he, when time allowed, went through a stage of reluctant twisting of lines and quantities to make the drawing satisfactory.'[20] Remarking on this passage, John Dixon Hunt writes: 'Rossetti arranged the real world after a vision of his ideal beauty. Which explains why his various models – Elizabeth Siddal, Mrs. Morris, Fanny Cornforth . . . – all leave the impression of being the same woman.'[21] If Pierston is a composite aesthete, then surely Rossetti is one of his components.

Reductiveness in the novel functions as well with Hardy's mockery of a particular kind of light, conventional novel. Hardy creates a kind of no-novel in which the usual novelistic conventions of time (genealogy), place (geography), and character are sought to be reduced into an unchanging sameness. Time in this novel would like not to move; the present seems to repeat the past. Action is only the repetition of previous action. The place of the novel, the island, masquerades as immutability. Pierston's character and his appearance – albeit only in a certain light – is as static as time or the island. He is the eternally 'Young Man', and Avice, of course, is always the same old Avice. The novel, finally, is a bit unbelievable, mocking its own prosy boredom, but that, it seems, is how Hardy wanted it to be.

Hardy's mockery of Platonism, aestheticisms, and the conventional novel come together at the end of the novel. There, all of the continuities – of Temperament, of art, of genealogy, of geography, of the Beloved – are broken, and Hardy inserts enough ironic twists to guarantee that they cannot be repaired. Pierston loses his aesthetic Temperament and gives up art. Genealogical tradition is broken in his marriage to Marcia, a kimberlin. He finally regains a lost love, but, ironically, it is the wrong one. The Beloved ceases with his desire for her.

As for the undermining of geographical continuity, we see it functioning at the novel's close within Hardy's mockery of aestheticism. In the Preface, he had warned of a threat to the island's stony hegemony: 'Yet perhaps it is as well that the artistic visitors do not come, or no more would be heard of little freehold houses being bought and sold there for a couple of hundred pounds – built of solid stone, and dating from the sixteenth century and earlier, with mullions, copings, and corbels complete' (p. viii). Throughout the novel, in a reductive way, these cottages are portrayed as being one with the island: 'Like the island it was all of stone . . . framed from mullions to chimney-top like the isle itself, of stone' (I, 1 [p. 4]; II, III [p. 75]). Pierston, the native of natives, ends by destroying these cottages, and hence, the island's continuity with itself: 'He was also engaged in acquiring some old moss-grown, mullioned Elizabethan cottages, for the purpose of pulling them down because they were damp; which he afterwards did, and built new ones with hollow walls, and full of ventilators' (III, VIII; p. 218). Hardy makes fun of the aesthete, the 'artistic visitor' whose appreciation turns to a desire to improve.

Hardy's attack on the conventional novel appears in the end as Pierston's marriage to Marcia, what Hardy calls 'the regulation finish that "they married and were happy ever after"':[22] 'It chanced that a day or two before the ceremony . . . Marcia's rheumatism suddenly became acute. . . . and as they thought it undesirable to postpone their union for such a reason, Marcia, after being well wrapped up, was wheeled into the church in a chair' (III, VIII; p. 216: ellipses mine). The word 'union' can only be ironic within the context. The implication seems to be that the only marriage suitable for popular fiction is one in which sex is a bygone possibility.

The final paragraph of the original version of the novel is much more obviously ironic than the later version: '"I-I-it is too, too droll - this ending to my would-be romantic history!" Ho-ho-ho!'[23] Pierston seems to be talking about the novel itself as a would-be romantic history. This self-consciousness seems doubled by the narrator who gets in the last laugh at Pierston's expense – 'Ho-ho-ho!' In the later version, Hardy seems to succeed in preserving this self-consciousness: 'At present he is sometimes mentioned as "the late Mr. Pierston" by gourd-like young art-critics and journalists; and his productions are alluded to as those of a man not without genius, whose powers were insufficiently recognized in his lifetime' (III, VIII; p. 218). The 'gourd-like young art-critics' could be a reference to the gourd-like Wilde, who, at that time, would have been mourning the death of the late Mr Pater. More importantly, the narrator's ironic attitude towards Pierston turns back upon himself. By revealing his own historical position ('At present') he undermines his own former omniscience. This opens the possibility of an autobiographical gesture.[24] Considering that this is the last sentence of the last novel Hardy will ever write, it is as if he were talking of a late version of himself who used to write novels, but 'whose powers were insufficiently recognized in his lifetime'.

NOTES

1. Thomas Hardy, 'Candour in English Fiction', *New Review*, II (January 1890) 15.

2. Thomas Hardy, *Life's Little Ironies* (London: Macmillan, 1912) p. vii.

3. 'An Imaginative Woman', *Life's Little Ironies*, p. 25.

4. The one critic I have found who treats the novel's irony in any depth is Joseph Warren Beach: 'There is in the treatment of Pierston's obsession a note of levity, of light irony, rather well sustained' (*The Technique of Thomas Hardy* [Chicago: University of Chicago Press, 1922] p. 131).

5. J. I. M. Stewart, *Thomas Hardy: A Critical Biography* (London: Longman, 1971) p. 159.

6. Hardy, 'Candour', p. 17.

7. Florence Emily Hardy, *The Later Years of Thomas Hardy, 1892–1928* (London and New York: Macmillan, 1930) p. 59.

8. Florence Emily Hardy, *The Early Life of Thomas Hardy, 1840–1891* (London and New York: Macmillan, 1928) p. 284. This diary entry is found adjacent to an entry about *The Well-Beloved*: ' "February 6. (After reading Plato's dialogue 'Cratylus'): A very good way of looking at things would be to regard everything as having an actual or false name, and an intrinsic or true name, to ascertain which all endeavour should be made. . . . The fact is that nearly all things are falsely, or rather inadequately, named." '

9. For a detailed discussion of topical references in the novel, see Michael Millgate, *Thomas Hardy: His Career as a Novelist* (London: The Bodley Head; New York: Random House, 1971) pp. 293–307.

10. Given by Stewart, p. 158.

11. Hardy, 'Candour', p. 18 (ellipsis mine).

12. Hardy, 'Candour', pp. 19–21 *passim*.

13. *Early Life*, p. 284.

14. Given in an appendix in Thomas Hardy, *The Well-Beloved: A Sketch of a Temperament*, ed. J. Hillis Miller (London: Macmillan, 1975) pp. 216–17 [paperback edition] (ellipsis mine).

15. See also Edward Mendelson's annotations of Hardy's references to mythological figures, in Miller's edition of *The Well-Beloved*, pp. 207–14 *passim*.

16. For a discussion of the repetition of names and the use of dithematic names in Wessex, see Henry Bosley Woolf, *The Old Germanic Principles of Name-Giving* (Baltimore: Johns Hopkins Press, 1939) pp. 70–94.

17. Hardy writes of *The Well-Beloved* in the *Early Life*: 'The story of a face which goes through three generations or more, would make a fine novel or poem of the passage of Time. The differences in personality to be ignored' (p. 284).

I have already noticed Hardy's puns in Pierston's name. The same is true of Avice Caro. At one point in the *Life* he suggests that he chose *Caro* because it means 'dear' (*Later Years*, p. 60), but he says nothing of *Avice* except that it is a name common to the island. *Avice*, or *Avis*, is also an obsolete form of *advice*, hence *aviso* means an intelligence or advice. An old form of *advise* is *avise*, which comes from the Latin *advisum* – view or opinion. *Vision*, of course, derives from *videre*, to see, and is therefore related to the *visum* of *advisum*. The first meaning of *advice* is 'the way in which a matter is looked at', and the first meanings of *advise* are 'to look at, view, observe', 'to bring a thing into view', and 'to look at mentally, to revise'. From *spicere*, the other Latin verb for seeing, we get *aspect* – look, view, appearance. To see, perceive, appear, seem are all notions bound up in the Greek word *eidolon*, meaning image, likeness, form, or apparition. And this word is linked to *eidos* (form, or shape) – Plato's idea, which also means the aspect of the thing as it appears to vision. *Eidos* implies *helios*, the sun, that which allows things to be seen. By a somewhat circuitous, but etymologically valid, route, we move thus from *Avice* to *eidos*, from the 'dear vision' to the 'dear idea'.

In the *Cratylus*, Plato says about the Greek word for name: 'The word ὄνομα seems to be a compressed sentence, signifying ὄν οὗ ζήτημα (being for which there is a search), as is still more obvious in ὀνομαστον (notable), which states in so many words that real existence is that for which there is a seeking (ὄν οὗ μάσμα); ἀλήθεια is also an agglomeration of θεία ἄλη (divine wandering), implying the divine motion of existence' (trans. Benjamin Jowett [1871]; in *The Collected Dialogues of Plato*, ed. Edith Hamilton and Huntington Cairns, Bollingen Series LXXI [1961; rpt. Princeton: Princeton University Press, 1973], p. 456). In reading this, one should keep in mind the original title of the novel – *The Pursuit of the Well-Beloved*. The name *Avice* might be highly significant in this pursuit or search, for it might name both a person and the object of the pursuit – *eidos*. What is named in the Greek word for name is what the Beloved is doing most often – wandering. The being for which Pierston searches, then, is the name – *eidos*/Avice.

At the end of the dialogue, Socrates rejects the Heraclitan flux in favour of his own version of how and what we know: 'Then how can that be a real thing which is never in the same state? For obviously things which are the same cannot change while they remain the same, and if they are always the same and in the same state, and never depart from their original form, they can never change or be moved. . . . But if that which knows and that which is known exist ever, and the beautiful and the good and every other thing also exist, then I do not think that they can resemble a process or flux' (pp. 473–4). We recognise in this the model of Pierston's idealism. Here we are also given the cause of its demise in Heraclitus' infamous notion. The overthrow of Pierston's idealism is in many ways a reversal of the end of Plato's dialogue. Flux overcomes that which wishes to remain the same.

18. Michael Millgate notes: 'It appears from a passage deleted from *Later Years* that Hardy believed *The Well-Beloved* had simply been made the pretext for a pre-determined onslaught: "It made him say, naturally enough, 'What foul cess-pits some men's minds must be, and what a Night-cart would be required to empty them!' " ' (p. 295).

19. *Later Years*, p. 60.

20. W. Holman Hunt, *Pre-Raphaelitism and the Pre-Raphaelite Brotherhood* (London: Macmillan, 1905) I, 341.

21. John Dixon Hunt, *The Pre-Raphaelite Imagination 1848–1900* (Lincoln: University of Nebraska Press, 1968) p. 187.

22. Hardy, 'Candour', p. 17.

23. *The Illustrated London News*, 17 December 1892, p. 775. In the appendix of the New Wessex Edition of the novel, the marks closing the quotation were changed so that the final 'Ho-ho-ho!' is included within Pierston's speech (p. 249 [paperback]). In the original serial version, the marks come after 'history!', thus placing the final laugh in the narrator's voice.

24. Helmut E. Gerber discusses the bitterness of the last two pages of the novel in relationship to Hardy's decision to give up novel-writing in his 'Hardy's *The Well-Beloved* as a Comment on the Well-Despised', *ELN*, 1 (1963) 48–53.

11 *Jude the Obscure*: Pessimism and Fictional Form

DAVID LODGE

We can all agree, perhaps, that *Jude the Obscure* is about frustration and failure in two areas of life – sex and education. It is about Jude Fawley's failure to get to the University, and about his disastrous relationships with women. But as soon as we ask what is the meaning of these themes as presented in the narrative, doubt and disagreement commence.

Some readers interpret the novel as an indictment of the society that made it impossible for a working man to obtain higher education and that punished any deviation from conventional norms of sexual behaviour. And there is some justification in the text for such a reading, which sees Jude and Sue as martyrs in the cause of progress and enlightenment. 'Our ideas were fifty years too soon to be any good to us', says Jude at the end. But is it true that he and Sue would have been happier in the age of the Open University and the Permissive Society? Hardly. If we look closely at the narrative we see that Jude's failure to get to the University is largely the result of his own character and his involvement with Arabella and Sue. There *were* very real social and economic forces working against a man in his position and with his aspirations, but they are only portrayed in the margins, so to speak, of the story; and Jude never puts them seriously to the test. When he realises the hopelessness of his academic ambitions, this realisation is presented in terms of awakening from a delusive dream and perceiving his own folly and impracticality. 'Well, all that was clear to him amounted to this, that the whole scheme had burst up, like an iridescent soap-bubble, under the touch of a reasoned enquiry' (II, vi; p. 136). Jude then recognises that his destiny lies among the ordinary working people of Christminster, and there is some suggestion that this could be a valuable and fulfilling life — more so than the lives of scholars and students. 'He began to see that the town life was a book of humanity infinitely more palpitating, varied, and compendious than the gown life.' This sounds hopeful, yet one could scarcely say that it is confirmed by the rest of the novel. In so far as the ordinary people of Christminster are presented — and it is not very far — they are a rather unpleasant and unsympathetic group, whose lives seem mean, narrow and monotonous rather than 'palpitating, varied, and compendious'. There is in fact no fulfilling community available to Jude.

If we turn to the sexual theme, we find the same ambiguity and negativity. In its own day the novel was seen as an attack on the institution of marriage, but again this is a very marginal implication. Neither Jude nor Sue finds much difficulty in obtaining the dissolution of their ill-advised marriages, but divorce does not solve their problems. Social disapproval of their irregular union is not the most important of these problems. Sue is in fact incapable of making Jude happy either inside or outside marriage because of her sexual frigidity and because (as we are frequently reminded) they are cousins in a family with a sombre history of marital problems. The story confirms this suggestion of a hereditary weakness where matrimony is concerned. Sue's marriage and remarriage to Phillotson are contracted in obedience to her own peculiar neurotic drives, just as, in marrying and remarrying Arabella, Jude is essentially a dupe and victim, a Samson to her Delilah (a picture of this Biblical couple ominously decorates the wall of an inn they visit during their courtship).

In short, there is no suggestion, in the novel, that the protagonists could have achieved happy and fulfilled lives. Their ideals and aspirations prove to be vain, impracticable illusions, and when they try alternative courses of action these too prove to be disappointing, or worse. Jude and Sue are trapped in a maze of unhappiness, from which there is no escape — except death. The last words of the novel, spoken by Arabella about Sue after Jude's death, are: 'She's never found peace since she left his arms, and never will again till she's as he is now!' This saying, as Michael Millgate has observed,[1] echoes a sentiment from one of Hardy's favourite texts, the *Oedipus Rex* of Sophocles: 'Call no man happy ere he shall have crossed the boundary of life, the sufferer of nought painful.' Perhaps more significantly, it agrees with an authorial comment very early in the novel about the boy Jude's abnormal sensitivity. This is a typical sentence of Hardy's in that it is full of small surprises or shocks; it keeps going on after you expect it to stop, becoming more and more daunting: 'This weakness of character, as it may be called, suggested that he was the sort of man who was born to ache a good deal before the fall of the curtain upon his unnecessary life should signify that all was well with him again' (I, II; p. 13).

Jude the Obscure is, by general agreement, Thomas Hardy's bleakest, most pessimistic, most depressing novel. What I want to examine in the rest of this essay is the way the form of *Jude* works to articulate and reinforce the pessimism of its vision of life. I use the word *form* in its widest sense to include all the means of literary presentation from the largest to the smallest in scope: the design of the plot, the point of view of the narration, the tone of the narrator, symbolic action, figurative language, right down to the construction of the simplest sentences. In one sense everything in a novel is form, since it is only by virtue of having form that a novel communicates at all. But we become conscious of form, as readers, through the perception of recurrence and repetition (and the negative kind of repetition which is contrast) in the stream of apparently random or historically 'given' particularity that, in the realistic novel tradition to which Hardy belonged, creates the illusion of life. In practice, Hardy was often prepared to risk breaking realistic illusion for the sake of an expressive effect. In this respect he had a kinship with American rather than European novelists of the nineteenth century, such as Hawthorne and Melville. But *Jude*, his last work of fiction, is a highly patterned novel which rarely strains the reader's credulity, with the exception perhaps of the murder of the children and some of the dialogue that is put into the characters' mouths. On the whole *Jude* combines a Sophoclean sense of tragic fate with the scrupulous verisimilitude of nineteenth-century realism and naturalism. No wonder it makes uncomfortable reading.

In a famous passage of Proust's *A la recherche du temps perdu*, Marcel, putting forward the theory that every novelist's work has a secret signature which makes it unmistakably *his* creation, refers to what he calls the 'stone-mason's geometry' which gives Hardy's novels their special character.[2] By this phrase he means the elaborate concern for parallelism and symmetry with which Hardy constructed his novels – a trait that Marcel attributes to Hardy's training and professional experience as an architect. The idea seems particularly illuminating with regard to *Jude the Obscure*, and not merely because the hero is himself a stone-mason by trade. The plot, for instance, considered in its bare outline as a design or structure, is strikingly symmetrical: the two marriages, the two divorces, the two remarriages. As Jude changes from religious belief to scepticism, so Sue changes from scepticism to religious belief. As Arabella changes from worldliness to religiosity and back to worldliness, so Phillotson changes from conventionality to unconventionality and back again to conventionality. This intricate pattern of shifting relationships between the two couples, which leaves them all, in the end, as they began, trapped with uncongenial and incompatible partners, embodies the idea which I find central to *Jude* – that life is a closed system of disappointment from which only death offers an escape.

Such a permutation of relationships between two couples could, of course, have provided the basis for a comedy. It doesn't, in this case, because the human consequences are tragic and painful, because the tone of the narrative is grave, and for several other obvious reasons. In the form of a novel, all the components are interdependent. Its effect is cumulative, and every word makes its contribution. I can best illustrate the point, however, by talking about larger units of meaning than words and sentences – by talking about scenes, or incidents or gestures. Most of the incidents in the novel belong to a series or 'set', all the items of which are related to each other either by similarity or by contrast. Indeed most incidents can be placed in more than one such series, and it is this complexity and multiplicity of cross-reference that prevents the elaborate patterning of *Jude* from seeming too obviously willed by the novelist. We have, rather, the sense of an inevitable destiny underlying the apparently gratuitous particularity of the stream of experience.

Let us first took at a specific example – the famous, or notorious, scene in which Jude first meets Arabella. The young Jude is walking along a country road, meditating enthusiastically upon his academic ambitions, oblivious to the provocative cry of 'Hoity-toity' from Arabella and her two companions, who are washing chitterlings in a stream behind the hedge.

> ' . . . I can work hard. I have staying power in abundance, thank God! and it is that which tells. . . . Yes, Christminster shall be my Alma Mater; and I'll be her beloved son, in whom she shall be well pleased.'

In his deep concentration on these transactions of the future

Jude's walk had slackened, and he was now standing quite still, looking at the ground as though the future were thrown thereon by a magic lantern. On a sudden something smacked him sharply in the ear, and he became aware that a soft cold substance had been flung at him, and had fallen at his feet.

A glance told him what it was – a piece of flesh, the characteristic part of a barrow-pig, which the countrymen used for greasing their boots, as it was useless for any other purpose. Pigs were rather plentiful hereabout, being bred and fattened in large numbers in certain parts of North Wessex. (I, VI; p. 41)

The symbolic and prophetic function of this incident need not be laboured. The seduction of Jude by the coarsely sexual Arabella is to be the first major check to Jude's academic ambitions, and this could scarcely be more vividly foreshadowed than by making her hit him on the ear with the sexual organ of a pig[3] at the moment when he is rapt in his dream of scholarly achievement. What may not be so obvious is that this particular incident, vivid and expressive in its own place, also has parallels before and after in the narrative.

To begin with, it belongs to a series of moments of disillusionment, or 'rude awakening', which in their constant recurrence make up the primary rhythm of Jude's life. I have already referred to one such moment: when Jude's scheme to study at Christminster 'burst up, like an iridescent soap-bubble, under the touch of a reasoned enquiry'. The shock of Arabella's missile is clearly a premonition of that later rude awakening, for the simile of the soap-bubble, applied to Jude's plans, is matched by the image of the magic lantern in the earlier passage. It is important to recognize that the throwing of the pig's pizzle does not only reflect upon the thrower – it also represents the reality principle breaking in upon illusion.

A more obvious parallel appears in the second chapter of the novel, when Jude, in a mood of sympathetic identification with the rooks whom he is being paid to frighten away, encourages them to eat the corn, and suddenly receives a smart blow on the buttocks from the irate farmer. Other moments of disillusionment and deflation include: Physician Vilbert's failure to remember his promise to supply Jude with Latin and Greek grammars; Jude's bitter disappointment on discovering that there is no quick method of learning those languages; Phillotson's failure to recognise Jude when the latter seeks him out in the spirit of a disciple visiting his old master; the crass materialism of the composer of the hymn that had moved Jude so deeply that he made a pilgrimage to meet him; Jude's discovery on his wedding night that Arabella wears false hair; and his realisation, when Sue leaves Phillotson and elopes with him, that she does not want to consummate their love. One could multiply examples.

Going back to the first encounter of Arabella and Jude, it is worth noting that she throws the pig's pizzle in order to attract his attention, because she is separated and concealed from him by a hedge and a stream. As the scene proceeds they exchange a few words, then Jude breaks through the hedge and he and Arabella walk along the two opposite banks of the stream until they reach a small footbridge where they can meet. The scene thus belongs to another series which runs through the whole of Hardy's fiction, but which is particularly marked in *Jude the Obscure*. J. Hillis Miller has described them as scenes 'which . . . dramatise some form of obstructed relationship',[4] because in them, communication takes place across window-sills, through doors, across streams, or by letter. It is an indication of Sue's neurotic sensibility that she actually prefers obstructed or oblique communication to a direct encounter. One remembers the extraordinary exchange of notes between herself and Phillotson in their school in which she begs to be released from their marriage. And when Jude visits her shortly before that episode at Shaston, she dismisses him, and then, as he is going through the garden, opens the window and calls him back. 'I can talk to you better like this than when you were inside', she says; and the narrator, or Jude, observes: 'Now that the high window-sill was between them, so that he could not get at her, she seemed not to mind indulging in a frankness she had feared at close quarters' (IV, I; p. 246). Arabella, in contrast, always seeks the direct encounter, in which she can bring her physical presence into play. When Jude discovers her serving in the Christminster pub, they talk across the bar for a while, but she insists on meeting him outside, where she immediately takes his arm and, by the end of the evening, she sleeps with him; just as at their first meeting she talked to him across the stream, but exerted her sexual allure upon him at close quarters on the footbridge.

That there is something coarse, degrading and, to a fastidious sensibility, disgusting about Arabella's sexuality, is suggested by her close association with, of all animals, pigs. It is with a pig's sexual organ that Arabella first attracts Jude's attention; it is with the botched killing of a pig that their marriage reaches its crisis and breakdown; and it is in the living quarters behind a squalid pork-butcher's shop that she finally succeeds in recapturing him.

In trying to account for the peculiarly bleak and depressing effect of *Jude the Obscure*, we can reasonably point to the fact that it is the least pastoral, most urban of the Wessex novels. Much of the action takes place in towns and cities, in railway trains,[5] on streets and pavements, or indoors; and these settings are described on the whole perfunctorily and reductively. The interiors are mostly dingy and uncomfortable, and the exteriors of buildings, even the colleges of Christminster, are grimy, decayed and forbidding. But the lowering effect of these drab urban and domestic settings is intensified by the fact that the country, in so far as it is described at all, is equally *dreary*, to use a word that frequently appears in *Jude*. The very first chapter describes Marygreen, where Jude grows up, as a village totally lacking in charm or character, swathed in an oppressive clammy mist; and in the following chapter the ploughed field in which Jude is working calls from him the murmured observation, 'How ugly it is here!' (p. 10). Readers of *Jude the Obscure* are made to feel that there is not much to choose between town and country as environments, that they are both equally drab and unattractive. Again we encounter the peculiarly negative quality of this novel – the cancelling out of alternatives which makes the pursuit of happiness by the protagonists seem a vain endeavour. It is clearly part of Hardy's deliberate avoidance of anything approaching the quality of pastoral idyll, in *Jude*, that the only rural activity to be portrayed in any detail is the rearing of pigs. It makes *Jude* the antithesis of a novel like *Far from the Madding Crowd*, with its loving, lyrical descriptions of the seasonal tasks of the land, and a considerably bleaker novel than *Tess of the d'Urbervilles*, which has the beauty of the valley of the Great Dairies to balance the harshness of Flintcombe-Ash. Instead of milking, sheep-shearing, haymaking and harvesting, we have in *Jude* the painfully convincing scene in which Jude kills the pig, 'a dismal, sordid, ugly spectacle' as it is justly described by the narrator – who adds, however, the qualification: 'to those who saw it as other than an ordinary obtaining of meat' (I, X; p. 75).

This ambiguous rider is characteristic of Hardy. Is Jude admired, or mocked, for his distress over the pig's death? The episode certainly belongs to another set or series in the novel, concerned with animals and human attitudes towards them: there are the rooks which the young Jude fails to frighten away, the earthworms which he takes care not to tread on, the trapped rabbit which he mercifully kills, and the pigeons which Sue impulsively frees after they have been sold to a poulterer at an auction of her and Jude's effects. 'Why should Nature's law be mutual butchery!' (V, VI; p. 371), Sue complains on this occasion; while Jude earlier perceived from his experience with Farmer Troutham, 'the flaw in the terrestrial scheme, by which what was good for God's birds was bad for God's gardener' (I, II; p. 13). Again we encounter what might be called the heads-you-win-tails-I-lose syndrome in Jude the Obscure. There is, it appears, no morally irreproachable attitude towards the butchering of a pig.

To perceive how Arabella's throwing of the pig's offal belongs to the same set as the pig-killing scene, which itself recalls Jude's tenderness towards the rooks, which in turn is connected, through the parallel of the blow on the buttocks and the blow on the ear, with the pig's offal scene – to perceive these cross-references is to get some idea of the intricacy of Hardy's 'stone-mason's geometry' in Jude the Obscure. And we have far from exhausted the ramifications of the passage with which we started. Jude's last recorded thought just before he is hit on the ear is: 'Yes, Christminster shall be my Alma Mater; and I'll be her beloved son, in whom she shall be well pleased.' This, of course, is an allusion to the baptism of Christ by John the Baptist in the New Testament, when a voice from heaven was heard to pronounce these words of approval and a dove descended upon the head of the Saviour. That Jude is standing beside a stream at this point strengthens the parallel, though what descends upon him out of the sky is not a dove but a pig's pizzle. This ironic, almost blasphemous religious allusion again belongs to a series which runs through the whole novel. It was presumably not fortuitous that Hardy chose to call Jude's childhood home Marygreen, and Oxford Christminster. Certainly, Jude's ill-fated return to the city in Part Six is heavy with scriptural allusion, especially to Christ's passion. Seeing Phillotson in the crowd waiting for the Remembrance Day procession to pass, Sue remarks: 'He is evidently come up to Jerusalem to see the festival like the rest of us.' A little later she says that 'leaving Kennetbridge for this place is like coming from Caiaphas to Pilate' (VI, I; pp. 396, 397). Jude's speech to the waiting crowd – a 'sermon' as it is called by one of the auditors – and his scathing comment on the ill-treatment of the cab-horse, which brings down upon him the disapproval of authority in the person of a policeman, may be said to recall Christ's preaching in Jerusalem immediately before his Passion, as recorded in Matthew, Chapters 22–5. Jude's own passion is the horrific death of his children and the estrangement this causes between himself and Sue. 'Then let the veil of our temple be rent in two from this hour!' (VI, III; p. 427), he says when she refuses to sleep with him. In this context Jude's casual exclamation to Sue at the time of their elopement, 'There, dear; don't mind. Crucify me if you will!' (IV, v; p. 290) seems ominously prophetic.

It is clear that by identifying Jude with Christ, Hardy did not mean to confer on his hero's suffering any aura of redemptiveness or transcendence. Rather, the parallels are reductive and ironic, underlining the futility of Jude's sufferings, and the irrelevance of the Christian myth and its consolations to his plight. Whatever its sources in Hardy's personal experience, *Jude the Obscure* is, in its profound pessimism, very much a novel of its time – the period of *fin de siècle*. God is dead, and according to the doctor who attends the murdered children, there is a 'coming universal wish not to live'. 'All is trouble, adversity and suffering', Sue tells Little Father Time. As readers of *Jude the Obscure* we cannot avoid the challenge of Hardy's pessimism because of the form of the novel, in which every incident is not merely revealing and expressive in its own place, but also reinforces the meaning of innumerable other incidents, all carrying the same general implication. For the reader, as for Jude and Sue, there is no escape.

NOTES

1. Michael Millgate, *Thomas Hardy: His Career as a Novelist* (London: The Bodley Head; New York: Random House, 1971) p. 324.

2. Quoted by J. Hillis Miller in *Thomas Hardy: Distance and Desire* (London: Oxford University Press; Cambridge, Mass.: Harvard University Press, 1970) p. 206.

3. As the scene continues, there are several explicit references to this object in the text of the first edition (1895) which Hardy removed in revising the novel for the edition of 1903, and did not restore subsequently. This belated bowdlerisation of a scene which had caused great offence on the novel's first publication (one reviewer described it as 'more brutal in depravity than anything which the darkest slums could bring forth') is rather to be regretted. See 'Note on the Text' in the New Wessex Edition of *Jude the Obscure*, ed. Terry Eagleton (London: Macmillan, 1975) p. 424 (p. 439 in paperback edition).

4. Miller, p. 158.

5. The railway, which is extending its steel tentacles into Wessex in *The Woodlanders* and *Tess of the d'Urbervilles*, seems to enclose completely the terrain of *Jude the Obscure*, and provides the typical mode of travel for its characters. Indeed, so much attention is given to the use of the railway, especially by Jude, to the problems, ironies, and frustrations of such travel – waiting for connections, missing trains, planning cross-country journeys – that it does not seem fanciful to interpret the railway (a 'closed system' which allows its users a strictly limited mobility) as a symbol for life itself in this novel.

12 Hardy's Absences

JAMES R. KINCAID

Criticism of Thomas Hardy is marked by more than its share of brilliance and also of heroic ingenuity. Probably one is best advised to avoid both, and for many of us the first prohibition creates no hardship. But there may be a mere ingenuity, heroic or not, in the recurrent attempts to create either a univocal or a muddled Hardy, one who 'explained' and formed perfectly or one who offers texts already deconstructed. I think it is possible (and by no means unique) to occupy a middle ground, recognising the large and the local gaps, the 'open spaces', in Hardy texts without succumbing to the old itch to find a covering formula for the text's 'unity' or to the new itch to ignore such traditional organising patterns as there are and proclaim that the meaning of the text is indeterminate. We now acknowledge more fully the tentativeness and inconsistency of a typical Hardy narrator and the ambiguity of the action. What is not so clear are the theoretical implications of these facts or, more modestly, the effects they have on our actual reading experience.

My thesis is that our response to Hardy's narratives depends to an important degree on what is not explicitly there, on crucial absences, often emphasised *as* absences, that become present by implication in our reading. In a way, then, we generally deal not with 'open spaces' but with incongruous solidities. Not every signal possible is given by the text, and thus we have something more like formal incoherence[1] than indeterminacy. Usually, in fact, the organising patterns that we perceive are quite clear; it is only that they are multiple and contradictory. This is not to deny the complexity or subtlety of the fiction; I seek only to explore a few of the devices by which the narratives create definite but incompatible expectations, not exactly frustrating any set of expectations but refusing to allow us to fulfil our rage for order and coherence by satisfying any one set of expectations exclusively.

To approach this task and also to define more exactly what that task is, I would like to juxtapose three statements: the first by the narrator of *Jude the Obscure*, the second by Roland Barthes, and the third by John Bayley – a fittingly incoherent company:

> Events did not rhyme quite as he had thought. Nature's logic was too horrid for him to care for. That mercy towards one set of creatures was cruelty towards another sickened his sense of harmony. (I, II; p. 15)

> For these moderately plural (i.e., merely polysemous) texts, there exists an average appreciator which can grasp only a certain median portion of the plural, an instrument at once too delicate and too vague to be applied to univocal texts, and too poor to be applied to multivalent texts, which are reversible and frankly indeterminable (integrally plural texts).[2]

> [In some novelists] differentiations all work like a team, the members of which are mutually supportive, and aware of each others' duties.
>   Diversity in Hardy is quite unlike this. As with the poems, component parts of the prose seem unconscious of each other's presence. . . . It seems to be our own activities among the constituent parts of the writing that give us our sense of what is going on.[3]

The passage from *Jude* seems to support, in context, the 'radical disunity' Bayley so superbly defines;[4] it also seems to fit what Barthes would term a 'moderately plural (i.e., merely polysemous)' text, in that its meaning does not appear to be 'frankly indeterminable'.[5] Often in Hardy we find characters out to make events 'rhyme', equipped or cursed with a sense of 'harmony' that discordant nature refuses to countenance. That one act should result both in cruelty and in kindness violates any coherent approach to life or to fiction, but it does violate in discernible, determinate ways. There are clear stabilities in Hardy, generally, and somewhat surprisingly, basic moral stabilities. The passage from *Jude the Obscure* does not, after all, question what is 'cruel' and what is 'kind'. The disunity is established not only in reference to the expectation of unity but in reference to certain other givens, certain unities of effect. It may be, as Jude states later in the novel, that plans must not be judged by their 'accidental outcomes' but by 'their essential soundness' (VI, I; p. 393), and the divorce of will and action creates an enormous and interesting

problem for judgement. But even here we are not lost in indeterminacy: Jude assumes that there is a distinction between 'sound'
and 'unsound' plans, and he also assumes that outcomes are definite
and comprehensible. Thus, his denials are also affirmations that give
us a means for locating precisely what the disunity may be, how it
arises, and what effects it has.

Having said this, one must admit that things are by no means this
simple. The senses of harmony possessed by Hardy characters differ
markedly and may alter within a single character as situations vary.
The narrator also adds to the cacophony by the subtlety of his
associations and by his inconstancy. Not everything apparently
absent in Hardy is absent all the time. That which is solid as an
apparent absence – kindness, harmony, nature's beneficence in this
case – may become slippery by being made explicitly present.
Nature, for instance. Nature, we had been told, was possessed of a
'logic', though the contradictory effects of actions may make the
term 'logic' feel more than a little ironic. However, we are tempted to
suppose that there is some coherent logic, some reason behind the
kindness-cruelty contradiction and that the problem is caused by the
clash of this coherence with the expectations of a more benign
coherence, that is, with Jude's 'sense of harmony'. But a few lines later,
after allowing Jude to indulge in notions that the horror of this
disharmony, this 'rattling', would become worse as he grew older
and that therefore he had better not grow up – a coherent sequence of
reasoning, we notice, quite at odds with a universal denial of
coherence – the narrator blandly states, 'Then, like the natural boy,
he forgot his despondency, and sprang up' (I, II; p. 15). 'The natural
boy'! How are we to take the connection between 'Nature' and
'natural'? Are they two different things entirely? Impossible, but how
are they to be distinguished so as to make smooth the transition from a
'logic' in Nature that is vile to the suggestion of a 'natural' healing and
flexibility? Is it that the term 'logic' was, from the start, totally ironic,
that the whole passage constitutes a playful frustration of our desire
for univocality? Surely not that exactly, since we are able still to locate
a possibility for distinction: human nature is not the same, necessarily,
as Nature (a point coincident with the original statement), nor is
Jude's natural ability to forget the same thing, necessarily, as healing.
Not necessarily, but the whole scene does tend to swim a little in our
minds. Still, this unfocused quality is possible only because so much is
clearly focused: there is an expectation of harmony; there are acts
which are kind and cruel. No reader can doubt, here at least, that

Jude's response to Nature is serious and acute. It signals the respect we must give to his sensitivity; it asks for a painful apprehension of his vulnerability; it makes us clearly anticipate impending doom.

Such solidity as there is, in other words, makes us anticipate a tragedy. But is a tragedy what we get? Hardy, of course, hoped that 'certain cathartic, Aristotelian qualities' might be found in his fable (Postscript to *Jude The Obscure*), but there are, as many critics have noted, at least as many uncathartic, violently un-Artistotelian qualities that get in our way. Jude's humble origins may not be a problem, but his obscurity certainly is. Where is there any resonance, even significance, to his action? Who even observes it? Where is there an Ishmael or Horatio? Where is that 'epiphany of law' Frye talks about?[6] Tragic heroes do not do such undignified things as jumping up and down on unyielding ice, trying to get themselves dead and failing. Tragic catastrophes are not brought about by such purely external means as are employed with Father Time; tragic deaths are not described in such a concrete, half-comic way as 'the bumping of near thirty years had ceased' (VI, XI; p. 490). Tragedies end with a glimpse of restored order, with somebody like Fortinbras taking control, not with some animal like Arabella out to repeat her chaotic entrapments.

The tragic action is disrupted in a million ways; tragic form is demonstrably not there. But why do we, all the same, feel that it *is* there, and why is it possible to construct equally convincing arguments for its presence?[7] One way to explain this contradiction is to use Northrop Frye's mythos of winter, irony, to describe the shape of the plot. One might say that the irony works in this case as a parody of romantic tragedy, making us expect a tragic action and then consistently frustrating those expectations. The action is made 'universal', but there is a certain aimlessness to that universality that keeps its significance from being felt in the plot itself. That is, we are continually being directed toward a pattern of action that is being inverted. It could be said, however, that the novel gains its power only by the discrepancy between these two patterns: the tragic pattern being completed in our minds and the ironic action insisted on by the words on the page. The absence of tragedy thus becomes a presence.

There is, thus, a way in which Hardy teases us with dichotomous solidities, organising patterns that are supported by plenty of evidence but which are mutually contradictory. The scene in which Jude and Arabella kill a pig is a good example. Generally speaking, the scene might be seen as functioning in two opposite directions: first, it can reinforce Jude's tragic sensitivity, his heroic insistence on a universal harmony that is not there; or it can parody that elevation, making it appear not only jejune but actually insensitive, the situation, put crudely, of a man perfectly willing to eat ham but unwilling to face the fact that pigs must be slaughtered to provide that food. What are we to make of Jude's resistance to nature's law of mutual butchery? In this particular scene the question really centres on what we are made to feel for the pig. It is not that simple, but Hardy's use of the pathetic fallacy here will give us a handle.

In the chapter just preceding our scene, Arabella has confessed, if that's the word, that she isn't pregnant after all. Jude, in anger, says directly that he certainly would not have tied himself down with Arabella had he known: 'I shouldn't have hurried on our affair' (I, IX; p. 70), a curiously pettish way of putting it. Arabella, with her usual exasperating blandness, ignores this and, in an ironic anticipation of Jude's later citation of the *Agamemnon* (VI, II; p. 409), says, 'Don't take on, dear. What's done can't be undone.' The tragic potential of this trap for Jude is thus undercut in advance, though such potential can only be undercut if it is, at the same time, present. In any case, Jude awakes the next morning to muse on the tragic wrong of a 'social ritual' that, without fault on anyone's part, has created 'a gin which would cripple him, if not her also, for the rest of a lifetime'. Why, this gin robbed a man of his 'one opportunity of showing himself superior to the lower animals'. Pigs, say.

The text thus sets up a problematic union-division between Jude and Arabella. Since we know more of her tricks than does Jude at this point, we are inclined to think of him as trapped not by any fundamental law or even social ritual but by his dimple-manufacturing wife, surely one of 'the lower animals'. I suspect that we are likely to overlook his outburst and the rather ungenerous reflection on the fact that he is certainly trapped – and maybe Arabella is too. He seems pretty much separated from her, that is, in reference to the distinction between a sensitive human and 'the lower animals', and feels cheated by the marriage-funeral of the chance to demonstrate that conviction.

The scene that follows both confirms and denies Jude's feeling, exalts it and makes it grotesque. The chapter (I, X) opens as follows: 'The time arrived for killing the pig which Jude and his wife had fattened in their sty during the autumn months, and the butchering was timed to take place as soon as it was light in the morning, so that

Jude might get to Alfredston without losing more than a quarter of a day' (p. 72). The focus on Jude is revealing. He 'and his wife' have been fattening the pig for the purpose of killing it, and the butchering has been scheduled so that he can lose as little money as possible. 'Poor folks must live', as Arabella says, and killing the pig is not simply a general family necessity but a necessity for Jude. Imagine the difference if instead of 'Jude and his wife' the text had presented 'Arabella and her husband' or even 'Jude and Arabella'. The family unit Jude has created (or been trapped into) makes slaughter inevitable, and there is a suggestion here of mere squeamishness. Jude has, we see, been involved in all that leads up to the butchering, so that his sudden reluctance in the face of death must strike us as incongruous. He participates eagerly enough in the morning's preparations, saying that he prefers scalding to singeing: 'I like the way of my own county.' How are we to read this? Does it suggest that Jude has participated before in such practices, that he has brutal ties we hadn't suspected, that he is drawn sentimentally to old county traditions?

The first sign of Jude's separation from the gory ritual is given when he lights the fire that will heat the water, he having won the scalding-singeing debate. He feels the cheer of the warm fire, 'though for him the sense of cheerfulness was lessened by thoughts on the reason of that blaze.' All very well, but what did he suppose was going to climax all those months of fattening he 'and his wife' were promoting? The separation between Jude and Arabella does, how-ever, become more insistent when Arabella says she has, as is the custom, starved the pig for the last day 'to save bother with the innerds'. Arabella's flat acceptance of such gruesome details and such suffering is contrasted now with Jude's generalised pity: 'Poor creature!' (p. 73).

Here the narrator enters, pathetic fallacy ready, to tell us about those 'lower animals' referred to earlier. First, a robin flies away, 'not liking the sinister look of the scene', a scene, we might note, in which Jude is participating. Since Arabella has already offered to do the killing, why doesn't Jude follow the lead of the robin? That robin, after all, flees, 'though hungry'. The implications are clear: one may, like the robin, reject this sinister life and heroically choose not to be. But Jude ignores this tragic opportunity because of some feelings of manliness, we later learn. But if manliness is to be defined as the ability to overcome compassion, it appears that the 'lower animals' are, in fact, more human than man and that Jude's attempt to make a distinction between himself and that lower form is ironically confirmed.

Jude then nooses 'the affrighted animal', whose voice turns from 'surprise' to 'rage'. Arabella opens the door and she and Jude 'together' hoist 'the victim' on to the stool. Jude holds him so that Arabella may bind him, the animal's tone changing from 'rage' to 'despair'. The significant point in this description, again, is that all human emotions are given to the animals: the robin and the pig. The presumably human actors – Jude and Arabella alike – are denied human feelings. Jude, thus, inevitably caught up with his wife in this mess, can escape only by being one with the animals, denying his manliness and inverting the distinction he had tried to maintain.

We see all that and respond to such touches as Jude's scraping the bristles from the pig's neck 'as he had seen the butchers do'. But Arabella's reprimand – 'Don't be such a tender-hearted fool' – is bound to sound callous, not primarily because of any specific signals of callousness here but because of an external referent: Jude's attempts to escape the brutality of this situation, however futile such attempts might be, seem dignified and human, despite the irony invested in the scene. And, of course, there are contradictory signals supporting Jude within the scene, again given to us by the pig. The versatile pig changes its tone once more, not to a note of 'harmony' but to a 'shriek of agony', this time, however, directed not at his killer, Jude, but the accomplice: 'his glazing eyes riveting themselves on Arabella with the eloquently keen reproach of a creature recognizing at last the treachery of those who had seemed his only friends' (pp. 74–5); and 'friends' continues the ironic unification of Jude with Arabella, but the pig knows at last who his real enemy is and in his tragic recognition scene singles out Arabella for his ocular eloquence.

Jude then performs a bit of inappropriate slapstick, knocking over the pail that had caught the blood. The narrator, however, as is usual with him, counteracts – or appears to – the ludicrous aspects of this image by drawing our attention to the 'dismal, sordid, ugly spectacle' of the blood on the snow and, by implication, of the whole episode. It is , however, 'a dismal, sordid, ugly spectacle' only 'to those who saw it as other than an ordinary obtaining of meat'. The curious distance implied in 'obtaining of meat' contrasts with all the grisly naturalistic details. How are we, in the end, to take this? Surely there is a dominantly ironic perspective that insists on the impossibility, even the absurdity or cowardice, of the attempt to separate oneself from this obtaining of meat. But there is also a sense, mostly there by implication, that it is the very ordinariness of such a process that denies what we think of as human qualities and creates a callousness that can be avoided only by such inner resistance as Jude possesses. It is primarily the absence that creates our sense of tragic potential in this scene. We see mostly the absurd side of resistance; we sense, however, the noble side. It is what we sense in conflict with what we see that makes this scene so powerful, a paradigm of the strong incoherence that controls the entire novel.

The effects of this absence seem to me dominant throughout Hardy's fiction, though such contradictions are brought into being by very different means. Few readers have found *A Pair of Blue Eyes* to be a very coherent text, judging from the criticism,[8] but it may be that Hardy simply 'bares the device' more ostentatiously here, bringing his absences more prominently before us. The dominant plot of 'The Maid's Tragedy' is played off against a shadow plot of 'The Maid's Treachery'. Elfride is both the victimised innocent and the devious female who gets what she deserves. Beyond this, Hardy plays with the very authenticity of his text, asking whether this text or any text can truly be 'read'. The narrator constantly teases us by hinting at a solidity and a coherence that might lie behind the manifestly vaporous and contradictory text. This hint of a determinable pattern for the events is given immediately on the opening of the novel. We are told that Elfride's emotions, lying very near the surface, were to be known 'only to those who watched the circumstances of her history' (I; p. 1). Since we are about to receive an account of those circumstances, clearly we ought, then, to be able to 'know'. That is the promise, but it turns out that such knowing requires a good deal more than just watching. Elfride, the next paragraph says, had a 'charming power of preventing a material study of her lineaments'; 'you did not see the form and substance of her features' while looking at her. We are told that the interest in her rested in 'the combination of very interesting particulars', not 'in the individual elements combined'. There is, then, 'a form and substance', a 'combination' that is more than an aggregation of parts, but Elfride is so formed that we are prevented from reaching that combination. 'Watching her', then, will not, in itself, break down the text. It may all be coherent, but forces are at work to deny us access to that coherence.

The games with 'reading' continue throughout. Elfride, says Swancourt, has been formed by 'reading so many of those novels' (I; p. 3), one of which she has been writing. Stephen, also according to Swancourt, possibly picked up his manners from watching plays (IX;

p. 91). In part created by texts, then, these characters struggle to read one another by the same means. They fail, of course, and their failure is reflected in our own. Mrs Swancourt informs Elfride that her temporary 'companionless state' will give her, 'as it does everybody, an extraordinary power in reading the features of our fellow-creatures here [in London society]. I always am a listener in such places as these – not to the narratives told by my neighbours' tongues, but by their faces – the advantage of which is, that . . . they all speak the same language' (XIV; p. 153). But of course they do not speak anything like the same language, nor are their features any more open to easy reading than Elfride's own. She is finally a surrogate for the reader's similarly hubristic quest for discovering coherent meaning.

When Knight comes on the scene, having read Elfride's novel severely, she struggles anxiously to inform him of her '*real* meaning' (XVII; p. 175), the secret behind the words. But this is impossible, since Knight is a very bad reader of her: 'He could pack them [women] into sentences like a workman, but practically was nowhere' (XVIII; p. 193). This suggests that there is, in experience, something more substantial than words, a reality that a good reader can find. Knight is said to lack 'the trick of reading truly the enigmatical forces at work in women' (XX; p. 226). Elfride, similarly, suggests that her problem with Knight stems from inadequate powers as a reader: 'I suppose I must take you as I do the Bible – find out and understand all I can; and on the strength of that, swallow the rest in a lump, by simple faith' (XIX; pp. 208–9). Well, the swallower gets swallowed, as it turns out, but is this because she did not read as well as she should? One is teased by that possibility, but one is also teased by the possibility that there is no substance behind words, that all is a verbal texture concealing – perhaps nothing. Knight, for instance, returns after some immersion in real experience, so he thinks, to his earlier essays on women, love, and marriage: he is able, 'reading them now by the full light of a new experience, to see how much more his sentences meant than he had felt them to mean when they were written' (XX; p. 213). In this textual world, words are or seem to be impossible to escape and impossible to comprehend fully. Knight finds that his words mean 'more' but not something different. That is, he is confirmed by what he has written, not changed, and the raw experience, that solidity that presumably lies behind words, is made problematic. Knight is no more able to live outside words than is Elfride.

But are we able to do so, to escape the ambiguous snow-blindness engendered by the hopeless attempt to read? Are we, to take one case, able to read Knight any better than does Elfride? There are so many inconsistencies in the presentation, so many empty spaces. Nowhere are these gaps so apparent as in the cliff-hanging scene and in what follows from that apparent climax. Everyone recognises that Elfride's action in saving his life as she does is in some sense a literal anti-climax. She rids herself of any attachment to Stephen and commits herself, emotionally and sexually, to Knight. That appears to be a positive and heroic act, and we are bound to wonder why it turns out not to work as we feel it should. What we receive is a subtle non-explanation, contradictory directions for reading the climax that turns into a catastrophe. The usual critical manoeuvre is to look back from the conclusion of the novel and fill the gap with a coherent reading of Knight's consistent sexual morbidity, his 'pathological' obsession, his 'tremendous sense of sexual inadequacy'.[9] Blaming Knight and reading the scene ironically is a way of closing what is open and creating coherence: 'The irony of his physical rescue is that his psychological condition cannot be helped by her.'[10] The suggestion, to complete the irony, is that Knight, far from responding fully to her act of love, is driven to think that having acted passionately now she has surely done so in the past. He is spurred on to jealousy, to distance rather than closeness.

These readings fill in the gap plausibly enough, but only if we regard the novel's close as settling all the issues of how to read. Elfride, for instance, is made sympathetic at the end, and the narrator issues many diatribes against men: 'Clinging to him so dependently, she taught him in time to presume upon that devotion – a lesson men are not slow to learn' (XXX; p. 349). But such attacks must be matched against many earlier comments on Elfride's 'inconstancy' and against the snide reflections on women's general inferiority that pepper the novel for three-quarters of its length. The fact is that the scene on the cliff gives out contradictory signals as to both Knight and Elfride and conceals from us the definite information we need to read coherently.

When Knight, clinging perilously to the rock face, sees Elfride return, his eyes speak silently 'the whole diapason of eloquence, from lover's deep love to fellow-man's gratitude for a token of remembrance from one of his kind' (XXII; p. 246). This surely does not appear cold-blooded or morbid. His concern for her safety during the rescue is similarly touching. He thinks of a good plan for saving his own skin – Elfride tying her underwear-rope around her own waist – but is silent on that. Well, the truth is that he is nobly silent on that until she says that it was her plan all along, at which point he ignobly protests not at all.

After she hauls him to safety, Elfride and Knight exchange a glance in which 'each told a long-concealed tale of emotion.' Elfride, apparently reading badly as always, thinks 'perhaps he was only grateful, and did not love her', and it is true that he does not kiss her, due to his 'peculiarity of nature' in respecting the unfair advantage he has gained. Perhaps he is already beginning his icy reversal of what we think the scene should accomplish? Perhaps not, too, since we are told that he releases her from the kissless embrace 'reluctantly' and that, cold and wet as he is, he is still 'glowing with fervour'. Then follows a frustratingly neutral description of his gathering together her linen fragments and chasing down the banker's receipt she had received from Stephen. That banker's receipt is surely meant to recall to us Elfride's treachery, however understandable, and to put Knight in the place of a deceived lover, whose only reaction to the receipt is an affectionate thought of Elfride as 'impractical'.

Where does all this leave us? With several possibilities for explanation, all conceivable and supportable, but none available for dominance over the others. The text pushes us in several different directions and then frustrates us by contradictory explanations or, more prominently, by none at all. The scene then shifts abruptly for the next four chapters to Stephen, who, of course, can tell us nothing about the effects of this on Knight. Such a perspective does, however, almost necessarily put the heroic Elfride in a negative light. We are told that 'perhaps' she had a 'proneness to inconstancy', that, like most women and unlike most 'sensible men', she had misread Stephen's modesty and tendency to disparage himself (XXVII; p. 288). Her father adds ammunition to this attack by quoting Catullus to the effect that 'a woman's words to a lover are as a matter of course written only on wind and water' (XXVII; pp. 292–3). Swancourt is hardly a reliable guide, to be sure, and there are many hedges, even here, against an accurate local reading.

We do not see Knight again until the masterful scene in the vault, where he, unaware of the emotional charge between Elfride and Stephen, carries on in a ponderous, half-comic manner, mouthing sentiments all too banally appropriate to the occasion: 'How much has been said on death from time to time! how much we ourselves can think upon it!' (XXVII; p. 298), followed with some lines from the Hundred-and-second Psalm.

The narrator, however, does something to protect him, saying that, though not so handsome as the others, he had an integrity that lent to his features 'a dignity not even incipient in the other two'. Even his 'obtuseness' is said to come from his total inability to deceive others, rather than from 'any inherent dulness in him regarding human nature'. On Elfride, the narrator is careful to confuse, to conceal while appearing to reveal:

> It is difficult to frame rules which shall apply to both sexes, and Elfride, an undeveloped girl, must, perhaps, hardly be laden with the moral responsibilities which attach to a man in like circumstances. The charm of woman, too, lies partly in her subtleness in matters of love. But if honesty is a virtue in itself, Elfride, having none of it now, seemed, being for being, scarcely good enough for Knight. (XXVII; pp. 299–300)

The apparent sharpness of the sentences here, implying that Elfride is blankly dishonest and incapable of bearing moral responsibility, is modified by all the conditional terms and the expressions of doubt. And it is not long before the narrator is using very different formulae to describe Elfride's plight: 'Elfride was burdened with the very intensity of her love' (XXXI; p. 351). When this happens, we are given alternative possibilities concerning Knight: 'Perhaps Knight was not shaped by Nature for a marrying man' (XXXII; p. 366). Perhaps, but what do we do with that glowing fervour he had felt earlier or with the statement that Knight 'was at once the most ardent and the coolest man alive' (XXVIII; p. 315)? As to all these possibilities, and others, the narrator answers, 'One cannot say' (XXXII; p. 366).

One cannot say, then, to what extent Knight's pathological morbidity provides a coherent explanation for the anti-climax, just as one cannot say how adequate our reading of the novel can be. It is the virtue of Hardy's art that these non-explaining explanations continue to haunt us, that he is able to use the power of absence to effect a brilliantly incoherent art.

NOTES

1. This term is meant to refer to a state in which a reader perceives competing patterns for organising details in the text, no one of which can be made to dominate the others. The incoherent text, then, is determinate but not univocal. For a further discussion of formal incoherence see my 'Coherent Readers, Incoherent Texts', *CI* III (1977) 781–802.

2. Roland Barthes, *S/Z: An Essay* (1970), trans. Richard Miller (New York: Hill & Wang, 1974) p. 6.

3. John Bayley, *An Essay on Hardy* (Cambridge: Cambridge University Press, 1978) p. 118 (ellipsis mine).

4. Bayley, p. 40.

5. Barthes's categories are, of course, open to question, particularly as regards the distinction between the text with limited indeterminacy and the one with total indeterminacy. His own demonstrations suggest that there is no real distinction between these two, that there is no 'classic text'. It may follow from this that all texts are indeterminate, but I am trying to cling to some formalist assumptions, to the possibility that plurality may be limited and thus determinate.

6. *An Anatomy of Criticism: Four Essays* (Princeton: Princeton University Press, 1957) p. 208.

7. See, for example, the subtle and persuasive argument in Dale Kramer's *Thomas Hardy: The Forms of Tragedy* (London: Macmillan; Detroit: Wayne State University Press, 1975) pp. 136–63.

8. J. Hillis Miller's suggestive treatment, in *The Form of Victorian Fiction* (Notre Dame: University of Notre Dame Press, 1968) pp. 7–16, is noteworthy. Of course, criticism being what it is, most try to find a formula for coherence in the novel. I think it is significant, however, that the most distinguished analyses articulate that formula as a consistent general pattern of what I would call incoherence. Michael Steig's 'The Problem of Literary Value in Two Early Hardy Novels' (*TSLL* XII [1970] 55–62) argues that there is 'a consistency to be found in the very pattern of setting up expectations and then disappointing them' (p. 59). Arthur K. Amos, in 'Accident and Fate: The Possibility for Action in *A Pair of Blue Eyes*', *ELT* XV (1972) 158–67, says that the presence of an 'if-plot' – an alternative plot in which characters make different choices and are rewarded instead of punished' creates an integrated and coherent 'negative *exemplum*' (pp. 163, 166).

9. The 'pathological' tag is repeated by many critics, J. I. M. Stewart, for example, in *Thomas Hardy: A Critical Biography* (London: Longman, 1971) p. 65. The second quote is from Steig's 'The Problem of Literary Value', p. 60. It should be noted, however, that Steig is fully alert to the contradictory attitudes signalled towards Knight. He points out 'the apparent unsureness of Hardy's attitude toward Knight' (p. 61), for instance.

10. Bayley, *An Essay on Hardy*, p. 141; also see Ronald Blythe's 'Introduction' to the New Wessex Edition of the novel (London: Macmillan, 1975) pp. 19, 29 (paperback edition).

Index

Page numbers in *italics* indicate major entries.